THE ECONOMICS OF EXCESS

THE ECONOMICS
OF EXCESS

▌ADDICTION, INDULGENCE,

AND SOCIAL POLICY ▌

HAROLD WINTER

STANFORD ECONOMICS AND FINANCE, AN IMPRINT OF
STANFORD UNIVERSITY PRESS ▌ STANFORD, CALIFORNIA

Stanford University Press
Stanford, California

Special discounts for bulk quantities of Stanford Economics and Finance are available to corporations, professional associations, and other organizations. For details and discount information, contact the special sales department of Stanford University Press. Tel: (650) 736-1782, Fax: (650) 736-1784

Printed in the United States of America on acid-free, archival-quality paper

Library of Congress Cataloging-in-Publication Data

Winter, Harold, 1960- author.

   The economics of excess : addiction, indulgence, and social policy / Harold Winter.

     pages cm

   Includes bibliographical references and index.

   ISBN 978-0-8047-6147-5 (cloth : alk. paper) — ISBN 978-0-8047-6148-2 (pbk. : alk. paper)

  1. Substance abuse—Economic aspects. 2. Substance abuse—Government policy. 3. Social policy—Economic aspects. 4. Economics—Psychological aspects. I. Title.

  HV4998.W56 2011

   362.29—dc22   2011004557

Typeset by Newgen in 10/14 Minion

❚ TO THOMAS MICHAEL WINTER, FOR TEACHING ME THE TRUE MEANING OF PATERNALISM. I HOPE YOU ENJOY ALL YOUR FUTURE EXCESSES. ❚

CONTENTS

PREFACE

Do cigarette taxes make smokers happier? This unusual question comes from the title of the research paper (Gruber and Mullainathan, 2002) that started me on the journey of writing this book. I thought the authors were being sarcastic with their title, and the answer to their question would obviously be no. I was wrong. The idea that taxation makes smokers happier is at odds with the traditional economic model of consumption. A tax raises the final price a consumer must pay for a good, and a price increase is usually thought of as making a consumer worse off. Do you feel happier when there are price increases for the products you enjoy consuming? I had a very hard time wrapping my mind around the idea that smokers *welcome* increased taxation. To make matters worse, even if smokers don't welcome increased taxation, some economists argue that these smokers are better off having their behavior controlled *even if they don't realize they are better off.* Within this framework, it is not difficult to justify social policy designed to protect people from themselves.

Protecting people from themselves has traditionally not been much of a concern to economists. The more traditional justification for social control policies such as taxation is to protect people from *others.* Smokers harm not only themselves but others, with their secondhand smoke. Drinkers who drive while under the influence put others at risk. Adverse health outcomes caused by smoking, drinking, and overeating impose health insurance costs on others who belong to the same social or private insurance pool. Countless research papers and books have been written about the pros and cons of numerous social policy options designed to control behavior that is costly to others. This book, instead, focuses mainly on the more controversial justification (at least among economists) for social control policy—to protect people from themselves.

A relatively new field of economics known as *behavioral economics* challenges the standard economic premise that people are fully rational. As briefly explained in the introduction of an important volume on the applications of behavioral economics to various fields of economics:

> Over the last decade or so, behavioral economics has fundamentally changed the way economists conceptualize the world. Behavioral economics is an umbrella of approaches that seek to extend the standard economics framework to account for relevant features of human behavior that are absent in the standard economics framework. Typically, this calls for borrowing from the neighboring social sciences, particularly from psychology and sociology. The emphasis is on well-documented empirical findings: at the core of behavioral economics is the conviction that making our model of an economic man more accurate will improve our understanding of economics, thereby making the discipline more useful. (Diamond and Vartiainen, 2007, 1)

In essence, behavioral economics contends that people are far from perfect, and depending on the context, it is these imperfections that provide justifications for social policy to protect people from themselves.

In this book, I discuss both standard and behavioral economics applied to addiction, indulgence, and social policy. Although these issues are related, they can also be quite segmented according to how economists approach them. In chapter 1, I provide a thorough discussion of economic models of addiction, both standard and behavioral. The model I develop in most detail takes into account both approaches. And even though this is the most challenging material in the book, it is highly instructive, especially for students. Fortunately, for the more casual reader, all the key concepts are developed in simpler examples so that when they are referred to later in the book they can easily be understood.

In the next three chapters, I examine specific indulgences: smoking (chapter 2), drinking (chapter 3), and overeating (chapter 4). The vast majority of economic research on these topics does not explicitly take into account models of addiction or behavioral economics, but the standard models still offer interesting insights into the ways economists approach these issues. Throughout these three chapters, I try not to present material that is overly redundant. It would be easy to write a specific section on smoking, and then in the next chapter use the same material and simply replace the word *smoking* with the word *drinking*. For example, in the smoking chapter I discuss how smokers perceive the health risks of smoking. The key material is on how economists approach risk misperception, and that can be applied to any type of risk. Once discussed in terms of smoking, it is not necessary to repeat all that material again. I try to keep these chapters reasonably separated and focused on unique issues. By necessity, there is some overlap, but not much. Thus, if you are familiar with this material and read just one of the chapters, you may feel that I have not been complete. My goal is to make the three chapters work as a whole and to complement each other, not to substitute for one another.

Social policy is the focus of chapter 5. Because the standard model of rational behavior does not lend itself well to justifying social policy to protect people from themselves, this chapter is largely concerned with the behavioral economics approach to social welfare analysis. My goal is to present a careful and thought-provoking discussion of the pros and cons of using behavioral economics to justify social control policy, especially policies relating to addictive and indulgent behavior. This chapter also offers a concise discussion of *neuroeconomics* (the application of neuroscience to the discipline of economics), an exciting and controversial new field many behavioral economists are enthusiastically embracing. Finally, in chapter 6, I briefly summarize some of the main points made throughout the book, and discuss the role of economic analysis in advising social policy.

The primary target audience for this book is undergraduate students with little or no background in economics, but the material may also be of interest to a broader audience. There are no mathematical equations, no graphs, and no tables and only a few numerical examples that facilitate the discussion when necessary. The goal is to make a large scholarly literature accessible to those who lack the training, or the time, to read the source material themselves. That being said, this book does not offer an extensive scholarly survey designed to aid researchers in the field. As much material as there is discussed here, far more is not addressed. A thorough list of references and comprehensive chapter-ending suggested readings aid the interested reader in delving further into the material.

In choosing material to review, this book focuses almost exclusively on economic research. Many disciplines are concerned with addiction, indulgence, and social policy, and they all offer many interesting and relevant insights, but these other approaches are well beyond the scope of this book. In no sense am I trying to convey that economic reasoning presents the only way to think about these issues, or the best way, but it is the way I have been trained to think about them. My hope is that this book can be part of an interdisciplinary reading list in *any* public policy course, regardless of the discipline, but it is not meant to be interdisciplinary in and of itself.

In terms of which papers I choose to discuss, my bias is toward recent research as opposed to older (and even possibly seminal) research. Many of the papers discussed are empirical studies, and I treat this material as if the reader has no background in statistics or econometrics. The key debates in the empirical work involve methodological issues that typically lead to conflicting results across studies. I am mostly interested in the questions raised in these studies, the qualitative results, and occasionally the quantitative results; I am *not* trying to formally address these methodological concerns. While I do not discuss any formal statistical issues, if you use this book as a text and your students have the appropriate background, all the original papers are well referenced and easy to acquire.

One last note: I do not include a dedicated chapter on the topic of the economics of drugs. This may seem an unusual decision in a book about addiction and social policy, but I have reasons for doing this. First, much of the theoretical and policy discussion throughout this book can be applied to *any* addictive good, and after covering smoking, drinking, and overeating, there isn't much material remaining that is unique to drugs. Second, the difference between drugs and the other topics is that drugs are illegal and controlled through the criminal justice system. A proper discussion of drugs, then, would require some detail on the economics of crime and punishment, a topic that I recently covered in another book that includes a dedicated chapter on drugs (Winter, 2008).

Acknowledgments

For many reasons, this book turned out to be far more difficult and time-consuming to write than I anticipated. Throughout all the turmoil, my editor at Stanford University Press, Margo Beth Crouppen, was infinitely patient and understanding. I owe her a great deal of gratitude. I also want to thank Jessica Walsh, Rebecca Logan, Judith Hibbard, Mary Ann Short, and everyone else at SUP and Newgen involved with this project I do not know by name.

Several friends, colleagues, and reviewers offered helpful comments on various portions of this book. I would like to think Gwill Allen,

Ariaster Chimeli, Joni Hersch, Jody Sindelar, and William Neilson for their suggestions.

Over the past three years, I have had an army of students assist me with various aspects of completing this book. I would like to thank Graham Bowman, Jessica Cherok, Nick Cobos, Todd Holbrook, Jane Krosse, Kari Lehmkuhl, Jonathan Leirer, David Plumb, Rebecca Schueller, and Thomas Ruchti. A very special thanks goes to my enthusiastic and incredibly helpful research assistant Chris Matgouranis. This time, I'm not forgetting to thank BPW and HKPW, but I do apologize and offer thanks to anyone I have forgotten.

Finally, I'd like to thank all my family members, who supported and encouraged me throughout some difficult times. No one deserves more thanks than Jenn, who put up with far more than anyone should ever have to put up with from me. Thank you for sticking it out.

Suggested Readings

Two excellent collections of papers on behavioral economics are by Loewenstein and Rabin (2003), and Diamond and Vartiainen (2007).

THE ECONOMICS OF EXCESS

THE ECONOMICS OF ADDICTION

When discussing addictive behavior we need a clear definition of the term *addiction*. It is not difficult to find definitions of addiction. The truly difficult task is deciding which of the phenomenally similar, but not identical, definitions to present. Here are two examples:

- a physiological and psychological compulsion for a habit-forming substance. In extreme cases, an addiction may become an overwhelming obsession (http://www.personalinjuryfyi.com/glossary.html)
- a chronic, relapsing disease characterized by compulsive drug-seeking and use and by neurochemical and molecular changes in the brain (http:www.tobaccofreeqc.org/youth/glossary.php)

With words such as *compulsion*, *obsession*, and *disease* used to define it, addiction is certainly not considered to be a beneficial activity. Even healthy activities such as exercising or eating well acquire the label *exercise nut* or *health nut* for those who practice them excessively.

The American Psychiatric Association offers a more thorough definition:

Answer yes or no to the following seven questions. Most questions have more than one part, because everyone behaves slightly differently in addiction. You only need to answer yes to one part for that question to count as a positive response.

1. Tolerance. Has your use of drugs or alcohol increased over time?

2. Withdrawal. When you stop using, have you ever experienced physical or emotional withdrawal? Have you had any of the following symptoms: irritability, anxiety, shakes, sweats, nausea, or vomiting.

3. Difficulty controlling your use. Do you sometimes use more or for a longer time than you would like? Do you sometimes drink to get drunk? Do you stop after a few drinks usually, or does one drink lead to more drinks?

4. Negative consequences. Have you continued to use even though there have been negative consequences to your mood, self-esteem, health, job, or family?

5. Neglecting or postponing activities. Have you ever put off or reduced social, recreational, work, or household activities because of your use?

6. Spending significant time or emotional energy. Have you spent a significant amount of time obtaining, using, concealing, planning, or recovering from your use? Have you spent a lot of time thinking about using? Have you ever concealed or minimized your use? Have you ever thought of schemes to avoid getting caught?

7. Desire to cut down. Have you sometimes thought about cutting down or controlling your use? Have you ever made unsuccessful attempts to cut down or control your use?

If you answered yes to at least 3 of these questions, then you meet the medical definition of addiction. (http://www.addictionsandrecovery.org/definition-of-addiction.htm)

Although less judgmental than the previous definitions, an underlying negative feel is still associated with this more complete definition.

In contrast, the standard economic definition of addiction is judgment free. Here is an example taken from the seminal work on the economics of *rational* addiction (Becker and Murphy, 1988):

> The basic definition of addiction at the foundation of our analysis is that a person is potentially addicted to a good if an increase in his current consumption of the good increases his future consumption of the good. (681)

That may not be an elaborate definition, but it has some strong points in its favor. Unlike many of the other definitions of addiction, the economic definition *describes* behavior, it does not *condemn* it. Quite simply, addictive behavior depends on how consumption in one period affects consumption in another period. If the more you smoke today, the more you want to smoke tomorrow, smoking is addictive. But likewise, if the more you exercise today, the more you want to exercise tomorrow, exercising is addictive. With this definition, you can consider the consumption of *any* good to be potentially addictive. Furthermore, there is no reason to identify or distinguish between physical addiction and psychological addiction. The only important trait to identify is a person's consumption pattern over time.

Thinking about addiction as a consumption issue allows us to raise the types of questions in which an economist specializes. How do price changes affect the consumption of addictive goods? What about income changes, information changes, or the costs of quitting? How do regulations or criminal laws affect consumption? More generally, we can challenge the premise that addicts are somehow "trapped" by their addiction. As we do with other consumer products, we can predict that addicts make rational choices when consuming addictive goods. In other words, an addict will rationally choose to trade off short-term benefits (getting high) with long-term costs (future health problems). If addicts are making these trade-offs, we must address precisely how they compare future costs to current benefits. This comparison lies at the heart of the economic theory of addiction.

The Subjective Rate of Time Preference

Consider the following thought experiment. You are asked to choose between the following two options: receive $1,000 today or receive $1,000 exactly one year from today. Which option would you choose, keeping in mind that there is no right or wrong answer? By far, the most common choice is the $1,000 today, and let's assume that's your choice also. How would you answer a follow-up question: Would you prefer $1,000 today or $1,100 one year from today? Still the $1,000 today? How about $1,200 in one year? Not enough? How about $1,300, $1,400, or as much as $1,500? What would it take to get you to choose the future amount? Eventually, we can find a future amount that you would choose over the current amount of $1,000. What this experiment is trying to demonstrate is that, dollar for dollar, we prefer current dollars over future ones. In fact, most of us must be paid a premium, perhaps a large premium, before we're willing to give up a current payment for a future one. More succinctly, most people tend to be *impatient* to some degree, while addicts are often thought of as being highly impatient.

Economists have a simple tool for numerically measuring a person's level of impatience—the *discount factor* (usually depicted by the symbol δ, the Greek letter delta). Using the hypothetical example from above, assume that you are *perfectly indifferent* as to whether you receive $1,000 today or $1,500 one year from today. What is meant by "perfectly indifferent" is that if you are offered $1,499 one year from today, you strictly prefer the current amount of $1,000, and if you are offered $1,501 one year from today, you strictly prefer the future amount of $1,501. At $1,500 one year from today, you truly don't see a difference between the current and the future options. In this case, because the current amount of $1,000 is equivalent to the future amount of $1,500, we can say that you discount the future amount by two-thirds (1,000 ÷ 1,500). Equivalently, we can say that you have a discount factor of two-thirds, or δ = .67, approximately.

In economic terms, the discount factor is a measure of a person's *rate of time preference.* How impatient is a person when considering current versus future trade-offs? As the discount factor becomes larger (closer to 1), the person is *less* impatient (or more patient). As the discount factor becomes smaller (closer to 0), the person is *more* impatient (or less patient). It is very important to recognize that the discount factor is a subjective measure of impatience. To a typical economist, there is no such thing as a right or wrong (or a good or bad) level of impatience. A rate of time preference is precisely that—a preference. Yet, when scholars discuss public policy justifications for controlling addictive behavior, addicts' supposed shortsightedness is often at the top of the list of justifications.

The concept of impatience is of paramount importance when discussing addictive behavior, and we examine it in careful detail. Typically, addicts are thought of as being more impatient than nonaddicts. In its simplest form, addiction is a trade-off between the current benefits the addict reaps from smoking, drinking, using drugs, and so on, and the future costs the addict will bear from poorer health or increased health care costs. Compared to their farsighted counterparts, shortsighted (or myopic) people place little weight on future outcomes, so the current benefits of drug use, for example, are given more weight than the future health costs. Farsighted people, on the other hand, place more weight on future health costs, making them less likely to indulge in excesses today.

Impatience is a crucial quality to consider when discussing many types of behaviors, not only addiction. Consider the war against terrorism. One of the most frightening weapons some terrorists use is themselves. How do we fight someone willing to strap on a bomb and detonate it in a public place? A suicide bomber is likely to have an extremely low discount factor—they place virtually no value on future events. This makes it very difficult to deter suicide bombers. If they don't care about the future, if they don't even care about tomorrow, the threat of future punishment has no effect on them.

In a similar vein, criminals in general are believed to be far more shortsighted than noncriminals. A typical criminal weighs the current benefits of committing a crime against the future costs of apprehension, conviction, and punishment. A very myopic criminal is not easily deterred by the threat of future imprisonment. Severe penalties, such as the three-strikes law that harshly punishes a third offense, or hard labor, or capital punishment, are often justified as necessary sanctions to discourage certain costly criminal behavior.

It is not uncommon, on the basis of these examples, for shortsighted preferences to be associated with behaviors that are often considered bad or costly, not only from a social perspective but from an individual perspective as well. It is sometimes suggested that education or information would help shortsighted people become more patient, and that very well may be true. But economists usually view myopia as a preference, and it is not a simple thing to change someone's preferences. In fact, economists typically take preferences as given, meaning that we have very little to say about them other than that they exist. We may be able to predict different behaviors according to different levels of impatience, but we don't often criticize preferences themselves.

The Rational Addict

Describing addiction as a rational act is a result of accepting preferences as givens and making no judgments. Precisely how does a rational addict behave? Assume you are deciding whether to begin smoking today. You know that if you start smoking, it will affect how much you want to smoke in the future. You also know that, whatever benefits you reap from smoking, eventually you will face adverse effects and long-term health costs. If you are fully informed about all the benefits and costs of smoking throughout your entire life, you can decide if your lifetime costs of starting to smoke today exceed the future benefits or if it is the other way around.

But knowing future benefits and costs of smoking is only the starting point. You can't just add up all the benefits, add up all the costs, and see which is the larger of the two. You must also consider your rate of time preference. Any costs or benefits that accrue to you in the future need to be properly discounted to be comparable in a current sense. A $1,000 cost 10 years from now is not the same, in a current sense, as a $1,000 cost 9 years from now, which is not the same as a $1,000 cost 8 years from now, and so on. The further into the future you expect to receive a benefit or cost, the less it is worth to you today. Thus, if most of the benefits from smoking are in the near future, and most of the costs, even if substantial, are in the far future, you may give more weight to the current benefits of smoking than the future costs.

For a proper rational calculation of all the benefits and costs, you must apply your subjective discount factor to all future values. Still, the fundamental cost-benefit analysis for you is basically the same. Once you calculate your *current value* of all the benefits and costs of smoking today, you can then decide your best course of action. Notice, with this reasoning, *both* decisions— to start smoking or to refrain from smoking—can be fully rational acts. Smoking is like any other activity. If you decide to smoke, it is because you believe it is in your best interest. It is not that there are no costs to smoking, it is just that those costs (properly discounted) are outweighed by the benefits (also properly discounted).

While the concept of rational addict has appeal as a theoretical construct, this simple representation has problems. Most obviously, why should we believe that you are fully informed about all the costs and benefits of consuming an addictive product throughout your life? It may not be difficult to believe you understand the benefits, as they are often largely subjective, but how well do you truly appreciate the long-term health risks of your addictive behavior? Do you fully understand the costs associated with excessive smoking, drinking, or eating? Informational deficiencies offer an important justification for social policy intervention to protect people from themselves, and this is discussed in later chapters. What is far more interesting, however, is that there may be shortcomings to the rational-addiction model even when you are fully informed. You may make a rational, fully informed decision to start smoking that is correctly based on every cost and benefit you experience throughout your life yet still end up regretting your decision. This is where the behavioral economists step in.

Printers, Rebates, and Time Consistency

Thinking about addiction in a rational framework presents a challenge for many people, as it may be difficult to accept economic results based on models in which a person *chooses* to consume harmful addictive goods such as drugs or cigarettes. Sometimes an example involving a product that everyone can easily relate to clearly illustrates key concepts. The decision to purchase a computer printer offers just such an example.

Let's assume Tim, Nate, and Sophia are all considering purchasing a specific computer printer. This particular printer has all the features they desire, but they find the price just a little too high. At the listed price, none of them choose to buy the printer. Fortunately for them, the company that produces the printer is offering a rebate special. A rebate deal involves actions in three distinct periods. In the first period, you decide whether to buy the printer. If you do buy it, in the second period you do whatever is necessary to qualify for the rebate. For example, you may have to fill in some paperwork, go to the post office, participate in an online or telephone customer service survey, and so on. In other words, you must bear a cost to submit the rebate request. If you submit the rebate request, in the third period you receive your rebate. How you approach a rebate deal depends on what type of person you are.

Let's start with Tim. Tim will pay the high price this period only if he plans on submitting the rebate request next period. He knows that, in the future, he will incur a cost of submitting the request, but further into the future he will receive a benefit. To make his decision, he asks himself a question: If I buy the printer this period, will I submit the rebate request next period? To answer that question, Tim has the ability to think of himself as being in the second period. From that perspective, he incurs a current cost but receives a future benefit, and when properly calculating the current value (that is, discounting the future benefit), he finds it in his best interest to submit the request. Knowing that he will submit the rebate request, Tim (in the first period) calculates the current value of buying the printer, submitting the request, and receiving the rebate. On the basis of his properly discounted cost-benefit calculation, Tim decides to buy the printer this period. He follows through and submits the rebate request next period, and he receives his rebate in the third period.

Now let's turn to Nate. Nate faces the same decision that Tim does, but Nate approaches the problem in a slightly different way. Nate does not have the ability to project forward and think of himself as being in the second period. Instead, Nate makes his decision from only the first period's perspective. So Nate discounts both the future cost of submitting the rebate request and the future benefit of receiving the rebate, and he finds that it is in his best interest to buy the printer with the intention of requesting the rebate. But there is a twist. After buying the printer and getting to the second period, Nate must now decide if he wants to incur the cost of submitting the rebate request. To do this, he calculates the current (second period) value of the future (third period) benefit, compares it to the current cost, and finds that the cost outweighs the benefit. In other words, when actually in the second period, Nate does not find it worthwhile to submit the rebate request. Nate ends up buying the printer, not submitting the rebate request, and not receiving a rebate. Thus, Nate ends up with a printer he does not value at the price he paid.

Finally, let's consider Sophia. Sophia is, in some sense, a combination of Tim and Nate. Like Nate, once she is in the second period, she will not find it in her best interest to incur the cost of submitting the rebate request. But like Tim, she can project herself into the second period while still in the first period and think about what she will do if she buys the printer. Sophia knows that if she buys the printer in the first period, she will not follow through and submit the rebate request in the second period. Thus, she decides *not* to buy the printer in the first period. Three different people, three different outcomes. What accounts for these differences?

One major difference among these people is *time consistency*, best explained with a simple numerical example, similar to the one used above to illustrate discounting. Suppose you are given the following choice: 12 months from today you can receive $1,000, or 13 months from today, $1,100. Which would you choose? Many people, making their choice today, choose the $1,100 option. The 1-month delay a year from now, from today's perspective, is worth the extra $100. But now consider the following choice: you can receive $1,000 today or $1,100 in 1 month from today. Which would you choose? Many people who preferred delaying for 1 month when that delay was far in the future now choose the $1,000 option. In the present, their impatience level is quite high when considering waiting a month for the extra $100. But between the two *future* periods, 12 months and 13 months from now, their impatience level is quite low.

When people are *time consistent*, the choice they make between two future outcomes will be the choice they still make when the future outcomes become *current* choices. Ask Tim today what he will choose in 12 versus 13 months from now and he will choose the $1,100. When the year passes and he faces the choice at that time, he is time consistent because he still chooses the $1,100. Nate and Sophia both choose the $1,100 from today's perspective, but when the year passes and they must choose at that time, they choose the $1,000. Nate and Sophia are *time inconsistent*. Their preferences for the two amounts change over time.

The reason for time-inconsistent behavior has to do with precisely how Nate (and Sophia) discounts future periods. Nate is relatively patient between two future periods, but relatively impatient between the current period and the next. Eventually, the future periods become the current period and the next one, and Nate changes from being relatively patient between them to being relatively impatient between them. This explains why he prefers the $1,100 option over the $1,000 option when *both* are in the future but prefers the $1,000 option when that is the current choice and only the $1,100 is in the future. Tim, on the other hand, is equally patient between two adjacent periods whether they both occur in the future or one is current and the other is in the future.

In the printer and rebate example, during the first period the cost of submitting the rebate request and the benefit of the rebate are both future choices. Tim and Nate are both relatively patient over those choices, meaning that they both place a fairly high weight on the future benefit compared to the future cost. But once in the second period, the cost of the rebate request is current and the benefit is in the future. Tim is still fairly patient between the two and places a high weight on the benefit, but Nate is now relatively impatient between the two and places a low weight on the benefit. This is why Tim follows through with his intention of submitting the rebate request, but Nate does not.

Another major difference between Nate and Sophia has to do with how they perceive their time-inconsistent behavior. Nate does not recognize that he is time inconsistent, but Sophia does. Using economic terminology, Nate is considered *naive*, while Sophia is considered *sophisticated*. This is why Sophia can anticipate that she will not follow through with submitting the rebate request and she avoids buying the printer altogether. Nate, however, believes that he is time consistent and fully expects to submit the rebate request, only to find when the time comes that he no longer believes it to be in his best interest. Thus, due to time inconsistency and their comprehension of it, Tim,

Nate, and Sophia each take a different path when considering purchasing a printer that includes a rebate deal.

Placing these behaviors into an addiction scenario is now easy. Assume that each of the three is considering whether to start smoking cigarettes today, with the intention of quitting 10 years from now. If Tim decides that it is in his best interest to start smoking and then quit, that is exactly what he will do. If Nate decides to start smoking with the intention of quitting, he will find that after 10 years pass he no longer wants to quit. He was not aware of his time inconsistency when he decided to start smoking. As for Sophia, she will decide not to start smoking because she is aware of her time inconsistency problem and doesn't want the prospect of not being able to quit in 10 years.

Once again, we have three different people and three different behaviors. Time-Consistent Tim chooses a consumption path and sticks with it. Naive Nate chooses the same consumption path Tim does, but he does not stick with it. And Sophisticated Sophia chooses a different consumption path from the other two. While this is only a simple addiction story, it nicely illustrates how addictive behavior depends on a number of factors. Not all addicts are the same, and that fact complicates the role of public policy designed to protect addicts from themselves.

At this point, you have the basics of the economics of addiction that will allow you to apply these concepts in later chapters, especially chapter 5. Yet the economic addiction model can be far more intricate, and while it is a challenging exercise to work through some of those intricacies, appreciating how economists model complex addictive behavior makes the effort worthwhile.

An Economic Model of Addiction

There are many ways to formally model addictive behavior. In one model of addiction (O'Donoghue and Rabin, 1999b), a person's consumption choices are spread over three periods, as we saw in the printer rebate example. In each period, the person has two choices to make: to *hit*, that is, to consume some of the addictive product that period, or to *refrain*, that is, to not consume any of the addictive product that period. Furthermore, he can face two conditions in each period: he can be *hooked* to the addictive product (that is, has taken a hit in the previous period), or he can be *unhooked* to the addictive product (that is, has refrained in the previous period). This means we have four possible situations to consider, and each situation has an associated outcome, known as a *payoff.* Although we won't be solving complicated numerical examples (but all the results are based on explicit calculations not presented), introducing some simple numbers can facilitate the discussion.

Let's rank the four situations from best to worst for the person by assigning arbitrary numbers. The best outcome is for him to be unhooked and to take a hit. This yields a payoff of, say, 35. The second-best outcome is to be unhooked and not take a hit. This yields a payoff of 25. The third-best outcome is to be hooked and take a hit. This yields a payoff of 17. And finally, the worst outcome for him is to be hooked and not take a hit. This yields a payoff of 0. The numbers are only reference points for comparing the four outcomes. The absolute magnitudes of the numbers mean nothing; it is their relative magnitudes that matter. But these numbers set up a very specific, and reasonably complex, story.

The first part of this story does not sit well with most people, and it has to do with the benefits of taking a hit. Notice that if the person is unhooked, he receives a higher payoff if he hits (35) than if he refrains (25). And if he is hooked, he also receives a higher payoff if he hits (17) than if he refrains (0). In other words, no matter what, if he has only a one-period decision, he would always choose to hit. For some, the model immediately seems silly. Why assume that it is always in the person's best interest to hit? Isn't it more realistic, when it comes to addictive goods, to assume that it is *not* in someone's best interest to hit? We set up the model this way for two basic reasons.

First, we are trying to model behavior of an addict, but if we set the baseline decision as never consuming the addictive good, what's to model? Having different people consume the good in different amounts allows us to compare behaviors across addicts. The second reason to make it in an addict's best interest to hit is to give significance to *self-control.* If it is never in an addict's best interest to hit, what would it mean to exhibit self-control? If he is not attracted to the addictive good in the first place, he has no reason to control his behavior. But if he prefers to consume the good, at least on a per-period basis, and he recognizes the effect of current consumption on future consumption, he may refrain from immediate gratification to help avoid future costs. If he refrains in the first period when it is in his best interest to hit, that is a meaningful illustration of self-control.

Addictive goods are typically thought of as being habit forming. This means that the more an addict has consumed in the past, the larger his current temptation to consume. For example, if he is initially unhooked, he gets 25 from refraining and 35 from hitting, a gain of 10. But if he is initially hooked, he gets 0 from refraining and 17 from hitting, a difference of 17. Being hooked, meaning that he consumed the good in the previous period, gives him a larger thrill, so to speak, from hitting in the current period than he would get from hitting if he is not currently hooked.

But addictive goods are also thought of as reducing the well-being of the addict. This means that the more an addict has consumed in the past, the lower his current level of well-being. In this example, an addict who hits when unhooked gets a payoff of 35 but when hooked only 17. An addict who refrains when unhooked gets a payoff of 25 but when hooked only 0. Being hooked, then, compared to being unhooked, leads to a lower well-being regardless of the person's current behavior.

This model presents a picture of a person who faces fairly complicated consumption choices for the addictive good. There is an initial single-period incentive for the person to hit, but this will make the addict hooked for the next period, reducing his future well-being and counteracting that initial incentive to hit. But if he is hooked, the addictive good provides a fairly large thrill, making it difficult to refrain from continuing to hit. Thus, the addict experiences across-period tensions whether hitting *or* refraining, and how these tensions play out over the three consumption periods depends on how he discounts future periods. We will see that the consumption path of a time-consistent person may differ from that of a time-inconsistent person. Furthermore, time-inconsistent behavior can vary depending on whether the person recognizes that he has the potential to make inconsistent decisions over time. We return to the behaviors of Tim, Nate, and Sophia.

Time-Consistent Tim

In this model, Tim represents the perfectly rational addict. In being time consistent, Tim is equally patient between two future adjacent periods or between a current period and the next one. In deciding on his consumption path across the three periods, Tim starts by asking himself the following question: If I were in the third period, should I hit or refrain? As we know from the numerical example, Tim knows he will benefit from hitting as opposed to refraining. Whether he is hooked or unhooked, in Tim's story the payoff from hitting exceeds the payoff from refraining. And because it is the very last period in which he is making a consumption decision, there are no future repercussions of currently hitting. The third-period decision, then, is an easy one. Tim will always hit.

The next step in Tim's decision process asks a question similar to his previous one: If I were in period 2, knowing that I will always hit in period 3, should I hit or refrain? This decision is a little more complicated. First, Tim must consider how his period 3 payoff will be affected by his period 2 behavior. Granted, he knows he will hit in period 3, but the payoff he gets will depend on whether he is hooked (that is, has hit in period 2) or unhooked (that is, refrained in period 2) when he enters the final period. Furthermore, the payoff he receives in period 2 depends on his past behavior. Will he be hooked or unhooked in period 2?

So what should Tim do in period 2, knowing that he will hit in the third one? If he enters period 2 unhooked, he can get his largest payoff (35) from hitting, enter period 3 hooked, and because he always hits in period 3, get his third-largest payoff (17) then. If he refrains in period 2 (when unhooked), he gets his second-largest payoff (25), enters period 3 unhooked, and gets his largest payoff (35) when he hits then. So his choice is between hitting and getting his largest payoff immediately and his third-largest payoff in the future, or refraining and getting his second-largest payoff immediately and his largest payoff in the future. Because Tim is fairly patient between periods 2 and 3, he prefers to refrain in period 2, when unhooked. He cares enough about the future to make entering period 3 unhooked in his best interest.

Now, what happens if Tim enters period 2 hooked? The line of reasoning is similar, but the payoffs are different. If he hits in period 2, he gets his third-largest payoff (17), enters period 3 hooked, and gets his third-largest payoff (17) again. If he refrains in period 2, he gets his worst payoff (0), enters period 3 unhooked, hits, and gets his largest payoff (35). Once again, because he is fairly patient between the two periods, he prefers to refrain in period 2 when hooked. It doesn't matter if Tim is unhooked or hooked in period 2— it's in his best interest to refrain in that period because he is patient enough to wait for the large payoff he will get in period 3 when he enters it unhooked and chooses to hit.

So now Tim has his final, and most important, decision to make. So far, all his decisions have been hypothetical: what will he do in the future? Now he must ask himself: What will I do in period 1 knowing that I will refrain in period 2 and hit in period 3? He realizes that how he behaves in period 1 will affect his period 2 payoff. If he hits in period 1 (assuming that he is unhooked in period 1), he will get his largest payoff (35) immediately, enter period 2 hooked, refrain, and get his lowest payoff (0) then. If he refrains in period 1, he gets his second-largest payoff (25), enters period 2 unhooked, refrains, and gets his second-largest payoff (25) again. As it turns out, again because he is fairly patient between periods, it will be in his best interest to refrain in period 1, so as to enter period 2 unhooked.

In actuality, what we are doing is looking at the current-value (that is, properly discounted) payoffs of all of Tim's possible consumption paths. He knows that current behavior affects future payoffs, and he knows exactly how he will behave in the future given all the possible paths he can follow. In this example, Tim's best consumption path is to refrain in period 1, refrain in period 2, and hit in period 3. Not only is this a rational decision from period 1's perspective, but because Tim is time consistent, he will follow through and make the future consumption choices he currently plans on making. He can exhibit self-control in the first two periods even when, *on an isolated per-period basis*, it is in his best interest to always hit. The behavioral link across time allows Tim to curb his addictive urges, at least early on.

Naive Nate

Nate is time inconsistent. This means he is more patient between two future adjacent periods than he is between a current period and the next one. And this isn't the only difference between Nate and Tim. In thinking about his future consumption path, Nate asks himself a different starting question than Tim asks. Nate asks himself: From *period 1's* perspective, should I hit or refrain in period 3? It is important to recognize the difference between Tim's and Nate's questions. Tim has the ability to think of himself as being in period 3 and deciding what he should do. He starts at the end of the consumption path and works backward. Nate lacks this ability. Nate does think about what to do in the future, but he thinks about it from the current period 1 perspective. So when Nate compares period 2 and period 3, for him they are *both* future periods. When Tim compares period 2 and period 3, he can think of period 2 as the current period and period 3 as the *only* future period. This difference in how they think about their consumption paths will lead to a slight difference in how they behave.

When Nate thinks about period 3 from period 1's perspective, he recognizes that, by the nature of the example, he will want to hit no matter what. So as of today, he expects to hit in period 3. Now he needs to think about what to do in period 2. At this point, he must make an almost identical calculation to Tim's. Without going through all the comparative payoffs again, we know that Nate is fairly patient between periods 2 and 3 because he thinks about them as two future periods. As with Tim, that patience gives him the incentive to refrain in period 2 and enter period 3 unhooked and receive the largest payoff (35) from hitting then.

Now Nate gets to make his period 1 decision. From his calculations, he believes he will refrain in period 2 and hit in period 3. And even though he is fairly impatient between periods 1 and 2, if he enters period 2 hooked, he gets the lowest payoff (0) when he refrains then. Thus, it will be in Nate's best interest to refrain in period 1. Putting it all together, Nate believes his best consumption path is to refrain in period 1, refrain in period 2, and hit in period 3.

From period 1's perspective, Nate believes he will follow the same path that Tim follows. So at this point in the story, Tim and Nate are making the same consumption choices. But there is a key difference. By being time consistent, Tim *correctly* believes he will follow through and make the choices he planned on making. Nate, on the other hand, *incorrectly* believes he will follow through and make the choices he planned on making. Because he is time inconsistent, he will discover, to his dismay, that he changes his plans when the future becomes his present.

Nate does refrain in period 1 and enters period 2 unhooked. If he refrains again, he gets the second-largest payoff (25) in period 2, and the largest payoff (35) in period 3 when he hits. If he hits in period 2, he gets the largest payoff (35) then, enters period 3 hooked, hits, and gets the third-largest payoff (17). But when actually in period 2, period 3 is now the next period for him, and he heavily discounts between his current period and the next one. In this case, Nate finds that the immediate gratification of hitting in period 2 outweighs the future gratification of entering period 3 unhooked and getting the largest payoff. Nate finds it in his best interest to hit in period 2 and does *not* follow the consumption path he initially planned on following.

In period 3, Nate hits no matter what (as does everyone in this example). This has Nate following a consumption path of refraining in period 1, hitting in period 2, and hitting in period 3. Nate ends up hitting more often than Tim, who hits only in period 3. In period 2, Nate realized it was no longer in his best interest to stick to the plan he made for himself in period 1.

Sophisticated Sophia

Sophia has a little bit of Tim and a little bit of Nate in her. Like Nate, she is time inconsistent. Like Tim, she can think about future choices from the future's perspective, and this allows her to recognize her time-inconsistency problem. But being sophisticated doesn't mean she will consume less of the addictive product than Nate. She actually may be the heaviest user of the three.

Sophia begins her decision process as Tim does. She thinks of herself as being in period 3 and asks if she should hit or refrain, and as we know, she is best off hitting in period 3. Now she thinks of herself in period 2, knowing that she will hit in period 3. At this point, she has the same decision to make that Nate does when he is in period 2. She discounts the next period heavily, so she lacks the incentive to refrain in period 2. Instead, she hits, enters period 3 hooked, and hits again. Her immediate gratification in period 2 weighs heavier for her than her future gratification would have had she entered period 3 unhooked.

Knowing that she will hit in period 2 and again in period 3, how does Sophia behave in period 1? Unlike Nate, who incorrectly believes he will refrain in period 2, Sophia *knows* she will hit in period 2. If she refrains in period 1, she will get the second-largest payoff (25), enter period 2 unhooked, hit, and get the largest payoff. But because she is time inconsistent, she heavily discounts period 2 when she is making her decision in period 1. If Sophia hits in period 1, she gets a large payoff (35) immediately and a smaller payoff in period 2. But the instant gratification is important to her. Furthermore, the habit-forming properties of the addictive good mean there is even less reason for her to refrain in period 1. If she enters period 2 unhooked, hitting gives her only a little more payoff. But if she enters period 2 hooked, hitting is more tempting to her. And she knows she is going to hit in period 2 anyway. Sophia's consumption path is to hit in period 1, hit in period 2, and hit in period 3. Of the three in this example, she is the only one who exhibits no self-control in any period.

Why does sophistication lead to enhanced addictive behavior compared to naiveté? The reason involves the concept of pessimism among sophisticated addicts. Because the payoffs from consuming the addictive good depend on behavior in other periods, Sophia recognizes that because she will hit in the future, it is in her best interest to hit currently. This may seem unusual. Why should Sophia be pessimistic about the future? Why can't she merely avoid hitting in future periods? Remember, in this model, each person is rational in the sense that he or she chooses the action that yields the greatest (properly discounted) current payoff. By the nature of the numerical example, it is in Sophia's best interest to hit in periods 2 and 3, thus making it in her best interest to hit in period 1. By understanding her future behavior, her current optimal choice is to consume the addictive good. Nate, on the other hand, incorrectly believes he will refrain in period 2, so from period 1's perspective, he isn't so pessimistic about the future. He *believes* it is in his best interest to refrain in period 1, even though his belief turns out to be false. Nate's naiveté leads him to consume less of the addictive good than Sophia's sophistication does.

So far, Tim uses the least amount of the addictive good, Nate uses more, and Sophia uses the most. While it may seem that time-inconsistent behavior enhances the use of an addictive good compared to time-consistent behavior, that is the result of only this example. Many other possible scenarios can be considered. In general, however, Nate will tend to consume more of the addictive good than Tim will. Nate's naive belief about good future behavior often has him consuming too much in earlier periods. But Sophia, like Tim, may also end up being a light user. By recognizing her time inconsistency, she may exhibit self-control in her current behavior to avoid bad future outcomes, as she did for the printer rebate. But this may not always be the case.

Sophisticated Sophia faces a very intricate trade-off across periods. By the definition of rational addiction, an addictive good is one in which current and future consumption complement each other. Sophia recognizes two contradictory patterns. On the one hand, an increase in her future consumption of the addictive good may lead her to increase her current consumption as well. This is the pessimism effect discussed above. On the other hand, a reduction in her current consumption may lead to a reduction in her future consumption, giving her an incentive to practice self-control. Which effect dominates depends on the story we want to tell, but both are possible. The conclusion, regardless, is that addictive behavior can vary across addicts, and this will have important public policy implications.

More Addiction Theories

Economic models of addiction often use the time-consistent rational addict as the jumping-off point for more elaborate models of behavior. While time inconsistency is the challenge most often made to the standard rational-addiction model, it is not the only one. This chapter concludes with brief discussions of some of these alternative models.

Learning and Regret

Another model of addiction (Orphanides and Zervos, 1995) accounts for regret being experienced by a time-consistent addict. Rational addicts are often fully informed of all the costs and benefits of their actions, in the present and in the future. But what if they do not have perfect foresight? Inexperienced smokers or drug users, for example, may not truly appreciate the full impact of their current behavior on their future health. As they consume the good, however, they may develop a better understanding of its effect on themselves. The more they use the good, the more they learn about its potential harm.

In this model, the good does not become addictive until a critical amount of it is consumed. For example, if you smoke one cigarette a day, even for many years, you may never experience the habit-forming and reduction-of-well-being properties of a typical addictive good. But if you work your way up to a pack or more a day, then the common properties associated with addiction may kick in. Furthermore, this model assumes that addiction is strictly a harmful activity.

The authors consider three types in this framework. The first type is fully aware of the addictive nature of the good and of the critical level required for the addictive properties to kick in. This type chooses to be a light user of the good, meaning that he or she never consumes beyond the critical level. The second type is not, at first, aware of the addictive nature of the good or of the critical level. But with continued use that falls short of the critical level, this type may learn in time to slow down or reverse consumption of the good. The third type does not learn of the good's addictive nature before the critical level is reached. This type may unknowingly become harmfully addicted to the good, thus experiencing regret over past consumption decisions.

Projection Bias

In the previous model, the person could be uncertain about the degree of the harmful effects of the addictive good and of the critical level of consumption that has the addictive properties of the good kick in. But this is not the only type of uncertainty. In another model (Loewenstein, O'Donoghue, and Rabin, 2003), it is extremely common for preferences to change over time, not only in the long run but also in the immediate short run. People may anticipate these preference changes, but how accurate are these anticipations? An example can illustrate this point.

You take your family to a nice restaurant. You are all extremely hungry as you think about how much food to order. You know that as you eat your meal you will start to feel less hungry. Thus, your preferences for eating will change throughout the course of the meal, and you recognize the direction of that change. What you don't anticipate, however, is the magnitude of the change. Because you are very hungry now, you may believe that you will be hungrier in the future than you actually will be. You tend to exaggerate the degree to which your future preferences will resemble your current preferences. This is known as *projection bias*. The implication of such bias in this setting is that you may order more food at the start of your meal than you will be hungry for at the end of your meal.

In the context of addiction, projection bias has two key effects. First, an addict may understand that her future well-being may deteriorate as she continues to consume the good, but she may underestimate how much it will deteriorate. Second, an addict may understand the habit-forming properties of an addictive good but may underestimate the strength of this effect. Both of these biases can lead to overconsumption of the addictive good.

Projection bias with addiction may also help explain some of the difficulties in trying to quit consuming the addictive good. Imagine a short-run change in your preference for smoking. You have a stressful event in your life, and you increase your current consumption. Using the economic definition of addiction, this current increase in consumption leads to an increase in future consumption, long after the stressful event has passed. But projection bias may enhance this effect. Because you are experiencing greater cravings now, you may believe your future cravings will be greater, even though they may be much less. Because of the pessimism effect, your biased anticipation of future cravings may discourage you from trying to slow down or quit now.

The bias effect can also work the other way around. If you currently experience very low cravings for the addictive good, you may believe you will experience lower cravings in the future than you actually will. This bias may encourage you to attempt to quit, but you have an increased chance of relapsing when you discover your future cravings turn out to be higher than you anticipated. In all, projection bias can seriously alter an addict's consumption path for an addictive good.

Temptation and Self-Control

In the standard rational-addiction model, a time-consistent addict does not have to take any particular measures to control himself from consuming the addictive good. He doesn't have to flush his cigarettes down the toilet or avoid walking into stores that sell cigarettes. If he feels it is in his best interest to smoke, he will. If he feels it is not in his best interest to smoke, he won't. As we saw above, even when the payoff from hitting exceeds the payoff from refraining on a *per-period* basis, the time-consistent addict may not hit in every period because he recognizes that being hooked reduces future payoffs. He exhibits self-control in the sense that he may refrain in the present to enhance his future well-being.

In a refinement to the standard model (Gul and Pesendorfer, 2001), a time-consistent person may plan on exercising self-control by committing in an earlier period to avoid future temptations. Another restaurant example can help explain this concept. Consider a two-period story about deciding where to eat lunch. You wake up in the morning (period 1) and commit at that time to where you will go for lunch (period 2) later that day. You have three choices: the restaurant that has an all-vegetarian menu, the restaurant that has an all-hamburger menu, or the restaurant that has both vegetarian meals and hamburgers on their menu. You have a preference ranking for the three restaurants. As you are trying to be good and watch your weight, you prefer the vegetarian restaurant over the hamburger place. Furthermore, because the restaurant that offers you both options allows you still to be good and not eat a hamburger, you prefer that restaurant to the hamburger place. The interesting preference comparison is between the vegetarian restaurant and the one that offers both options. If you can eat a vegetarian meal at either restaurant, is there a reason to prefer the one that restricts your choices, or are you indifferent between the two (assuming the food is the same price and equally good at both places)?

In the typical economic model, adding an irrelevant choice to a menu should have no effect on preference. You want to eat a vegetarian meal, so why should it matter if there are nonvegetarian options on the menu? It shouldn't. But in this story, the hamburger presents a temptation to you. In the morning, when thinking about where to eat lunch, you may have your mind set on having a vegetarian meal. But at lunchtime, when you are at the restaurant, the availability of a hamburger on the menu may tempt you away from the vegetarian meal. In this setting, you can exhibit two types of self-control.

The first type of self-control occurs in period 2. If you go the restaurant with both food options, you may still resist temptation and consume the vegetarian meal. But resisting temptation imposes a cost on you because it forces you to make a difficult choice. Instead, you may commit to go to the all-vegetarian restaurant so you don't have the temptation of a hamburger. This form of self-control occurs in period 1. If you choose to commit in period 1 to avoiding the restaurant that offers both choices, you are demonstrating a preference for the narrow menu that includes only vegetarian meals over the broader menu that also includes hamburgers. In other words, you are clearly demonstrating that the addition of the hamburger to the menu makes you *worse off*, even if you can choose not to order it.

Committing in period 1 to avoid temptation in period 2 sounds a lot like something a sophisticated time-inconsistent person such as Sophia would do. Recall the computer printer rebate example. Sophia recognized that she would not follow through and submit the rebate request, so she avoided that problem by not buying the printer in the first place. In this restaurant example, Sophia may recognize that if she goes to the restaurant with the hamburger option, she may succumb to temptation even though she preferred not to from the morning's perspective. By committing to go to the all-vegetarian restaurant, she avoids facing that temptation. As for Nate, the naive time-inconsistent person, from his morning's perspective he may well believe he will resist temptation if he goes to the restaurant with both options, only to find he also succumbs. Nate does not commit to the all-vegetarian restaurant. Why should he? He naively believes he is time consistent.

This model of temptation, however, does not rely on the assumption of time inconsistency to motivate commitment in period 1. If you are time consistent and decide in the morning to have lunch at the all-vegetarian restaurant, that is where you will go for lunch. If you decide to go to the restaurant that offers both options and order the vegetarian meal, that is precisely what you will do. The key point to this story is that you may prefer to exhibit self-control in period 1, rather than in period 2, *even when you will consistently avoid the temptation in period 2*. This is an unusual result and bears repeating. Using the authors' own words:

> Decision makers with self-control will expend resources to remove tempting alternatives from their choice sets even if they do not expect to succumb to the temptation in the future. (Gul and Pesendorfer, 2001, 1420)

Thus, removing irrelevant alternatives, which are nevertheless tempting, has the potential to make you better off. You practice self-control in this case, not to avoid the temptation itself, but to avoid the cost of having to make the decision to avoid temptation.

Addiction and Cues

In another theory of addiction (Laibson, 2001), an environmental cue triggers the desire to consume an addictive good. For example, a recovering heroin addict may be successfully resisting her temptation to use the drug, but she one day bumps into old friends who used to abuse the drug with her. The interaction with these friends or the memories they recall trigger a desire to consume the drug again. In this setting, cues and current consumption complement each other. Cues related to past consumption may trigger a change in preference or behavior that affects current consumption. The sight of an opened pack of cigarettes, the sound of a bottle of beer being opened, the sight of a dessert tray as you enter a restaurant may each trigger a stronger desire to smoke, drink, or eat sweets than the desire felt just moments before.

Explicit acts of self-control are expected to play a role in this setting. By exhibiting self-control in avoiding certain cues, the addict reduces her craving for addictive goods. Avoiding social situations where addictive products are available or purposely not keeping cigarettes or alcohol or junk food in the house, even if it is possible to consume these goods in moderation, are examples of self-control methods. This is in contrast to the standard rational-addiction story in which the time-consistent addict always optimally chooses to consume or not consume addictive goods. For this addict, there is no reason to diverge from his consumption path by avoiding cues that trigger cravings. Any cravings for addictive goods are anticipated and rationally acted on.

Addiction as a Mistake

An interesting extension of the cue model of addiction (Bernheim and Rangel, 2004) has three premises. The first is that use by addicts is often a mistake. The second premise is that past consumption of an addictive good can sensitize an addict to environmental cues that trigger mistaken usage. And the third premise is that addicts, to some degree, are sophisticated in that they understand these cue-triggered mistakes and may attempt to exhibit self-control. This sounds similar to the preliminary discussion of cues above, with one key difference.

In the original cue model, the addict does not make mistakes. A cue in that case triggers a change in preference or behavior, but that change implies a different rational act caused by enhanced cravings, not a mistaken act. In the authors' own words:

> We argue that these premises find strong support in evidence from psychology, neuroscience, and clinical practice. In particular, research has shown that addictive substances systematically interfere with the proper operation of an important class of processes which the brain uses to forecast near-term hedonic rewards (pleasure), and this leads to strong, misguided, cue-conditioned impulses that often defeat the higher cognitive control. (Bernheim and Rangel, 2004, 1559)

What is meant by a *mistake* here is a divergence between choice and preference. To help explain their model, the authors provide the following analogy. It's not unusual for Americans visiting the United Kingdom to get hit by automobiles because they tend to look left to see approaching traffic, even though they know that in the United Kingdom traffic approaches from the right. They choose to look left, even though they must obviously prefer to look right. Thus, the decision to look left is a mistake. Basically, the brain is on automatic, with a lifetime of conditioning suggesting that looking left is the safe choice to make. In this case, the decision-making process is incredibly fast and possibly fatally wrong.

Many models of addiction allow for mistakes in the sense that the addict can come to regret past consumption decisions. An addict who is time inconsistent, or one who does not have perfect foresight of the harmful effects of the addictive good, can easily experience regret some time in the future. But in all of the models discussed above, rational behavior always underlies all decisions. Time-inconsistent people maximize their current discounted payoffs whenever they make a choice to hit or refrain. They make optimal choices in early periods, but as time progresses, they make different optimal choices that may veer from the original consumption path. Addicts who lack perfect foresight make optimal choices *given* the imperfect information they are considering.

In this model of addiction, the concept of a mistake is much stronger:

> Addicts often describe past use as a mistake in a very strong sense: they think that they would have been better off *in the past as well as the present* had they acted differently. They recognize that they are likely to make similar errors in

the future, and that this will undermine their desire to abstain. When they succumb to cravings, they sometimes characterize choices as mistakes *even while in the act of consumption*. (Bernheim and Rangel, 2004, 1560; emphasis in original)

This depiction of an addict's mistaken behavior provides a very strong challenge not only to the standard rational-addiction model but to pretty much every economic model of addiction that has at its core the notion of rational behavior.

Sophistication in this story has the addict taking strong measures to prevent herself from consuming the addictive good. Sophia, our sophisticated time-inconsistent addict, recognized her time-inconsistency problem and, in certain cases, exhibited self-control by not consuming the good. In this story, however, the sophisticated addict is much more proactive. She takes measures to avoid cues to circumvent cravings but realizes that cravings are inevitable. In this case, exhibiting self-control may mean the addict commits herself to an extended-stay treatment program to prevent access to the addictive good or has family and friends physically restrain her from consuming the good. At times the difference may be subtle, only in degree, between self-control to avoid a craving and self-control to deal with a craving that occurs.

With the existence of all the economic models discussed in this chapter (and the many others not discussed), public policy advice is often complex and conflicting. While some economists still rely on the standard rational-addiction model, others have attempted to refine and (in their opinion) improve on the standard model in many useful ways. And to a growing number of economists, truly innovative models that challenge economic reasoning at its rational core offer nothing short of a revolutionary approach to the economic analysis of addiction. In the next three chapters we will examine in detail specific acts of indulgence—smoking, drinking, and overeating—and then in chapter 5 examine how the economic theories of addiction can be used to justify real-world policy interventions meant to protect people from themselves.

Suggested Readings

The seminal paper on rational addiction is by Becker and Murphy (1988). The economic model of addiction presented in detail is drawn from O'Donoghue and Rabin (1999b). These last two authors have been influential in developing several formal models of addictive and related behavior. See O'Donoghue and Rabin (1999a, 2000, 2001a, 2001b, 2002).

The additional economic models of addiction discussed, and some related material, can be found in Orphanides and Zervos (1995, 1998), Loewenstein, O'Donoghue, and Rabin (2003), Loewenstein (1996), Gul and Pesendorfer (2001, 2007), Laibson (2001), and Bernheim and Rangel (2004).

Examples of models not discussed can be found in Dockner and Feichtinger (1993), Quiggin (2001), Carrillo (2005), Alamar and Glantz (2006), Beshears et al. (2006), Fudenberg and Levine (2006), Manzini and Mariotti (2006), Rasmusen (2008b), Wang (2007), and Glazer and Weiss (2007).

Other interesting papers on the economics of addiction are by Skog (1999), Ferguson (2000), Gruber and Koszegi (2001), Rogeberg (2004), and Yuengert (2006).

A discussion of time inconsistency and rebates can be found in Gilpatric (2009).

2

SMOKING CAN KILL YOU

While celebrity endorsements are extremely common, in modern times you don't see many celebrities endorsing cigarettes. In the 1950s, however, it wasn't uncommon to see a big star smiling at you from a magazine advertisement for cigarettes. Consider the advertisement in *Life*, June 27, 1955, featuring beautiful screen star Maureen O'Hara (of *The Hunchback of Notre Dame*, *How Green Was My Valley*, *Miracle on 34th Street*, *The Quiet Man*, and many other films) lying back, relaxing, with a lit cigarette in her hand and a big smile on her face. The copy reads:

> How's your disposition today? Feel cross as a bear? That's natural when little annoyances pile up. But the psychological fact is: pleasure helps your disposition. That's why everyday pleasures, like smoking for instance, are important. If you're a smoker, you're wise to choose the cigarette that gives you the most pleasure. That means Camel. As lovely Maureen O'Hara knows, it's wise to choose a cigarette for the pleasure it gives.

But did lovely Maureen O'Hara know precisely what chemicals were in her pleasurable cigarettes?

Cigarettes contain hundreds of chemicals, but let's just highlight a few of the more impressive-sounding ones: acetic acid, aconitic acid, ammonia, amyl alcohol, ascorbic acid, benzaldehyde, benzyl alcohol, butyric acid, caffeine, carbon dioxide, cellulose fiber, cuminaldehyde, decanoic acid, diethyl malonate, ethyl oleate, ethyl salicylate, geranyl acetate, glycerol, hexanoic acid, hexyl alcohol, isoamyl benzoate, isobutyl alcohol, lactic acid, linalool oxide, malic acid, menthyl acetate, octyl isobutyrate, palmitic acid, phenenthyl alcohol, phenylacetaldehyde, potassium sorbate, pyridine, sodium chloride, sodium hydroxide, tannic acid, terpinyl acetate, valeraldehyde, and so on (http://quitsmoking.about.com/cs/nicotineinhaler/a/cigingredients_3 .htm).

You may have no idea what most of these chemical are or how dangerous they are in the amounts found in cigarettes, but most of them don't sound particularly appealing. And of the over 4,000 chemical compounds emitted by a burning cigarette, 69 of them are known to cause cancer. Cigarettes may be the most notorious (legal) product sold today. Antismoking advocates are extremely vocal, and restrictions on smoking seem to increase daily. And why should this be surprising? Smoking is unhealthy, not only to the smoker but also to those exposed to secondhand smoke. More succinctly, smoking imposes substantial costs on the smoker and others. But with all this talk and worry about the costs of smoking, we never seem to hear much about the other side of the story—the benefits of smoking.

What about the Benefits?

To an economist, the words *costs* and *benefits* go together like hot dogs and hot dog buns. We can't think of one without thinking of the other. From a public policy perspective, cost-benefit analysis compares all the costs and benefits of a proposed policy to determine its ultimate usefulness. When asked, many people have a difficult time identifying the benefits of smoking. Yet approximately 22 percent of the world's adult population smokes, which is close to the US rate (Naurath and Jones, 2007). Some countries with the highest smoking rates are Cuba (40 percent), Kuwait, Chile, Russia, Belarus, Bangladesh (all 37 percent), Estonia, Latvia, Azerbaijan, and Indonesia (all 36 percent). Some countries with the lowest smoking rates are Nigeria (6 percent), El Salvador, Ghana (both 8 percent), Afghanistan, and Ethiopia (both 9 percent). With just that data, it is a daunting task to argue that there are *no* benefits to an activity that so many people undertake.

We could try to figure out precisely what the benefits are—the physical satisfaction a smoker experiences, the psychological satisfaction, or maybe the smoker simply looks good with a cigarette. To an economist, however, knowing why a smoker smokes is not of primary interest. Without precisely identifying the benefits of smoking, one simple fact allows us to know, without a doubt, that there are benefits: smokers buy cigarettes.

If Dick pays $4 for a pack of cigarettes, it must be the case that Dick values that pack at a minimum of $4. Dick may value his pack more, maybe even a lot more, but he can't value it less. If he did, he wouldn't pay the $4. Explaining why someone pays for something they don't receive any benefits from is a futile task. If they buy it, they value it, regardless of why they value it. And value is, always has been and always will be, a subjective concept. Jane may not value the pack of cigarettes at $4. She may not value the pack at 1¢. But it is not Jane's valuation that we are interested in right now. It is Dick's. It is quite common to look at other people's purchases and be critical of what they are buying. But the only value that matters is that of the actual purchaser.

From a cost-benefit perspective, there are legitimate ways to justify policy intervention to control smoking. First, after identifying and measuring as many costs and benefits as possible, one can argue that the costs of smoking exceed the benefits and restrictions are warranted from a social policy point of view. It doesn't necessarily matter how you measure the costs and benefits. It may be with very sophisticated statistical techniques, or it may be in a very casual manner. But if a weighing of the costs and benefits yields net costs, you have a simple justification for intervention.

Second, you may not care about the benefits of smoking and not include them in any cost-benefit calculations. Identifying costs and benefits is one thing, but deciding which costs and benefits matter to you is another thing entirely. What matters from a social policy perspective is subjective. Everyone's view of the world is his or her own view. Economists tend to be inclusive, often including all identifiable and measurable costs and benefits in any social policy assessment. But if you don't believe that a certain class of benefits, or a certain class of costs, is relevant for deciding on social policy, so be it. There is no such thing as a correct policy objective. If you don't care about smokers' benefits, then obviously you are far more likely to be in favor of smoking restrictions. But notice, not caring about smokers' benefits and not believing there are such benefits are two completely different things. If you argue that smoking has no benefits, you are factually incorrect. It is important to emphasize that nowhere in the literature on the economics of smoking does anyone argue that smoking is a healthy activity. Quite the contrary. What many economists do argue, however, is that smoking yields benefits to the smoker, and these benefits may very well more than offset the costs.

It's What You Know

So why do people smoke? They must believe that their personal benefits of smoking outweigh their costs, and they find it worthwhile to spend money on cigarettes. But one counter to this simple explanation of smoking is that, regardless of the benefits, smokers may smoke because they *misperceive* the true costs of smoking. If smokers believe smoking is less dangerous than it is, their personal cost-benefit calculation is done with imperfect information. This lack of perfect information is often used to justify social policy intervention to restrict smoking. Thus, it is important to examine the risk perceptions of smokers. Do they, on average, tend to underestimate the risks of smoking?

It is difficult to believe that smokers are completely unaware of the risks of smoking. Antismoking campaigns, funded by state and private institutions, are very common. With the vast majority of society made up of nonsmokers, smokers routinely face a severe social stigma, bringing constant reminders of the risks of smoking. Even cigarette packaging informs smokers of the risks. In the United States, cigarette packages contain one of four surgeon general warnings about the risks of smoking:

- Smoking causes lung cancer, heart disease, emphysema, and may complicate pregnancy.
- Quitting smoking now greatly reduces serious risks to your health.
- Smoking by pregnant women may result in fetal injury, premature birth, and low birth weight.
- Cigarette smoke contains carbon monoxide.

Each of these warnings is prominently preceded in capital letters by the words SURGEON GENERAL'S WARNING.

Cigarettes sold in Canada have a greater number of warnings, and they are more prominently displayed on the packaging compared to the US warnings. The title of this chapter is one of the warnings printed in large letters on Canadian cigarette packages. Currently, Canada has several other warnings, including the following:

- Cigarettes cause mouth diseases.
- Each year, the equivalent of a small city dies from tobacco use.

- Cigarettes cause strokes.
- Tobacco use can make you impotent.

In addition to the warning labels, Canadian packages display images to further warn of the health risks of smoking. The first warning above accompanies an image of a diseased mouth. The last warning has a flaccid cigarette. Many of the other images are striking, showing a diseased brain, a diseased heart, a dirty ashtray overflowing with cigarette butts, and so on. The images and labels cover 50 percent of the packaging.

Many other countries use similar mandatory warnings on their cigarette packages. Here are some examples:

- Smoking causes blindness. (Australia)
- Smoking shortens your life. (Croatia)
- Smoking makes your skin age. (Germany)
- Smoking can cause a slow and painful death. (Czech Republic)
- Smoking can damage the sperm and decreases fertility. (Finland)
- Cigarettes contain benzene, nistrosamine, formaldehyde and hydrocyanic acid. (Italy)

And this is only a very small sample of the warnings on cigarette packaging throughout the world.

In light of all these warnings, smokers must have at least some knowledge about the health costs of smoking. But having some knowledge does not preclude the possibility that smokers still *under*estimate the true health risks of smoking. And the implications of risk underestimation are quite serious.

In deciding to purchase a package of cigarettes, you not only pay an explicit monetary price but also an implicit health risk price. Let's say a pack of cigarettes costs $4 at the store. Furthermore, assume each pack of cigarettes imposes an additional $2 health risk on you. What this means is that if cigarettes increase your health costs, those health costs can be averaged out to $2 per pack. The full cost of the pack of cigarettes to you is $6, made up of the monetary costs and the implicit health costs. If perfectly informed, you would buy the pack of cigarettes only if you value it at a minimum of $6. This would be a well-informed rational decision by you.

But now let's say you underestimate the true health costs of a pack of cigarettes, believing it to be only $1 instead of the true $2. From your perspective, the full cost is only $5. If you value the pack of cigarettes at $5.50, for example, you will purchase it even though your value is less than the true, full cost of $6. You purchase the pack only because of your underestimation of the risk. It is precisely this sort of behavior that provides a justification for policy intervention to discourage you from smoking. Unfortunately, the problem of imperfect information has a flip side: What if you *over*estimate the true risk of smoking?

Let's say you believe the health risk is $3 a pack, instead of the true $2 a pack. From your perspective, the full cost of the pack of cigarettes is $7. If you value the pack at $6.50, for example, you will not buy it, even though you would if you understood the true, full cost of $6. Thus, overestimation of risk prevents you from buying the pack of cigarettes. In this case, an economist can ask an unusual question: From a social policy perspective, should you be *encouraged* to purchase the pack of cigarettes?

Public policies designed to discourage smoking are common, while policies designed to encourage smoking are nonexistent. Yet if the justification for the intervention is lack of perfect information, there may not be much sense to this asymmetric policy stance. If you are misinformed, and the objective is to have you behave *as if* you were perfectly informed, the only thing that remains is to determine precisely how you are misinformed. If you underestimate the risk of smoking, the perfectly informed you would smoke less. If you overestimate the risk of smoking, the perfectly informed you would smoke more. Because we do not see policies designed to encourage you to smoke more, it must be for one of two reasons: either you never overestimate the risk of smoking, or the objective is not to have you behave as if you were perfectly informed but to always encourage you to smoke less. So the key question is do smokers tend to underestimate or overestimate the true risks of smoking?

Smoking and Risk Perceptions

An early study (Viscusi, 1990) on assessing smokers' risk perceptions provides a good example of how survey data can be used to compare risk perceptions to true risk levels. In a sample made up of over 3,000 people, each was asked the following question: Among 100 cigarette smokers, how many of them do you think will get lung cancer because they smoke? The answer to this question was an average of 42.6, for a perceived lung cancer probability of 42.6 percent. At the time of the study, the true lung cancer rate was 5 to 10 percent. Thus, on the basis of this study, people tend to overestimate the true risk of smoking, as least with respect to the risk of contracting lung cancer.

Similar results are found for slightly different risk assessments. In asking about the overall mortality risk of smoking (deaths from lung cancer, heart disease, throat cancer, and any other fatal illness associated with smoking), once again people tend to overestimate the true risk of smoking. Also, when asked about life-expectancy loss due to smoking, people tend to perceive this loss as larger than the available scientific evidence suggests it is. Furthermore, this tendency to overestimate the risks of smoking holds true for both smokers and nonsmokers and for young smokers (between ages 16 and 21), who appear to overestimate the risks of smoking more than those in older age groups (Viscusi, 1991). While it may not be surprising that nonsmokers overestimate the risks, which is a possible explanation for their being nonsmokers to begin with, smokers themselves overestimating the risks suggests that they highly value smoking. They perceive the full price of a pack of cigarettes to be higher than the true, full price, yet they still purchase the pack.

The above assessment of risk perceptions has been seriously challenged, particularly in the writings of one scholar (Slovic, 1998, 2000a, 2000b). He finds four failings in the previous study's analysis. The first is that accounting for a risk assessment in terms of a smoker's probability of getting lung cancer in his or her lifetime is only part of the story. Smokers must perceive not only the probabilities of the risks they face but the severity of the risks. For example, let's accept as fact that the average smoker grossly overestimates the risk of getting lung cancer in his or her lifetime. This fact alone suggests that smokers are smoking too little compared to how much they would smoke if they understood the true risk. But what if the average smoker also grossly underestimates the true costs of getting lung cancer? By that fact alone, smokers may be smoking too much compared to how much they would smoke if they understood the true severity of lung cancer. In other words, overestimating the risk of lung cancer while underestimating its severity may leave the smoker overestimating, underestimating, or correctly perceiving the full cost of getting lung cancer from smoking.

The second failing has to do with *optimism bias*. The above survey question asks the respondent how many smokers out of 100 will get lung cancer. The question does not ask the respondent for the probability that she herself will get lung cancer from smoking. When a person believes his or her personal risk is less than the risk to others facing the same situation, that is known as optimism bias. You may believe 50 people out of 100 will get lung cancer if they are lifetime smokers but that you yourself have only a 5 percent probability. When the optimism bias is in effect, people overestimate the general risk of smoking but underestimate their personal risk.

The third failing is the most elaborate of the four. Even if smokers overestimate the risk of smoking at some point in their life, is there an earlier time (such as adolescence) when smokers don't appreciate how the risks of smoking are *cumulative* over their lifetime? Smoking can be thought of as a series of single acts, with one cigarette at a time eventually adding up to literally hundreds of thousands of cigarettes smoked in a lifetime. How do young smokers perceive the short-term risks of smoking, before the cumulative effect brings them into the long term?

Consider the following results of a survey of high school students in Oregon. The students are divided into three groups—nonsmokers, light smokers (five or fewer cigarettes a day), and heavy smokers (six or more cigarettes a day). When asked if smoking a pack of cigarettes a day will eventually harm a person's health, nearly every respondent in each group agreed with that statement. When asked if every single cigarette smoked causes a "little bit of harm," again nearly every respondent in each group agreed. But when asked about risks in the short term, the groups differed in their responses.

When asked whether there is really no risk from smoking in the first few years, or whether only the very next single cigarette will probably not cause harm, or whether the harmful effects of smoking rarely occur until a person has smoked for many years, a greater proportion of smokers (light and heavy) than nonsmokers agree with those statements. Thus, adolescent smokers are relatively more likely to deny short-term risks compared to nonsmokers, even though all the respondents recognize the long-term risks associated with smoking.

The potential failure of young smokers to recognize the short-term risks of smoking leads to the fourth and final failing. Recall the learning and regret model (Orphanides and Zervos, 1995) of addiction discussed in chapter 1. It is possible that a misinformed smoker may realize too late in life that he reached some critical amount of smoking that has now caused him to become addicted to cigarettes. Addiction can often lead to regret, even for smokers who tend to overestimate the risks of smoking.

But the debate does not end here. There have been responses to these concerns (Viscusi, 2000). While it is true that assessing probability and severity is important when studying risk perceptions, people generally have an implicit (if not explicit) understanding of the severity of lung cancer or other smoking-related illnesses. Whether they over- or underestimate the true severity of an illness such as lung cancer is an open-ended question, but it is unlikely many would classify lung cancer as a light illness.

Next, while the concept of optimism bias is interesting and has much empirical support in many settings, the key issue here is whether it comes into play when assessing perceived smoking risks. One interesting study (Khwaja et al., 2009) examines the risk perceptions of mature smokers—that is, those between ages 50 and 70. Among the issues the study examines, one is of great interest for our purposes: How accurate are smokers' beliefs compared to nonsmokers' about the mortality, disease, and disability risks of smoking? Can mature smoking behavior be attributed to differential risk perceptions?

The study finds that mature smokers are *not* overly optimistic in perception of future health risks. In this age group, smokers and nonsmokers have fairly accurate risk perceptions about their chance of surviving to age 75 and the physical difficulties they will encounter. Furthermore, they are highly pessimistic about their chances for serious chronic diseases, such as lung cancer, stroke, or heart problems. This study concludes that mature smokers have fairly objective risk perceptions about their behavior and often pessimistic perceptions, suggesting that they do not continue to smoke because of underestimation of risks. Of course, this does not rule out the possibility of optimism bias, especially for young smokers, but it does suggest that such bias is not necessarily exhibited by smokers.

On the other hand, another study (Khwaja, Sloan, and Chung, 2006) examines how smokers develop their risk perceptions of smoking. Using a sample of mature current or former smokers (ages 51 to 61 in 1992) with spouses of any age, the study determines how people assess, on the basis of adverse health shocks they or their spouse experience, their future survival expectations. Interestingly, when a spouse experiences an adverse health shock, the smoker does not perceive the risks to be any different than before and the smoker is not more likely to quit smoking. But when the smoker experiences an adverse health shock, the smoker reconsiders the health risks of smoking and is more likely to quit. In a way, this confirms the existence of optimism bias in that you may not be surprised when bad health outcomes occur in others, but your optimism is shattered when you yourself experience a bad health outcome.

The authors of the previous study suggest a policy implication of their result. They believe that antismoking messages are not likely to be effective in reducing smoking unless the messages can be presented in a manner that is interpreted as highly personal to the smoker. But another study (Hsieh et al., 1996), looking at social policies in Taiwan designed to greatly increase warnings of the adverse health consequences of smoking, finds that such policies have a negative impact on smoking participation rates. However, the authors are careful to point out that the male smoking-participation rate in Taiwan at the time of the study was among the highest in the world (over 50 percent in their sample), and even greater use of antismoking messages would likely reduce the smoking participation rate only to a threshold that is in line with many developed countries (closer to 20 percent). In other words, the effectiveness of antismoking campaigns is likely to be limited.

Yet another study (Hammar and Johansson-Stenman, 2004) approaches risk perception in a totally different way. This Swedish study uses experimental evidence to determine how much smokers are willing to pay for risk-free cigarettes. Each subject is presented with the following scenario:

> Imagine that you have been randomly chosen to try a new type of cigarette that has been developed by Swedish researchers. Everybody else will continue smoking ordinary cigarettes and unless you do not want to, no one will know that you now use a new totally risk-free type. The risk-free cigarette has the same taste as the cigarette you normally smoke. It also looks the same, gives you the same feeling of satisfaction, and neither you nor those around you can distinguish it from an ordinary cigarette. Further, it is also addictive in the same way as ordinary cigarettes and is perceived in the same way by those around you in terms of smoke, smell, eye irritations, etc. However, it is completely harmless for you as well as those around you. Note that it has been proven that the new cigarettes are totally harmless. If you think that this sounds unrealistic, we ask that you answer as if you accept this as a fact. The only problem with the new cigarette is that it is more expensive than the ordinary one.

Then respondents are asked questions relating to how much extra they would be willing to pay for the risk-free cigarettes.

The study offers two main conclusions. The first is that the smokers who participated in their experiment tend to underestimate the risks of smoking. This was determined by their low willingness to pay for the risk-free cigarettes to get the health benefits that would accrue from switching. In other words, smokers likely did not perceive the true risk of smoking, because if they had, they would have been willing to pay more for the risk-free cigarettes. The second conclusion was that optimism bias was likely to have been present at the time the person decided to start smoking. This was found by the response to the following question: When you started smoking, did you believe that you would still be smoking today? As many as 86 percent of the respondents answered no.

As for the cumulative-risk criticism of risk assessments, this depends on one's perspective. What do researchers agree on? There is some consensus that smokers have a good understanding that there may be substantial long-run health costs to smoking. But it's more complicated than that. Let's return to the Oregon high school students who nearly unanimously agreed that every single cigarette smoked causes a "little bit of harm." Is this an accurate perception of the risk of smoking? What is the correct scientific reference point? One estimate considering a pack-a-day smoker for 40 years puts the average mortality rate per cigarette at less than one in a million. Is this a little bit or a lot of harm? Because they agree that each cigarette smoked causes a little bit of harm, does that suggest these Oregon students overestimate or underestimate the long-run risks of smoking? Simply believing that an activity is harmful does not in itself address misperceived risk assessments. There must be a comparison of perceived risks versus true risks.

But even with an understanding of the long-term risks of smoking, do smokers, especially adolescents, underestimate the cumulative risk of smoking because they underestimate the short-term risks? What about the Oregon student smokers who appear to deny the existence of short-term health costs of smoking? They believe that health costs accrue only to people who smoke for many years and that there is little or no cost to smoking for a few years or to smoking the very next cigarette. But does this tell us these students underestimate the short-term risks? Not at all, unless we know what the true short-term risks are. It is very possible that a young healthy body can tolerate smoking for several years with no long-term adverse health effects. And do you believe there is much of a health cost in smoking just one more cigarette? Is it even a meaningful question if there are many next cigarettes to be smoked?

One serious issue can arise because of a belief that smoking poses little or no short-term cost: Can smoking, especially for adolescents, lead them to become addicted? If a young smoker believes smoking has few short-term risks, either correctly perceived or underestimated, this may encourage the initial act of smoking. But what causes the initial act to turn into an addiction? As discussed above and in chapter 1, a smoker may misperceive the risk of a critical threshold that, once reached, leads to a harmful addiction. It is often mentioned that many young smokers, when surveyed, say they are well aware of the difficulties in quitting smoking once begun. But this doesn't mean they are aware of exactly how much smoking can lead to addiction. So a misperception of the risk of becoming addicted, which can be different from a misperception of the health costs of smoking, may be leading to addiction. But there is another explanation that has nothing to do with risk perception. What if young smokers tend to be time inconsistent and naive?

Naive time inconsistency can lead a young smoker to begin smoking with a perfect understanding of all the current and future health costs of smoking yet still become addicted and regret the initial decision to smoke. Naive Nate, from chapter 1, may begin smoking with the sincere intention of quitting in a few years. Recall that he is patient between those future periods, but impatient between the current and the next period. Quitting is the rational choice from an early perspective, but when the future arrives his impatience about the next period discourages him from quitting. So starting to smoke when young with the intention of quitting may involve some risk misperceptions, but it may involve time inconsistency. And these are two very different explanations, especially from a social policy perspective.

If a misunderstanding of the risks of smoking is causing people to begin to smoke, or to smoke too often, or to become addicted, social policy may try to provide information to help smokers reevaluate the risks. But if it is a time-inconsistency problem, providing information about the risks of smoking will not be helpful. There are three types of smokers: those who underestimate the risks of smoking, those who overestimate the risks, and those who are fully informed. There are also various types of addicts: time-consistent ones, naive and sophisticated time-inconsistent ones, and those who may be making mistakes when smoking. Social policy is difficult enough when considering only people who are fairly similar in their behavior, but the tremendous difference across smokers makes it far more intricate and complicated.

Rational Taxation?

In the United States, all 50 states apply an excise tax to cigarettes. Rhode Island leads the way, with the highest tax rate of $3.46 per pack (as of October 2009).

South Carolina has the lowest tax rate, 7¢ per pack. Does this have anything to do with South Carolina being a major tobacco-producing state? Most likely, as the major tobacco states (Georgia, Kentucky, North Carolina, South Carolina, Tennessee, and Virginia) have an average tax rate of 40¢ per pack, compared to the average for the rest of the states of $1.47 per pack. But before you decide which state you want to live in on the basis of cigarette tax rates, you may want to check on other local taxes. For example, New York City adds a $1.50 tax to the New York State tax of $2.75, for the nation's highest state and local tax rate of $4.25 per pack. And as you move around the country trying to avoid high cigarette taxes, don't forget the federal tax rate of $1.01 per pack, raised to that rate from 39¢ per pack by President Barack Obama in 2009 (for cigarette tax information, see http://tobaccofreekids.org).

Cigarette excise taxes are a common policy tool used by governments around the world, and there is often political and social pressure for countries with relatively low tax rates to increase those rates. For example, smoking rates in China are among the world's highest, with 36 percent of China's population above age 15 being smokers. The real (inflation adjusted) price of cigarettes in China has fallen substantially since 1990, leading to increased smoking and increased mortality and health costs. Cigarette tax rates in China are 40 percent of the retail price (as of 2008), which is the lowest rate compared to nearby countries such as Singapore (69 percent of retail price), Philippines and Thailand (63 percent), and Hong Kong and Korea (60 percent). Anti-smoking advocates often point to China as having one of the world's least effective policy stances against smoking (see http://tobaccofreecenter.org).

From an economic perspective, taxation traditionally serves two main public policy goals. The first is to generate revenue for the state to sustain its governing bodies and to enact whatever policies it wishes to enact. The second is to protect others from the harm caused by certain private activities that have social costs associated with them. For example, cigarette taxes certainly raise revenue, yet they also can be justified as protecting nonsmokers from the adverse health consequences of secondhand smoke. Yet a third less traditional policy goal of cigarette taxation, in line with the theme of this book, is that taxes can help protect people from themselves.

One interesting quirk about taxation as a method to control addictive behavior is that addicts are commonly thought of as being trapped by their addiction, unable to make rational consumption decisions. Yet if this is true, what role can taxation play in affecting their behavior? If addicted smokers need to smoke, regardless of the price of cigarettes, it will be very difficult to control behavior through tax policy. So, ironically, rational tax policy to control cigarette consumption *necessarily* requires some amount of rationality from smokers. While it is well accepted that consumption and price are inversely related—the higher the price, the lower the consumption—the key question is how sensitive is the consumption of an addictive good to increases in price? To an economist, this question can be reworded: What is an addictive good's *elasticity of demand*?

Elasticity of demand directly measures the sensitivity of consumption to price. For example, assume that the price for a pack of cigarettes increases by 5 percent. We expect to observe a reduction in consumption, but will that reduction be greater than 5 percent or less than 5 percent? (The reduction may also be exactly 5 percent, but we can ignore this possibility for ease of discussion.) If the reduction in consumption is greater than 5 percent, we say that the demand for the cigarettes is *elastic*. This means that a small percentage price change leads to a larger percentage consumption change. If the reduction in consumption is less than 5 percent, we say that the demand for the cigarettes is *inelastic*. This means that a small percentage price change leads to an even smaller percentage consumption change.

To further elaborate, if price increases by 5 percent, assume that consumption falls by 10 percent. This implies that the consumption effect is twice the price effect, or the elasticity of demand is −2.0 (the minus sign represents the inverse relationship between price and consumption). If consumption were to fall by only 2.5 percent, this implies that the consumption effect is half the price effect, or the elasticity of demand is −0.5. When the elasticity of demand is less than −1 (such as −2.0), the demand is elastic. When the elasticity of demand is between −1 and 0 (such as −0.5), the demand is inelastic. Using tax increases to control smoking, then, will be more effective the more sensitive cigarette consumption is to price. So what is the elasticity of demand for cigarettes?

An industry of economic studies has attempted to estimate the elasticity of demand for cigarettes, examining three fundamental types of smoking behaviors. First, how do cigarette price changes affect smoking *initiation*? Increased cigarette taxes, for example, may discourage some potential smokers from becoming actual smokers. This is important when discussing youth smoking behavior. Second, how do price changes affect smoking *cessation*? It is possible that some smokers will completely quit because of increased prices. Finally,

how do price changes affect cigarette *consumption?* Current smokers who remain smokers after the price change may reduce their consumption of cigarettes. Thus, a distinction can be made between the smoking-participation
rate and the smoking-consumption rate in these studies.

While the studies differ in methodologies and data, and there is a wide
range of results, the conclusion is that smokers vary their consumption of
cigarettes according to price changes. In general, estimates for a broad range
of the elasticity of demand is between −0.14 and −1.23, which means the
elasticity can be inelastic or elastic. But more narrowly, many of the studies
find the elasticity of demand to be between −0.3 and −0.5, which is strictly inelastic. Researchers who rely on these studies commonly say that the elasticity
of demand for cigarettes is −0.4. This means that, on average, a 10 percent increase in the price of cigarettes leads to a 4 percent reduction in consumption.

To fine-tune the elasticity estimates, many researchers have focused on
partitioning the data into narrower demographic groups. Although there are
a variety of studies, with some conflicting results, a brief overview of some of
the most common results will adequately convey that not everyone responds
to cigarette price changes in the same manner.

Various Demographic Groups

One study (Farrelly et al., 2001) covers many of the main demographic groups.
They find that women are more likely to quit smoking in response to an increase in cigarette prices but men are more likely to reduce their consumption. Adults in lower-income groups are more price responsive than adults in
higher-income groups. Young adults (ages 18 to 24) are more price responsive
than older adults. And African Americans and Hispanics are more price responsive than whites.

Another study (Hersch, 2000) finds that income has a greater impact
on smoking-participation rates than on the number of cigarettes smoked.
Higher-income groups are less likely to smoke, and the author attributes this
to the common perception that as one gets wealthier one is less willing to bear
risks. Better-educated people are also less likely to smoke. Employment status
influences smoking rates. Compared to people not in the labor force, white-
collar workers are less likely to smoke, blue-collar workers are more likely to
smoke, and unemployed workers smoke the most.

Yet another study (Czart et al., 2001) focuses on the smoking behavior
of college students. College students, away from home for the first time in

their lives, may be more likely to experiment with smoking, drinking, and drugs and not be very responsive to policies designed to control their behavior. But this study finds that cigarette price increases affect college students in terms of reducing both the number of cigarettes smoked and the smoking-participation rates.

Related to smoking behavior of college students is the question of how education affects smoking behavior. As just briefly mentioned, better-educated people are less likely to smoke. But exactly why is this the case? Is it that more education allows a person to be better informed about the health consequences of smoking, thus discouraging unhealthy behavior? Or is it because the same factors that encourage someone to pursue more education also encourage that person not to smoke? For example, if a person is relatively patient, that strong concern for future outcomes may be leading to choices that promote future good health and enhanced educational opportunities. If this is the case, education in and of itself does not discouraging smoking; it is simply correlated with another factor that discourages smoking.

To sort out this observational equivalence problem, one interesting study (Grimard and Parent, 2007) attempts to draw a direct link between educational attainment and smoking behavior. The trick is to find a way to observe increased education caused by a factor that does *not* also affect smoking behavior. One such factor is attending college to defer military draft. During the Vietnam War, a young man could avoid the draft by attending college. Many young men did just that. Compared to young women, who were not eligible for the draft, these men obtained more education for a reason that likely had little to do with their preference for smoking. Thus, as these two groups faced different educational attainment levels over this draft eligibility period, their smoking behavior may also have differed from what it would have been without the draft. The study finds that increased education did reduce the probability of becoming a smoker, but it did not increase the probability of quitting smoking for those who previously smoked. Thus, the study finds a direct link between more education and lower smoking rates.

Youth

Many studies tend to focus on youth smoking behavior. It is commonly accepted that youth smokers are very likely to become adult smokers, and so policies designed to control youth smoking initiation and cigarette consumption may provide substantial long-term benefits. One study (Carpenter and Cook, 2008) finds that cigarette tax increases reduce the participation rate of youth smokers (grades 9 through 12). With their data, they find that a $1 increase in tax per pack of cigarettes would reduce the youth participation rate (having smoked at least once in the past 30 days) by 10 to 20 percent. They also find that the tax increase would reduce the number of youths who are *frequent* smokers (smoked on at least 20 out of the last 30 days). They also briefly address the *mechanisms* by which tax increases reduce youth smoking.

Smokers in high school are generally too young to legally purchase cigarettes. If you can't buy cigarettes, how are you responding to price changes? An obvious answer is that the laws banning sales to youths are not well enforced, and therefore many youths face the same retail price as adults. But even with strong enforcement of the age restriction laws, youths may get older friends or family to purchase their cigarettes and reimburse them at the higher prices. Even if cigarettes pass to youths for free, the tax increase may reduce the number of cigarettes available to be shared.

There also may be an important *peer effect*; that is, if older friends and family are smoking less often (because of a tax increase, for example), youths, from a social interaction perspective, may also smoke less often. One study (Powell, Tauras, and Ross, 2005) takes advantage of a rich data set based on 1996 survey data of high school students in the United States. The data include detailed information on individual smoking behavior, student and parental demographics, and school identifiers (for public, private, and parochial schools). With this survey data tobacco price and policy control variables are merged. The results of the study offer strong support for peer effects influencing youth smoking behavior. For example, the study finds that moving a high school student from a school where no one else smokes to a school where 25 percent of the students smoke increases the probability that the student smokes by approximately 14 percent. Thus, the authors conclude, increased cigarette prices can directly (through the price effect) and indirectly (through the peer effect) reduce youth smoking rates.

Another study (Powell and Chaloupka, 2005) examines parental control and youth smoking behavior. In addition to policy controls such as taxes and restrictions to access, parental influence has a significant impact on controlling youth smoking behavior. The study finds that improvements in parent-child communications, home smoking rules, and parental smoking behavior itself can all affect the probability of a youth smoking.

To measure smoking-participation rates, surveys ask if the respondent has had at least one cigarette in the last 30 days. A yes identifies the person as a smoker. Although it is pragmatic to keep survey questions as straightforward as possible, in this case the question does not capture other key aspects of smoking behavior, especially at the youth initiation stage.

Youth initiation can be quite complex. Young people who have smoked recently may be only experimental smokers. If asked whether they intend to be a regular smoker in the future, a yes suggests the youths may be further along the smoking *uptake process* than those who answer no. The youth uptake process tries to distinguish between different levels of youth initiation. In addition to future smoking intentions, actual past smoking behavior also predicts future behavior, as does the ability to refuse a cigarette from a friend in the face of peer pressure. Thus, intentions, past behavior, and the ability to handle social interactions all place youths in various stages of the uptake process.

One study (Ross, Chaloupka, and Wakefield, 2006) examines how cigarette prices affect youth smokers at various stages in the uptake process. The main finding is that higher prices have an increasing impact on reducing smoking the further along the uptake process is the youth. Early in the uptake process, when a smoker is only experimenting, price will not be much of a factor in the smoking decision. But as the smoker progresses to more persistent smoking, price effects matter more. Another finding is that age restriction laws strongly discourage progress to higher stages on the uptake process. Thus, the effectiveness of public policy to control youth smoking depends on not only whether the youth has smoked a cigarette in the past 30 days but also the smoker's location in the uptake process.

Another study (Fletcher, Deb, and Sindelar, 2009) separates the two basic types of youths—those who respond to increased cigarette prices and those who do not. While the former group is the larger of the two, the existence of the unresponsive group suggests that cigarette taxation may not be the best way to control youth behavior. What is interesting about this study is that the authors attempt to distinguish between the two groups by attributes of self-control and time preference. The study uses survey questions to measure these attributes. One question asks respondents to rank, from "strongly agree" to "strongly disagree" (with three rankings in between), the statement "When making decisions, you usually go with your gut feeling without thinking too much about the consequences of each alternative." A respondent's ranking indicates his or her self-control. Another question asks respondents to choose from "almost no chance" to "almost certain" (with three rankings in between) in response to "What do you think are the chances you will live to age 35?" This provides a measure of time preference. The study finds that it is clearly those youths who are the most impulsive and the least patient (in terms of not expecting much of a future life span) who are the least responsive to cigarette price changes.

In further examining the impact of future life expectancy and smoking behavior, one study (Adda and Lechene, 2001) takes advantage of a data set from Sweden. The study asks, for both youths and adults, how does life expectancy influence a person's decision to smoke? The basic trade-off is that those who expect to live long lives have more to lose (compared to those who do not expect to live long lives) from adverse future health costs from deciding to be current smokers. Although not specifically concerned with youth behavior in terms of distinguishing between different youth groups, the authors find that at young ages a person's smoking behavior does not depend on life expectancy. At older ages, however, life expectancy is an important determinant of smoking behavior. Those who expect to live longer lives are less likely to smoke, are more likely to quit at an earlier age, and if they do smoke, tend to consume fewer cigarettes. In fact, the authors conclude that life expectancy is a major factor in explaining differences in smoking behavior.

Mental Illness

It appears that people who are suffering, or have suffered, a mental illness are, proportionally, heavy users of addictive substances. One study (Saffer and Dave, 2005) finds that people with a history of mental illness are 89 percent more likely to smoke (and 26 percent more likely to consume alcohol and 66 percent more likely to consume cocaine) compared to those without mental illness. The study then examines how responsive those with a mental illness are to cigarette price changes.

Obviously, the first step in such a study is to define what is meant by *mental illness*. Without going into much detail, the authors categorize persons as having mental illness if they responded to detailed survey questions that they exhibited any of one of the following 12 psychiatric disorders (see Saffer and Dave, 2005, appendix B, p. 245, for definitions): generalized anxiety disorder, social phobia, simple phobia, panic attack, panic disorder, agoraphobia, post-traumatic stress disorder, major depression, dysthymia, bipolar disorder, mania, or nonaffective psychosis. (There are also disorders specifically related to drug and alcohol abuse, but these are not included in this study to avoid having to work with a highly biased sample.) In this study's sample, 24 percent of the respondents have experienced mental illness in the past year, and 43 percent have experienced it in their lifetime.

The study finds that smokers who exhibit mental illness respond to cigarette price changes in the same way as smokers who do not exhibit mental illness do. The elasticities lie between −0.5 and −0.7 for both groups, and this is consistent with many of the standard studies that estimate a cigarette elasticity of demand. Another study (Tekin, Mocan, and Liang, 2009) confirms this result but looks specifically at adolescents (students in grades 7 through 12), some known to have mental illness and some known not to suffer from mental illness. These students are responsive to cigarette price changes, and the response is similar to that found with adolescents who do not suffer from mental illness. Thus, taxation may be one way social policy can control smoking by the mentally ill, but because mental illness itself is a predictor of smoking, treating the illness may be another way to control smoking.

Developing Countries

It has been hypothesized that cigarette taxes would reduce smoking more in less developed countries (LDCs) than in more developed countries, such as the United States. An early plea for policy makers in LDCs to embrace more aggressive cigarette tax policies (Warner, 1990) suggests that the greater price responsiveness will be due to two main reasons. First, smokers in LDCs are likely to have very limited financial resources, making cigarette price increases more constraining. Second, if it is true that smokers in LDCs consume fewer cigarettes per day than, for example, their US counterparts, they are less likely to suffer nicotine addiction and may be able to reduce their consumption with greater ease.

One early study of cigarette price effects in an LDC (Chapman and Richardson, 1990) used data from Papua New Guinea, a small country (population 4 million) just north of eastern Australia. In 1987 Papua New Guinea ranked 48th in the World Bank's ranking of poor countries. The little evidence on smoking behavior that existed at the time showed some extremely high participation rates in certain parts of the country for both men (85 percent) and women (80 percent). Tobacco products ranked fifth in household expenditures (behind rent, beer, rice, and transport). The study's finding supported the hypothesis that, in at least one LDC, smokers were more responsive to price increases than those in the United States.

A much more recent study (Kostova et al., 2010) examines the relationship of cigarette prices and youth smoking in several developing countries (which are usually countries with per capita incomes in the low to mid range). Using data from 20 countries (South Africa, Egypt, Jordan, Kuwait, Morocco, Pakistan, United Arab Emirates, Poland, Russia, Brazil, Chile, Costa Rica, Mexico, Peru, Venezuela, India, Indonesia, Sri Lanka, China, and Philippines) and survey results from respondents between ages 9 and 19 (average age approximately 14), the study examines the effect of cigarette prices on smoking participation rates and smoking intensity. In addition to survey data on smoking participation and intensity, respondents answer questions relating to the level of antismoking sentiment, the prevalence of cigarette advertising and antismoking messages, and the perceived effectiveness of age restriction tobacco policies.

The results show price effects for both smoking participation and intensity, with the participation effect being smaller than the intensity effect but both effects being larger than the usual results for US youth data. Thus, the authors conclude that the price responsiveness of youth smoking in developing countries is higher than in the United States, likely due to tighter income constraints in poorer countries and to the lower average age of respondents in this study relative to past studies on youth smoking behavior. Furthermore, the authors find that youth smoking participation in these developing countries is affected by antismoking sentiment, cigarette advertising, and age restriction policies but that the intensity of smoking is not affected by these factors. However, they find that antitobacco media campaigns reduce both participation rates and intensity.

Another study (Lance et al., 2004) estimates the elasticity of demand for cigarettes in China and Russia, two countries with high smoking participation rates, especially among men, and fairly lax social policies to control smoking. The study is interested in determining the potential effectiveness of more aggressive cigarette taxation policies in each country. In contrast to the previous study, the findings for both countries are that the elasticity is small, generally indistinguishable from zero. This suggests that price increases through taxation are likely to have little impact on cigarette consumption in China and Russia.

The authors offer some explanations for this result. For both countries, the study uses a sample of men over age 13, whose smoking participation rate is extremely large—55 percent for China and 58 percent for Russia. They interpret these high participation rates as possibly indicating high addiction rates. Furthermore, the addictiveness of cigarettes in both countries may be enhanced by the general lack of regulatory controls on nicotine levels. They also point to cultural and institutional differences with countries such as the United States that may account for the lack of price responsiveness in China and Russia. For example, there may be much less antismoking sentiment in these countries and less social policy support to facilitate quitting (subsidized quitting aids, government antismoking campaigns, and so on).

Cigarette Taxes and Adverse Side Effects

One side effect of increasing cigarette taxes is that, as smokers respond to the price increase by smoking fewer cigarettes or quitting completely, they may begin to indulge in other addictive goods, for example, food (chapter 4 examines the connection between cigarette taxes and obesity rates). If increased taxes reduce smoking but increase obesity rates, the initial goal of improving the health of the smoker is partially or completely offset by changed eating behaviors. Similarly, what if increased cigarette taxes reduce smoking but increase use of smokeless tobacco products?

There are two main types of smokeless tobacco—chewing tobacco and snuff. Chewing tobacco is in the form of loose leaf, plug, or twist. Snuff is a finely ground tobacco that can be dry or moist or packaged in sachets. In whatever form, a user places the smokeless tobacco between cheek and gum. The Centers for Disease Control and Prevention (CDC) reports that smokeless tobacco contains 28 cancer-causing agents; is associated with leukoplakia (precancerous lesions in the mouth), recession of the gums, gum disease, and tooth decay; and can lead to nicotine addiction. As of 2009 in the United States, 3.5 percent of adults (age 18 or over), 6.1 percent of high school students, and 2.6 percent of middle school students were smokeless tobacco users (CDC, 2011).

While not many studies have examined the impact of cigarette prices on smokeless tobacco use, the few that have offer mixed results. One study (Oshfeldt, Boyle, and Capilouto, 1997) finds a small effect for increased cigarette prices increasing snuff use and an even smaller effect for it increasing chewing tobacco use. Another study (Tauras et al., 2007) concludes that for male high school students, increased cigarette prices lead to *reduced* use of smokeless tobacco products. The authors attribute the difference between their result and the one from the previous study to the younger students in their sample. It is likely that younger smokers and smokeless tobacco users are still experimenting with these products, so they may tend to be used in more of a complementary manner as opposed to being substitutes. Whatever the case, it is certainly important to consider conflicting effects when pursuing a policy objective.

Another potential offsetting effect works against the health benefits of smoking fewer cigarettes. As taxes make it more expensive to smoke, smokers may indeed smoke fewer cigarettes, but they may switch to a brand of cigarettes higher in tar and nicotine. Indeed, two studies (Evans and Farrelly, 1998; Farrelly et al., 2004) find that smokers do switch to brands with greater concentrations of tar and nicotine when cigarette prices increase. They conclude that using taxes to curb smoking may have the perverse effect of inducing some smokers to smoke more harmful cigarettes, even if smoking fewer. They suggest cigarette taxes should be scaled to the tar and nicotine levels of the cigarette.

But even if smokers don't switch brands, and even if they do smoke less because of the increased taxes, there may still be a perverse effect if smokers smoke their cigarettes more intensely. For example, a smoker may put out a cigarette before it reaches the filter line, but if induced to smoke fewer cigarettes, that smoker may smoke the cigarette right down to the filter. This enhanced intensity increases the adverse health effect *per* cigarette, possibly more than compensating for the health benefit found from smoking fewer cigarettes.

One study (Adda and Cornaglia, 2006) examines the effect of taxes on smoking intensity to determine if offsetting behavior counteracts the intended policy goal of improving health outcomes for smokers. The authors have an interesting data set that includes information on *cotinine* concentrations. Cotinine is a chemical made by the body from nicotine, found in cigarette smoke. By knowing a person's cotinine level (in saliva, for example), we can get a good idea of how intensely the person smokes. This way of measuring nicotine intake is likely to be far more accurate than simply asking smokers how many cigarettes they smoke a day or how intensely they smoke. Survey responses may not always be truthful, and recall is not perfect. Even with accurate answers, key differences in smoking intensity levels may not be picked up by the questions.

For example, assume a survey asks the following question: How many cigarettes do you smoke a day? Consider two people who give identical answers of one pack a day. On the basis of that question alone, they would be considered to smoke with equal intensity. But what if one person smokes un-filtered cigarettes and inhales deeply with each puff, while another smokes filtered cigarettes, does not inhale deeply, and smokes only half of each ciga-rette? They may smoke the same number of cigarettes each day, but the first person is a more intense smoker, which a cotinine test would clearly show.

Cotinine has an in vivo half-life of approximately 24 hours, whereas nico-tine's half-life is about 30 minutes. Cotinine levels are lowest in the morning, due to no smoke exposure while sleeping, but for steady smokers cotinine levels reach a steady state and vary only about 15 to 20 percent throughout the day. Thus, a cotinine test provides an extremely useful measure for examin-ing the effect of public policy on smoking behavior.

The authors find that increased cigarette taxation does lead to increased smoking intensity. Quantitatively, they find that a 1 percent increase in ciga-rette taxes leads to an approximately 0.4 percent increase in intensity. Thus, taxation policy aimed at reducing smoking or reducing the onset of smoking or reducing both may not yield health benefits as high as previously believed. If smokers offset their reduction in smoking by smoking more intensely, taxa-tion will adversely affect their health. More troubling, the net health effect of the taxation can possibly be negative. At a minimum, the authors dem-onstrate that how smokers smoke cigarettes is important to consider when designing antismoking policy.

Taxes and Antismoking Sentiment

As the majority does not smoke, substantial public antismoking sentiments can affect smokers' behavior. Antismoking sentiment itself may not only reduce smoking but also be a confounding factor when trying to determine how price increases affect smoking behavior. For example, if antismoking sentiment is not properly taken into account, the impact of cigarette prices on smoking may be overestimated. That is, is it the increased prices that are reducing smoking or the antismoking sentiment? Or—what is most likely—is it both?

To measure antismoking sentiment, one study (DeCicca et al., 2008) uses a series of questions. The first six questions measure attitudes toward smok-ing in public places such as restaurants, hospitals, indoor work areas, bars and cocktail lounges, indoor sporting events, and indoor shopping malls. The next two questions measure attitudes about tobacco industry practices such as giving away free samples and advertising. The last question asks about rules for smoking at home. Data from three surveys between 1992 and 1999 were collected.

To provide an idea of the prevalence of antismoking attitudes, it is useful to present some survey results from one of the years (1999). Approximately 51 percent of the respondents believed that smoking should not be allowed at all in restaurants; 82 percent, in hospitals; 67 percent, in indoor work areas; 28 percent, in bars and cocktail lounges; 72 percent, in indoor sporting events; and 69 percent, in indoor shopping malls. Approximately 60 percent of respondents believed that tobacco companies should not be allowed to give away free samples, and 41 percent thought they should not be allowed to advertise their products. Finally, 60 percent of respondents lived in homes where smoking was not allowed. It is interesting to note that the antismoking sentiment increased over time, across all three surveys, for every question.

With this information, the authors ambitiously create a state-by-state (plus DC) antismoking sentiment measure. This measure, along with statewide variation in cigarette prices, allows the authors to examine the interaction of antismoking sentiment and cigarette prices on the smoking behavior of teens (eighth graders in this study). The statewide measure clearly demonstrates the politics of smoking viewpoints. Some of the lowest antismoking sentiments are found in the tobacco-producing states Kentucky, North Carolina, South Carolina, Tennessee, and Virginia. Two of the highest antismoking sentiment states are California and Utah.

The authors find that when taking into account antismoking sentiment, cigarette prices have little impact on youth smoking participation but some negative impact on smoking intensity. Thus, they find a price effect that reduces the daily consumption of cigarettes, but at the initiation stage the youths in this sample appear not to be price responsive. However, antismoking sentiment has a negative impact on youth participation, suggesting that peer effects and public sentiment are an important influence on younger smokers at the initiation stage. Perhaps there is some irony that a policy, in a state with a high antismoking sentiment, mandating increased cigarette taxes to reduce smoking may do little precisely because of existing strong antismoking sentiment.

Happily Controlled Smokers

Do you remember Sophisticated Sophia, the time-inconsistent addict from chapter 1? She recognizes that she has a self-control problem. She may be a smoker in the short term, planning on quitting in the near future. But as the future arrives, her time inconsistency has her change her mind and decide not to follow through with her intention to quit. As she is fairly patient between two future periods but fairly impatient between the current period and the next, she may never, regardless of her intentions, be able to quit smoking.

Because she's a sophisticated addict, Sophia may decide to take actions to help control her smoking. But any actions she tries to self-enforce may ultimately be fruitless. Maybe she decides not to buy cigarettes one day, only to run to the store when overcome by craving. Or she decides to fine herself one dollar every time she smokes, only to find she has saved enough by the end of the year to buy a new car. Recognizing a self-control problem and successfully dealing with a self-control problem are two different things. This is why a sophisticated addict such as Sophia may decide to support public policy intervention to control her smoking.

Sophia may be able to fine herself when she smokes, but she is not likely to be able to do that credibly. If she decides to smoke and not pay the fine, who will force her to pay? With taxation, however, the government forces higher cigarette prices on her. The thought of smokers being made happier by social policies that enforce restrictions on their smoking behavior can be a perplexing concept. Yet according to one study (Gruber and Mullainathan, 2005), smokers who face increased cigarette taxes are happier smokers. Economists don't normally think of taxation as a policy option preferred by those paying the tax. As the price of cigarettes rises, smokers are considered worse off because they must pay more for an activity they enjoy. Certainly, to the extent that smokers are time consistent, taxation must *necessarily* make them worse off. Thus, a study that demonstrates that smokers themselves are made happier by cigarette taxation implies that these smokers are *not* time consistent.

Unfortunately, the authors do not have access to data that directly measure smokers' preference for increased cigarette taxes. Instead, they tap into a nationally representative US survey known as the General Social Survey, which annually asks a series of question to respondents in approximately 2,000 households. The authors have data that cover 1973 to 1998, and among the many survey questions asked of respondents, the key question is this: Taken all together, how would you say things are these days—would you say that you are very happy, pretty happy, or not too happy?

To get a better feel for the data set, it may be useful to provide some more descriptive information. For example, approximately 35 percent of the sample are smokers, 84 percent are white, 57 percent are married, 19 percent are college graduates, 49 percent are full-time workers, and 3 percent are unemployed. As for the happiness variables, 32 percent report they are very happy, 56 percent are pretty happy, and 12 percent are not too happy. While happiness data is becoming more popular in the social sciences, its use is still considered a bit unusual to many scholars. Still, it is an interesting and legitimate data set to exploit in addressing certain issues.

To account for the impact of taxes on happiness, the authors use data on state cigarette excise taxes. The taxes vary widely, not only across states but also within states over the sample period. It is this variation that allows the authors to test their main hypothesis relating increased taxes to smokers' reported happiness levels. And their results are, in their own words, quite striking. They find that smokers are indeed happier when cigarette taxes rise. Furthermore, they confirm this result with a Canadian data set that uses a similar measure of happiness. Also, they demonstrate that other tax increases (such as a beer, gas, and sales tax) do not make smokers happier. Thus, it is not taxes themselves but cigarette taxes that smokers prefer.

The authors interpret their results as lending support to the existence of sophisticated time-inconsistent addicts. Recognizing their self-control problem, but maybe not being able to enact self-commitment measures, these smokers appreciate state policies that reduce their consumption of cigarettes. But the authors' result not only rules out time consistency but also casts doubt on the addiction-as-a-mistake model. If smokers consume cigarettes impulsively, that is, if their choice to smoke is distinct from their preferences, they should not be very responsive to price changes.

Another policy option for governments is to ban smoking, if not in its entirety, then in some venues such as restaurants, bars, and work areas. These bans may also be welcomed by smokers who recognize their lack of self-control. One study (Hersch, 2005) uses survey data to measure public support for smoking bans in several venues: restaurants, hospitals, indoor work areas, bars and cocktail lounges, indoor sporting events, and indoor shopping malls. (This is the same data used to measure antismoking sentiment in a study previously discussed.) Each respondent was asked the following question: In [fill in each venue one at a time], do you think that smoking should be allowed in all areas, in some areas, or not allowed at all? More than 200,000 responded to this survey, and in general, there was much support for complete smoking bans in all of these areas. The study found several interesting results.

First, respondents were grouped according to smoking behavior: never smokers, former smokers, and current smokers. Never smokers were more likely than former smokers to favor bans, and former smokers were more likely than current smokers to favor bans. For example, in 2002, 69.4 percent of never smokers favored bans in restaurants, compared to 57 percent of former smokers and 25.9 percent of current smokers. This is the general trend for all six venues in terms of smoking behavior, and it isn't too surprising.

Second, different venues yielded different responses from all three groups of respondents. The venue that received the most support for a smoking ban was hospitals. In 2002, 91.4 percent of never smokers, 86.3 percent of former smokers, and 74.2 percent of current smokers favored a smoking ban in hospitals. The venue that received the least support was bars and cocktail lounges, with 43 percent of never smokers, 30.8 percent of former smokers, and only 8.9 percent of current smokers favoring a ban.

Third, the trend toward favoring complete smoking bans steadily increased between 1992 and 2002 for all three groups of respondents and for all venues. For example, in 1992, 65 percent of never smokers, 56 percent of former smokers, and 31.4 percent of current smokers favored bans in indoor shopping malls. But in 2002 the respective percentages were 82.8 percent, 76.3 percent, and 59.8 percent.

While public support for bans was fairly pervasive, especially for never and former smokers, precisely how current smokers thought about smoking bans could be even further examined. Why a current smoker would favor a complete ban in public venues has two possibilities. First, in line with the theme of the addiction model and mentioned above, a sophisticated time-inconsistent smoker may welcome public bans to help restrict her own smoking. Second, it is possible that smokers themselves do not care for secondhand smoke. Maybe Sophia does not want to impose her smoke on others, or maybe she doesn't want her nonsmoking family and friends exposed to secondhand smoke. If the latter reason motivates current smokers to support smoking bans, it really has little to do with their self-control.

To try to distinguish between the two reasons, the study further partitions current smokers: smokers who have tried to quit in the past and plan to try again; smokers who plan to try to quit for the first time; and smokers who have no plans to try to quit. The idea here is that smokers who are failed quitters, and to a lesser extent smokers who have the intention to quit, may be more likely to support a ban, to help with self-control, than smokers who have no intention to quit. This is a clever way to see if some smokers recognize their self-control problems, as those who have unsuccessfully tried to quit in the past must realize that something is keeping them from quitting for good.

Consider the survey results for supporting smoking bans in restaurants. Of the smokers who have tried to quit in the past and plan on trying again, 24.4 percent supported a complete ban. Of those who plan to quit for the first time, 21.4 percent supported a ban. But of those who have no plans for quitting, only 12.4 percent supported a ban. These results suggest, to some extent, that smokers who are concerned about quitting are more supportive of restaurant bans than smokers who are not concerned about quitting. And these results are similar for the other venues. Thus, some evidence supports the idea that a subset of smokers are aware of, and concerned about, their self-control problems and favor government intervention to help them out.

Cigarette Advertising Bans

It is safe to say that advertising, as a marketing tool, has its critics. Certainly, many people find certain ads annoying, or not clever, or just plain silly. But advertising as a way to sell products is often criticized as being overly persuasive, even hypnotizing. How many people were seduced into smoking because of the lovely Maureen O'Hara advertisement that opened this chapter? How many teenagers took one look at the popular Joe Camel ads and immediately became lifelong smokers?

When considering criticisms of advertising, a very common one is that it makes people buy things they do not want or need. Before anything else, let's clear up one misconception. From an economic perspective, it is very difficult, if not impossible, to believe that advertising makes people buy things they do not want or need. Exactly what does it mean to buy something you do not want? If you don't want it, why buy it? That may sound simplistic, but it's a very tough question to answer. You may buy something and then wish you hadn't. That's a different issue involving regret as you gain experience with the product. But can you really argue that you didn't want it *at the moment you bought it*?

The role of advertising is to either create wants that did not previously exist, or to enhance wants that did exist. Cigarette advertising may bring first-time smokers into the market, or it may increase the amount of smoking by current smokers. It does not make people smoke who do not want to smoke.

As discussed earlier, that smokers are willing to pay for cigarettes *necessarily* implies that they benefit from smoking. Advertising may simply make some people willing to pay more for cigarettes. Of course, if the advertising is false or misleading, that is a different story entirely. But there are laws in place that discourage misuse of advertising, even though these laws are difficult and costly to enforce. Still, if a public policy goal is to discourage smoking, and if advertising encourages people to start smoking or to smoke more often, policies designed to reduce the amount of cigarette advertising may be an effective way to achieve that goal. This leaves an important empirical question to be addressed: Does cigarette advertising lead to more smoking?

Many studies have examined the link between cigarette advertising and smoking behavior. In a nutshell, these studies taken as a whole are extremely inconclusive. Owing to different data sets and different statistical methodologies, some studies find a positive link between cigarette advertising and smoking and some do not. But these conflicting results may also be due to cigarette advertising, *in theory*, not being expected to have the effect on smoking usually predicted.

Advertising enhances demand for a product through two basic channels: by increasing demand for the product in general or by increasing demand for a specific *brand* of the product at the expense of a competing brand. For example, Campbell's Soup introduced the advertising slogan "Soup is Good Food." This slogan may enhance the demand for Campbell's products and reduce the demand for its rivals' soups, or it may enhance the demand for all soups. When the milk industry uses the advertising slogan "Got Milk?" no brands are mentioned. The advertising is meant to increase the aggregate demand for milk. Cigarette advertising, if mostly used for brand competition, may do little for aggregate demand for cigarettes. On the other hand, cigarette advertising may increase aggregate demand, especially when the advertising is combating the numerous antismoking messages. Studies support both views of the effect of advertising on smoking, many finding an aggregate demand effect, many not finding such an effect.

In addition to looking at a demand effect, two studies (Gallet, 2003; Iwasaki, Tremblay, and Tremblay, 2006) focus on the potential *supply* effect of advertising restrictions on cigarette consumption. If restricting cigarette advertising enhances market power in the tobacco industry (that is, reduces competition in the industry), it may be that prices for cigarettes rise because of this impact on the supply side of the market. Although the studies take different approaches, they both find that advertising may reduce cigarette consumption. If firms with market power are selling a product that is associated with social costs, the higher prices associated with monopoly pricing, ironically, curtail the product's use. Restricting cigarette advertising, then, may be affecting smokers not because they are being less persuaded by the reduction in advertising but because the tobacco companies benefit from the policy's impact on their market power.

An interesting avenue of research takes a different approach in examining the link between advertising and smoking behavior. Instead of seeing how the amount of cigarette advertising affects the demand for cigarettes, one study (Saffer and Chaloupka, 2000) looks at how government regulation of cigarette advertising affects smoking. More specifically, one policy option for governments to pursue is to ban cigarette advertising in some or all media outlets. In 1971 the US government banned all cigarette advertising on television and radio. While broadcast media was the major outlet for cigarette advertising at the time, it certainly wasn't the only outlet. In addition to television and radio advertising, there was print advertising, outdoor advertising, point of purchase advertising, movie advertising, and sponsorship advertising (such as with sporting events). This study considers different degrees of advertising bans to determine how the banning policy's comprehensiveness affects cigarette consumption.

The authors create variables that take into account the degree of advertising bans in 22 countries, all members of the Organization for Economic Cooperation and Development (OECD). One of three variables is applied to each OECD country. Of the seven advertising outlets listed above, countries that ban cigarette advertising in two or fewer outlets are considered weak ban countries. If countries ban cigarette advertising in three or four outlets, they are considered limited ban countries. And finally, if cigarette advertising is banned in five or more outlets, they are considered comprehensive ban countries.

The data cover 1970 to 1992, and the progression in number of outlets banned during that time period is perfectly clear. In 1970, 19 countries were in the weak ban category, and 3 countries were in the limited ban one. None were in the comprehensive ban category. In 1980, 13 were in the weak ban category, 5 in the limited ban one, and 4 in the comprehensive ban one. And in 1992, only 7 countries were in the weak ban category, 9 were in the limited ban one, and 6 were in the comprehensive ban one. Thus, several countries more aggressively controlled cigarette advertising over time.

Another finding the study offers is how cigarette consumption compares across countries with different degrees of advertising bans. For example, in 1992, countries with a weak ban had a per capita consumption of 2,599 cigarettes; countries with a limited ban, 2,004; and countries with a comprehensive ban, 1,654. This was the typical trend—the greater the number of advertising outlets banned, the lower the per capita cigarette consumption. What the study concludes is that, as a policy option, advertising bans that are not comprehensive will not reduce cigarette consumption. But advertising bans that are comprehensive appear to reduce cigarette consumption, and this result suggests a positive link between cigarette advertising and smoking.

Applying the same methodology, another study (Blecher, 2008) confirms the above study's result for high-income countries but also looks at a subset of 30 developing (or lower income) countries. The study finds a similar trend over time for the developing countries: in 1990, 28 of the countries were in the weak ban category, 1 country in the limited ban category, and 1 country in the comprehensive ban category. By 2005 the respective numbers changed to 19, 0, and 11. So throughout the whole time period, several developing countries changed their policies from weak to limited to comprehensive bans. As for the effect of these advertising restrictions on smoking behavior, the author finds that for high-income countries only comprehensive advertising bans reduce cigarette consumption, but for developing countries both limited and comprehensive bans do. As discussed above, with respect to cigarette tax policy, these results further confirm that the effectiveness of advertising restrictions to control smoking depends on many factors.

Smoking and Economic Insecurity

A novel line of research is attempting to link smoking behavior to overall economic conditions. The basic idea is that smoking is a form of self-medication in response to financial insecurity. One study (Barnes and Smith, 2009) offers an intriguing explanation to account for this behavior, and it begins not with smoking but with a concern over future food supplies.

One explanation for a form of depression known as seasonal affective disorder (SAD) posits that it's a hibernation response—that the SAD sufferer believes food supplies will soon be scarce and preparations for this contingency are necessary. SAD is characterized by increased appetite, weight gain, and excessive sleep. The antidepressant drug bupropion manipulates dopamine and norepinephrine levels in the brain, and it counters the effects of SAD by causing appetite suppression, weight loss, and insomnia. But as an unexpected side effect, bupropion also suppresses the urge to smoke, and it is now the leading non-nicotine smoking cessation drug. If bupropion is a substitute for smoking, then it is possible that smoking is an antidepressant. Thus, the stress caused by economic insecurity may be a substantial factor in accounting for smoking behavior.

While it can be difficult to provide a precise measure of a person's own sense of economic insecurity, the authors offer three reasonable proxies. The first involves the person's probability assessment of being unemployed. The second involves the person's probability assessment that family income will fall below a specified poverty threshold. The final proxy measures the number of drops in annual (real) income the person experienced that were greater than 10 percent throughout the sample period (1983–1998). For each of these proxies in the study's data set, smokers are found to experience a higher level of insecurity than nonsmokers. The average unemployment probability is 0.05 for smokers and 0.028 for nonsmokers. The average probability of falling below the poverty threshold is 0.052 for smokers and 0.044 for nonsmokers. And the average number of large income drops is 3.12 for smokers and 2.83 for nonsmokers. The study finds that all three measures of economic insecurity positively affect the probability of smoking, and the authors conclude that "nicotine addiction may be more productively viewed as a symptom than a disease" (Barnes and Smith, 2009, 21).

In a similar vein, another study (Ayyagari and Sindelar, 2010) relates smoking behavior to job stress, particularly for older people (age 50 to 64). Using survey data, the authors have two measures of smoking, one that measures whether a person smokes or not, and one that measures the number of cigarettes smoked in a day. To measure job stress, one survey question asks each respondent to rank, from "strongly agree" to "strongly disagree," the statement "My job involves a lot of stress." The study finds that job stress is positively related to the decision to smoke and to the number of cigarettes smoked each day.

Smoking Early and Later in Life

One fascinating study (Eisenberg and Rowe, 2009) cleverly addresses the question of how smoking as a young adult affects smoking behavior in the future.

The common belief, and much evidence supports it, is that smoking early in life is highly correlated with smoking later in life. But that is different from considering whether smoking early in life *causes* smoking later in life. There are many reasons to smoke. For example, maybe one smokes early in life because of peer effects associated with friends or family members who smoke, and then one smokes later in life because of job stress, both reasonable explanations previously discussed. Then again, another reasonable explanation previously discussed is that cigarettes are addictive and so starting early in life does explain smoking later in life.

In this study, the authors take advantage of the Vietnam draft lottery to differentiate between two groups of young men: those who were drafted into the military and those who were not. Between 1969 and 1972, the Vietnam draft lotteries were held, and some men were randomly considered draft eligible while others were not. For the data used in this study, the men who were subject to the draft lottery were either 19 or 20 years old, and for those who served, the typical term of service was two years.

For those men who served in Vietnam, several factors increased their exposure to cigarettes. First, men who served were able to purchase cigarettes tax free and at wholesale prices at military bases and commissaries. Second, men in combat who were given food rations received free cigarettes as part of their rations. Third, peer effects were likely quite strong, as smoking was common among military men. Finally, military men were under a tremendous amount of stress, another predictor of increased smoking.

The study then compares smoking rates between men who were in the military service and those who were not. Looking at a period after the lottery (1978 to 1980), when the men were between 25 and 30 years old, revealed that men who were in the military were 35 percent more likely to smoke than those who were not in the service. Thus, the authors conclude, military service greatly enhanced the probability of becoming a smoker. But did this enhanced smoking effect lead to continued smoking later in life? Looking at a much later period (1997 to 2005), when the men were between 45 and 55 years old, the study finds no significant difference in the probability of smoking between those who served and those who did not.

What the results of this study suggest is that it is possible that increased smoking early in life does not necessarily lead to increased smoking later in life. Furthermore, when looking at the men between ages 45 and 55, those who served in the military did not seem to have worse health outcomes (as measured by self-reported health assessments and by the prevalence of cancer) at that stage in their lives compared to men who did not serve. In all, the authors offer a strong concluding comment:

> For health policymakers and consumers in general, our results can be viewed as an affirmation that smoking during young adulthood does not compel one into lifelong smoking, and by quitting in young adulthood one can substantially mitigate longer-term health consequences. (Eisenberg and Rowe, 2009, 29)

No doubt, this conclusion is at odds with commonly held beliefs about the ramifications of smoking when young, yet again demonstrating the theme developed throughout this chapter—smoking behavior is complex.

Suggested Readings

The main opposing viewpoints on smokers' risk perceptions can be found in Viscusi (1990, 1991, 2000), and Slovic (1998, 2000a, 2000b). Other papers on smoking and risk perception are by Hsieh et al. (1996), Sloan, Smith, and Taylor (2002), Clark and Etile (2002), Hammar and Johansson-Stenman (2004), Carbone, Kverndokk, and Rogeberg (2005), Khwaja, Sloan, and Chung (2006), Khwaja, Sloan, and Salm (2006), Lundborg and Andersson (2008), and Khwaja et al. (2009). Also see Hammit and Graham (1999).

Many papers examine how price changes affect cigarette consumption. Those focusing (for the most part) on adult behavior are by Becker, Grossman, and Murphy (1991), Chaloupka (1991), Townsend, Roderick, and Cooper (1994), Hersch (2000), DeCicca, Kenkel, and Mathios (2000), Czart et al. (2001), Farrelly et al. (2001), Gruber and Koszegi (2004), Gruber and Mullainathan (2005), Tauras (2005b, 2006), Stehr (2007), and DeCicca and McLeod (2008). Papers on price effects and mental illness are by Saffer and Dave (2005) and Tekin, Mocan, and Liang (2009). Papers that focus (for the most part) on youth behavior are by Chaloupka and Wechsler (1997), Gruber (2001), Emery, White, and Pierce (2001), DeCicca, Kenkel, and Mathios (2002, 2008), Tauras (2005a), Powell, Tauras, and Ross (2005), Powell and Chaloupka (2005), Ross, Chaloupka, and Wakefield (2006), DeCicca et al. (2008), Carpenter and Cook (2008), and Fletcher, Deb, and Sindelar (2009). Papers focusing on international behavior are by Warner (1990), Chapman and Richardson (1990), Lance et al. (2004), Wan (2006), and Kostova et al. (2010).

Two related papers on the impact of education on smoking behavior that use Vietnam draft avoidance data are by de Walque (2007) and Grimard and Parent (2007). Also see the paper by Card and Lemieux (2001) on how the draft affected the decision to attend college. One other paper that uses a similar data set to examine how smoking at a young age impacts smoking behavior when older is by Eisenberg and Rowe (2009).

Papers on the effects of cigarette price changes on smokeless tobacco use are by Ohsfeldt, Boyle, and Capilouto (1997), Chaloupka, Tauras, and Grossman (1997), and Tauras et al. (2007). Papers on price effects on tar and nicotine consumption and smoking intensity are by Evans and Farrelly (1998), Farrelly et al. (2004), and Adda and Cornaglia (2006).

Papers on smoking cessation and self-control are by Keeler, Marciniak, and Hu (1999), Hersch, Del Rossi, and Viscusi (2004), Hersch (2005), Hammar and Carlsson (2005), Kan (2007), and Jehiel and Lilico (2010).

Nelson (2006b) provides a succinct summary of the impact of advertising on cigarette consumption. Also see Goel (2009). For supply-side effects, see Gallet (2003) and Iwasaki, Tremblay, and Tremblay (2006). On the impact of advertising bans on cigarette consumption, see Saffer and Chaloupka (2000) and Blecher (2008).

Papers on smoking as a response to stress or economic insecurity are by Ayyagari and Sindelar (2010) and Barnes and Smith (2009).

Other papers examining a wide range of smoking issues are by Showalter (1999) on how firms behave in a market for an addictive product; Decker and Schwartz (2000) on the relationship between cigarettes and alcohol; Adda and Lechene (2001) on smoking behavior and life expectancy; Fenn, Antonovitz, and Schroeter (2001) on cigarette addiction and information; Cutler and Glaeser (2005) on differences in smoking (and drinking) behaviors; Stehr (2005) on cigarette tax evasion; Cook and Hutchinson (2007) on smoking and school continuation; Viscusi and Hersch (2008) on the mortality cost to smokers; Bitler, Carpenter, and Zavodny (2010) on clean indoor air laws and smoking behavior. Also see Heckman, Flyer, and Loughlin (2008), Weimer, Vining, and Thomas (2009), and Raptou, Mattas, and Katrakilidis (2009).

For a comprehensive survey on the economics of smoking, see Chaloupka and Warner (2000). For a discussion of tobacco regulation, see the papers by Viscusi (1998), Laux (2000), and Goel and Nelson (2006).

3

LET'S DRINK TO YOUR HEALTH

You have a drinking problem, and your behavior has many potential adverse health outcomes. You face a higher risk of heart attack or stroke. You are more likely to suffer hypertension, high blood pressure, Parkinson's disease, and even the common cold. And if that isn't enough, medical research has shown that your drinking problem increases your chances of developing diabetes, rheumatoid arthritis, osteoporosis, kidney stones, digestive ailments, stress and depression, poor cognition, hepatitis A, pancreatic cancer, macular degeneration (a major cause of blindness), erectile dysfunction, hearing loss, gallstones, liver disease, and several other serious ailments. Precisely what is your drinking problem? It's that you don't drink.

Research has shown that moderate drinking can have phenomenal health benefits (for a summary of the studies, see http://www2.potsdam.edu/ hansondj/AlcoholAndHealth.html):

- The risk of death from all causes is 21 to 28 percent lower among men who drink alcohol moderately compared to abstainers.
- Evidence from 20 countries demonstrates 20 to 40 percent lower coronary heart disease incidence among drinkers compared to nondrinkers.
- Abstainers' risk of stroke is double that of moderate drinkers.
- Women who consumed about a half drink a day had about a 15 percent lower chance of developing high blood pressure than women who abstained.

- Moderate drinkers were 30 percent less likely to develop type 2 diabetes than abstainers or heavy drinkers.

- A French study found moderate drinkers had a 75 percent lower risk for Alzheimer's disease and an 80 percent lower risk for senile dementia.

Many other studies demonstrate similar results for a wide variety of ailments.

While drinking in moderation appears to have tremendous health benefits, drinking in excess does not, so it is important to clearly differentiate between the two. Moderate drinking can be as little as a half drink to as many as three drinks a day, depending on a person's size. An average-size woman should drink approximately 25 percent less than an average-size man. As for the definition of "a drink," that can be 12 ounces of beer, 5 ounces of wine, or 1.5 ounces of liquor.

Slightly more than half (50.4 percent) of Americans age 18 and over are classified as *frequent* drinkers (at least 12 drinks in the past year). By gender, 60.1 percent of men and 41.5 percent of women 18 and over are frequent drinkers. Nearly 16 percent of youths ages 12 to 17 report having had at least one drink in the past month (CDC, 2009). On average, in 2003 American adults consumed 8.6 liters of pure alcohol a year. For an international perspective, the countries with the highest per capita consumption of alcohol are Luxembourg (15.6 liters), Ireland (13.7), Hungary (13.6), Republic of Moldova (13.2), and the Czech Republic (13) (http://apps.who.int/whosis/database/core/core_select_process.cfm).

In addition to persistent excessive drinking, there is also *binge drinking* to consider. Probably the most common definition of binge drinking is known as the 5/4 definition: binge drinking is consuming five or more drinks if you are a man, or four or more drinks if you are a woman, in a very short time (the definition of time length varies, but less than two hours is common). Another definition used by the National Institute of Alcohol Abuse and Alcoholism uses blood alcohol content (BAC) as the threshold: binge drinking is when a person reaches a BAC of 0.08 percent or higher. Another definition is based on the intention of the drinker: binge drinking is excessive drinking with the *goal* of becoming impaired.

Although the definition of binge drinking varies slightly from country to country, the prevalence of the behavior is an international phenomenon. In Australia in 2004–2005, among 18- to 24-year-olds, 49 percent of men and 21 percent of women binged at least once a week. In Denmark 60 percent of

15- to 16-year-olds reported binge drinking in the past 30 days (in a 2003 survey). In the United States, one study found that 44 percent of American college students (51 percent of men and 40 percent of women) in 1999 had engaged in binge drinking at least once in the past two weeks. In Russia binge drinking is often exhibited as two or more days of continuous drunkenness, and a 2006 study shows that 10 percent of men between ages 25 and 54 had at least one such episode in the past year (http://en.wikipedia.org/wiki/Binge_drinking).

What is unusual about binge drinking is that just a single episode can have severe *long-term* adverse effects. If you were to experience just one eating binge in your life, it is highly unlikely that you would suffer any adverse health effects after a few days at most. But with a drinking binge, you may do something while under the influence that will have lasting consequences. For example, binge drinkers have an increased probability of engaging in unprotected sex and contracting a sexually transmitted disease or causing an unwanted pregnancy. Or a binge drinker may have an accident that hurts himself or herself or others. And of course, repeated episodes of binge drinking may lead to the more traditional adverse health effects associated with alcoholism in general.

Social policy concerning drinking can be even more complicated than that for smoking, as the goal may be to *simultaneously* encourage moderate drinking yet discourage excessive drinking. A blunt policy tool such as increased taxes, then, can be problematic:

> Numerous states have recently increased their cigarette taxes, partly with the goal of reducing smoking and thereby improving health. Advocates for raising alcohol taxes also cite the public health argument, but few states have elected to do so in the last couple of years. While the explanation for this difference may have to do with the difference in political influence of the two industries, there is also an important difference in the nature of the public-health claims. For an adult to have a drink occasionally is not a health risk and may even confer a health benefit. Hence an increase in tax penalizes healthy as well as unhealthy drinking practices. On the other hand, smoking in any amount is detrimental to health. (Cook, Ostermann, and Sloan, 2005a, 3)

Thus, from a health policy perspective, smoking is considered unambiguously unhealthy, while drinking alcohol can be either healthy or unhealthy. This distinction makes for interesting policy analysis.

Control of Alcohol Consumption:
Taxes and Age Restrictions

The two most common forms of alcohol control policies are taxes and a minimum legal drinking age (MLDA) law. In the United States, the tax rates (per gallon) vary widely across states. For example, the spirits tax rate is $26.45 in Washington (the highest in the nation) but $11.41 and $3.30 in neighboring Utah and California, respectively. The table wine tax is $2.34 in North Carolina (the second highest, behind Alaska), but South Carolina's is less than half that at $1.08. The beer tax is $1.05 in Alabama (the second highest, behind Alaska again) but $0.43 in Mississippi (http://taxfoundation.org/publications/show/245.html). As explained in the previous chapter with respect to cigarettes, alcohol taxes are expected to reduce consumption by a large amount for consumers who are very sensitive to price changes (that is, they have an elastic demand) and by a smaller amount for consumers who are not very sensitive to price changes (that is, they have an inelastic demand).

In the early 1980s, the Reagan administration, in an attempt to reduce the incidence of drunk driving, recommended that states enforce an MLDA of 21. Although the federal government could not require the states to comply, it could encourage adoption by withholding federal highway funds from those that did not. Despite early resistance by some of the states, by 1990 every state complied. Most other countries also have age restriction laws for the purchase and consumption of alcoholic beverages. In some cases, these restrictions can be quite detailed. For example, in Austria the purchase and drinking age is generally 16, but there is some local variation:

> Upper Austria and Tirol prohibit the consumption of distilled beverages below the age of 18, while Carinthia and Styria prohibit drinks containing more than 12% or 14% of alcohol respectively in this age bracket. Carinthia additionally requires adolescents to maintain a blood alcohol level below 0.05%, while Upper Austria prohibits "excessive consumption," and Salzburg prohibits consumption that would result in a state of intoxication. Prohibitions in Vienna, Burgenland, Lower Austria and Vorarlberg apply only to alcohol consumption in public. Vienna additionally prohibits the consumption of alcohol in schools under the age of 18. (http://en.wikipedia.org/wiki/Legal_drinking_age)

The typical legal purchase and drinking age around the world is 18, with a handful of countries having the age at 16 or 21, and in some countries drinking is strictly prohibited for all. And while age restrictions do not perfectly keep alcohol out of the hands of those below the legal age, they are expected to reduce youth alcohol consumption by making it more costly for youths to drink.

It can be difficult to obtain direct data on drinking behavior, so many economic studies use data on alcohol taxes or on variations in the MLDA (before it became uniform in the United States at 21) instead. If it is found that taxes or the MLDA affects certain behaviors, you can conclude that the policy and behavior are indirectly linked by alcohol consumption. For example, if increased beer taxes reduce the number of sick days a person takes, it is not due directly to the taxes but indirectly to the reduction in alcohol consumption caused by taxes, with the reduced alcohol consumption reducing the number of sick days. Thus, it is key to examine whether alcohol taxes and an MLDA actually do affect alcohol consumption.

As with cigarette consumption, ample evidence negatively relates alcohol consumption to price. One study (Gallet, 2007) uses the results of over 130 other studies from 24 countries to do what is known as a *meta-analysis* (that is, a systematic procedure for statistically combining the results of many different studies) and finds that beer, wine, and spirit consumption are all sensitive to price changes. The study calculates an elasticity of demand for each beverage, finding it to be (on average) inelastic for beer (0.83) but slightly elastic for wine and spirits (1.11 and 1.09, respectively). Another study (Farrell, Manning, and Finch, 2003) finds that even heavy drinkers are sensitive to changes in the price of alcohol (finding an elasticity of approximately 1.33). The literature shows wide variation in alcohol price elasticities, from close to zero to reasonably elastic, but most agree that the expected inverse relationship between price and consumption does exist. The relationship between the MLDA and alcohol consumption, however, is not as well founded.

A substantial number of studies have examined the impact of MLDA laws on alcohol consumption and other alcohol-related issues (especially on traffic accidents). One very useful literature review (Wagenaar and Toomey, 2002) surveys 132 studies performed from 1960 to 2000, most from the United States but some from Canada, across a variety of disciplines, to determine if a consensus has been reached on the relationship between MLDA laws and alcohol consumption. The authors offer a succinct conclusion over their reading of the vast literature: the preponderance of the evidence indicates an inverse relationship between the MLDA and alcohol consumption. In other words, the policy has been effective at reducing drinking. However, the results can be interpreted quite differently.

Consider the authors' conclusion:

> The preponderance of evidence suggests that higher legal drinking ages reduce alcohol consumption. Of all analyses that reported significant effects, 87% found higher drinking ages associated with lower alcohol consumption. Only 13% found the opposite. The evidence is not entirely consistent: Almost half (46%) of the analyses found no association between the legal age and indicators of alcohol consumption. (Wagenaar and Toomey, 2002, 213)

It is difficult to accept the authors' main conclusion if we express their results differently. If almost half the studies found no association between the MLDA and drinking, and 13 percent of the approximately other half found a positive relationship, one can conclude that *fewer than half* found an inverse relationship between the MLDA and alcohol consumption. This does not seem to warrant the claim that "a preponderance of the evidence" indicates a lower MLDA reduces drinking.

The authors further divide the studies into what they classify as high methodological quality and low methodological quality. Focusing on only the high quality, they find that 33 percent found an inverse relationship between the MLDA and alcohol consumption, and 3 percent found a positive relationship. This leaves a large number (64 percent) that found no relationship at all. Again, what do these results suggest about the relationship between the MLDA and alcohol consumption?

Perhaps the authors are impressed with the minority of studies that find the MLDA reduces alcohol consumption, because as they point out, the MLDA laws are not strongly enforced and are easily circumvented. Many teens report in surveys that they find it easy to acquire alcohol. Many retail establishments do not request identification from underage purchasers, and some teens use false identification. Furthermore, a reasonably substantial number of high school seniors (approximately 10 percent according to one study in Wagenaar and Toomey's review) purchase from retailers who make home deliveries of alcohol. In addition to the ease of acquiring alcohol, the states often do not enforce the MLDA law against retailers and even less often against the teens themselves. Even when the law is enforced, sanctions are often not very severe. Because some studies find the MLDA law, despite light enforcement, reduces teen alcohol consumption, the authors conclude that stronger enforcement may further reduce teen alcohol use.

One study (Kaestner, 2000) specifically addresses the ambiguities associated with examining the impact of the MLDA on alcohol consumption. Using a statistical technique on a sample that includes both men and women ages 17 to 21, the study finds that raising the MLDA does reduce alcohol consumption. When men are examined separately from women, the result still holds for young women but not for young men. When looking at a higher average age group sample, ages 20 to 21, exactly the opposite is found: the result holds for young men but not for young women. When the author tries a completely different statistical technique, he finds that the MDLA has no significant effect on reducing alcohol consumption. Unlike the previous review that concludes that a preponderance of the evidence points to a negative relationship between the MLDA and alcohol consumption, this author offers a different conclusion:

> In the end, I believe the estimates presented in this article are not sufficient to decide either way, and my conclusion is that more research is necessary to establish definitively whether MLDAs have a deterrent effect on alcohol consumption. (Kaestner, 2000, 324)

Unfortunately, because of the nature of empirical analysis, it is doubtful whether a definitive conclusion can ever be reached. The more important point is that, when considering the results of these (or any other) empirical studies, one has to be aware of the inevitable inconsistencies.

One study (Laixuthai and Chaloupka, 1994) finds that either increasing alcohol taxes or raising the MLDA reduces alcohol consumption but argues that tax policy is likely the better choice from a cost-benefit perspective. First, enforcing the US MLDA law likely costs more than increasing taxes. Monitoring retailers (and consumers) to assure that they abide by the law, and punishing those that don't, requires a substantial use of resources. Second, taxes generate revenue that can be devoted toward other policy goals, but the US MLDA law has little potential for raising revenue. Third, to whatever extent alcohol consumption imposes costs on the drinker and others, a tax reduces consumption broadly across *all* drinkers and is not targeted at a specific age demographic. On the other hand, this also presents a downside of taxes over the US MLDA law. Taxes reduce moderate alcohol consumption benefits for all drinkers as opposed to just a narrowly targeted age demographic.

There is one other important consideration when comparing taxation to age restriction. The MLDA law may be played out, at least in the United States. Granted, the federal government can consider increasing the MLDA above 21, and individual states can do as they please, but that is unlikely to be politically feasible or desirable. Alcohol taxes offer tremendous flexibility in adjusting their levels. Strictly from a pragmatic perspective, then, taxation may be the more effective policy tool to reduce alcohol consumption, if that is the desired goal. And as we will see throughout the rest of this chapter, reducing alcohol consumption, especially among youths, is considered by many to be a desired policy goal.

Drinking and High School

One of the major concerns over teen drinking is how it affects high school academic performance and advancement. If drinking impairs students' ability to graduate on time or increases the likelihood of dropping out, teen drinkers may face long-term adverse consequences. As usual, a reverse causation problem needs to be considered. Perhaps other factors account for teen drinking and dropping out of high school, such as being myopic and not overly concerned about future outcomes. Or perhaps once students drop out and find employment, they now have disposable income to purchase more alcohol. Or maybe it is the stress of poor performance in high school that leads students to drink. Whatever the case, numerous studies have examined the link between teen drinking and high school performance.

In two related studies (DeSimone and Wolaver, 2005, and Chatterji and DeSimone, 2005), the authors find evidence that drinking has a negative impact on high school performance. In the first study, the authors find that drinking, especially binge drinking, lowers grades. This effect may be due to drinking taking time away from studying or drinking causing short-term impairment that increases absenteeism or makes it more difficult to concentrate on schoolwork. Although this effect involves, at first, a short-term cost, to the extent that lower grades reduce future academic advancement or reduce the likelihood of graduating, drinking may also impose substantial long-term costs on the student. The second study finds that for 15- and 16-year-old students, binge drinking and frequent drinking (having 14 or more drinks in the previous month) reduces the likelihood of currently being enrolled in or having completed high school four years later by approximately 11 to 13 percent.

Other studies find similar results. Two studies, by the same author (Renna, 2007, 2008), find that binge drinking by high school seniors reduces the probability of graduating with a high school diploma and increases the probability of receiving an exam-certified high school general equivalency diploma (GED). While both diplomas are often considered as counting for 12 years of completed education, and thus treated the same in many studies, there is evidence that GED graduates are more similar to high school dropouts than they are to high school graduates in terms of labor market outcomes such as wages and unemployment (Cameron and Heckman, 1993). Even for those with a high school degree, the author finds that binge drinking negatively impacts future earnings for students who graduate late because of their drinking behavior. Late graduation may signal poor performance to a potential employer, reducing the probability of securing a high-paying job. In fact, the author finds that in 1994 the annual earnings of men who graduated at age 19 were nearly $10,000 higher compared to men who graduated later in life. Furthermore, men who graduated late and those who dropped out of high school have virtually no difference in earnings.

But not all studies find that drinking adversely affects high school academic performance. One study (Dee and Evans, 2003) uses data from the 1980s, when there was state-to-state variation in the US MLDA. The first result is that teens who lived in states with a lower MLDA were substantially more likely to drink than teens in the higher MLDA states. But the second result is that the MLDA had virtually no impact on educational attainment measured by high school completion and college entrance. Thus, the authors conclude that teens who were more likely to drink were *not* less likely to graduate high school or enter college. In addition, the authors find evidence of reverse causation between drinking and educational attainment. Students who were not drinkers in their early high school years but were in their later years tended to be low academic achievers in their early years, suggesting that low academic achievement may lead to drinking as opposed to the other way around. Finally, a recent study (Sabia, 2010) finds that teenage binge drinking has very little impact on three measures of academic performance—grade point average, school suspension, and unexcused absences.

Drinking in College

We've seen some evidence showing that drinking in high school has adverse effects on academic performance. What does alcohol do to students who go on to college? Most college students reach the MLDA while in college, so that in itself can lead to increased alcohol consumption. But underage drinking while in college, just as in high school, can still be a concern. One study (Wolaver, 2002) finds that while being a binge drinker in high school has a small effect on *college* academic performance, concurrent drinking in college has a more significant impact, reducing grade point average, affecting choice of major (more likely to be a business major, less likely to be an engineering major), and reducing future earnings. The negative impact of drinking on college performance is more severe for students under age 21 than it is for those above the MLDA. A similar study (Powell, Williams, and Wechsler, 2004) finds that when considering a full sample of college students, freshmen through seniors, drinking does not affect two measures of academic performance—missing classes and falling behind in school. But the study finds that for upper-level students, that is, not freshmen, an increase in drinking (measured as one additional drink per drinking occasion) increases the probability of missing a class by about 8 percent and the probability of falling behind in school by about 5 percent.

Fraternity membership is often identified as a cause of college binge drinking. (Note that "fraternity" includes sororities in this discussion.) Approximately 15 percent of four-year-college students belong, and these students, on average, experience more binge episodes than nonmember students (DeSimone, 2007). Evidence suggests that students who did not binge drink before entering college are three times more likely to start if they join a fraternity compared to those who did not join one. However, binge drinking behavior no longer differed between members and nonmembers three years after leaving college. Fraternities may induce binge drinking behavior by creating strong peer pressure to drink or by threatening social ostracism of members who do not. Also, binge drinking may simply be considered as part of normal fraternity life, even without further explicit pressure. Finally, these groups may provide frequent and easy access to alcohol through numerous social events.

Yet these links may not be telling us that fraternity membership *causes* binge drinking. It is quite possible that high school students who are already heavy or binge drinkers may have a strong preference to join fraternities precisely because they provide environments that accommodate their preexisting behavior. It may be that even without fraternities these students would continue to binge drink throughout their years in college. Fraternities, in this case, do not cause students to binge drink but just provide a social venue to meet others who share their interests. One study (DeSimone, 2007) uses data from a 1995 survey that includes information on the drinking behavior of 18- to 24-year-old full-time four-year-college students. The study finds that fraternity membership does increase binge drinking behavior and suggests that alcohol control policies that specifically target fraternities and sororities may reduce such behavior in those groups.

Reducing fraternity membership may reduce binge drinking. A clever study (Sacerdote, 2001) examines roommate assignment at Dartmouth College and student behavior. In 1993 Dartmouth adopted a random (for the most part) roommate assignment system for incoming freshmen. In addition to gender, each freshman was distinguished by responses to four lifestyle questions involving smoking, listening to music when studying, keeping late hours, and neatness. Other than these distinctions, roommates were assigned randomly. One result of the study is that roommates affect each others' behavior, especially with regard to joining fraternities. If a student who is initially likely to join a fraternity is paired with someone who does not show an initial interest in joining one, the student inclined to join the fraternity tends to influence the roommate. Eliminating the possibility of this influence by using nonrandom roommate assignments—that is, matching likely fraternity members with each other—can reduce the number of students drawn to excessive drinking. Of course, fraternities and sororities could be banned altogether, but this extreme policy would eliminate the benefits such organizations provide students during their college years and throughout the rest of their lives.

Conventional social control policies, such as increased taxation, may not be too effective in reducing binge drinking, especially for college students. One study (Chaloupka and Wechsler, 1996) examines how increased beer taxes affect binge drinking rates of college men and women. While women are slightly responsive to beer prices, with higher prices reducing their binge drinking rate, men are not responsive at all. Furthermore, the slight responsiveness by women suggests that beer taxes would have to be substantially increased to have even a small effect on reducing binge drinking. For example, a doubling of the federal beer tax is predicted to reduce women's binge drinking rate by only 2 percent (with that rate approximately 40 percent at the time of the study). College students may not be very responsive to price because many students have access to free alcohol at parties or they enjoy discounted prices at local bars trying to attract students. Whatever the reason, if binge drinking in college is considered to be a serious social problem, unique policies may be required to deal with it.

On the other hand, using different data and fine-tuning their results, in a follow-up study the authors (Williams, Chaloupka, and Wechsler, 2005) look at how alcohol price changes and campus bans affect college student drinking intensity. They find that, as price increases, students are less likely to make the transition from abstainer to moderate drinker and less likely to make the transition from moderate drinker to heavy drinker. As for campus alcohol bans, they have more of an impact on discouraging an abstainer from becoming a moderate drinker than on discouraging a moderate drinker from becoming a heavy drinker.

Drinking and Sex

Many studies examine the relationship between drinking, especially heavy and binge drinking, and sexual activity with someone who is not a long-term partner. Among college student respondents in the 1995 survey, above, of college student behavior, 23 percent of four-year-college students who had ever had sex admitted to using alcohol or drugs before their last sexual encounter. This form of risky behavior can lead to serious long-term health costs if sexually transmitted diseases (STDs) are spread or if unwanted pregnancies occur. Once again, however, identifying the direction of causation between alcohol and sex is important before considering appropriate policy controls.

It may be the case that college students who enjoy drinking attend parties that serve alcohol to meet other students who enjoy drinking. Or some students may have strong preferences for many types of risky behavior, including binge drinking, unprotected sex, and drug use. In these situations, the alcohol is not what causes the risky sexual behavior but other factors. Then again, it may be that alcohol impairs the judgment of those who binge or lowers their inhibitions, thus creating a more direct link between excessive drinking and risky sexual behavior. One study (DeSimone, 2010) finds that while current binge drinking has little influence on students' likelihood of being sexually active (that has more to do with students having been sexually active in the past), it does have a direct relationship with sexual activity with multiple recent partners and with not always using condoms. In other words, the results of this study suggest that binge drinking doesn't make the student more likely to have sex but more likely to engage in risky sex.

Several other studies have looked at drinking and sexual behavior without regard to college attendance, especially for teens and young adults. The basic result found in the previous study often (but not always) holds—alcohol doesn't much affect probability of having sex, but it does affect probability of having unprotected sex. One study (Grossman, Kaestner, and Markowitz, 2005) examines alcohol and STDs. The authors look at how certain alcohol control policies affect STD rates. The idea is that if the control policies reduce alcohol consumption and if reduced alcohol consumption reduces the spread of STDs, then there is an indirect link between the policies and the spread of STDs. For example, the study finds that increased beer taxes and zero-tolerance laws reduce the male gonorrhea rate, but BAC laws in general and dry counties do not. (Zero tolerance is directed at underage drinking and allows young drivers to have a BAC of 0.02 percent or less, compared to an adult BAC limit of 0.08 or 0.10 percent.)

If alcohol consumption leads to an increased chance of unprotected sex, that not only spreads STDs but also increases unwanted pregnancies, especially among teens. In addition to the potential costs to the child of being born to a single teenage mother, the mother herself bears increased physical and possibly mental health costs, as well as increased difficulties in educational and occupational attainment. One study (Dee, 2001) examines how changes in the US MLDA throughout the 1980s affected teen pregnancy rates. The first set of results the author reports is that MLDA significantly affected pregnancy rates of black and white teens. Teens who lived in states with a low MLDA had a greater chance of becoming pregnant. But the author delved deeper.

As previously discussed, many unobserved factors that do not involve an MLDA could account for teen pregnancy rates across states. To try to correct for this, the author uses a control group of older women who, by definition, are not affected by the MLDA. Thus, if a variation in teen pregnancy rates is not also seen in the control group, the variation is likely due to the effect of the MLDA (and therefore, indirectly, alcohol consumption) on teen pregnancy rates. With this method, the author's more precise results are that increases in the MLDA do not affect white teen pregnancy rates but do affect black teen rates. An MLDA of 21 (before that became the law) would reduce black teen pregnancy rates by 6 percent.

Along similar lines, another study (Sen, 2003) examines the effect of beer taxes on teen birth rates and abortion rates. The results of this study are interesting, as the author finds that increased beer taxes reduce teen abortion rates but *not* teen birth rates. The implication of this finding is that increased beer taxes reduce unwanted pregnancies that would likely have been terminated through abortion rather than leading to increased birth rates. The author finds, however, that the effect is small. Quantitatively, if beer tax rates increased by 100 percent (a large increase), teen abortion rates would fall by only 7 to 10 percent.

Thus far, many studies have demonstrated that drinking, especially among teens and college students, can lead to all sorts of long-term costs. At their young age, the health benefits of moderate drinking are not yet realized and heavy or binge drinking may impair academic performance and lead to bad decisions. But for those students who do make it through college and find themselves gainfully employed, drinking may actually be career improving. We turn now to examining this unusual result.

The Drinker's Bonus

In the academic literature on drinking, economists often puzzle over a paradox that appears to be supported by a tremendous amount of empirical evidence: drinkers earn higher wages than nondrinkers. Why is this a paradox? How much someone earns is typically directly related to his or her productivity; that is, more productive people earn more. Alcohol is considered to be impairing, and impairment is expected to reduce productivity. From a commonsense perspective, then, drinkers would be less productive and earn less than nondrinkers. But if this is not the case, if drinking actually improves the productivity of workers, alcohol control policy may ultimately be detrimental to the economy as a whole. So it is important to carefully examine the paradox of the drinker's bonus to determine if it is valid or just a myth.

The first explanation to account for the drinker's bonus is that, as discussed above, moderate drinking provides health benefits relative to abstinence or excessive drinking. Healthy workers are likely to be more productive, both in terms of how they perform while at work and of being at work more often. If this is the explanation, we may be able to fine-tune the drinker's bonus to demonstrate that it is not being a drinker that yields the bonus but being a *moderate* drinker. One study (French and Zarkin, 1995) using US data finds evidence that those who have between 1.70 and 2.40 drinks per day have higher wages than those who drink less *or* more than those amounts. Another study using UK data (MacDonald and Shields, 2001) also finds that moderate drinking yields higher wages than abstinence, and these returns drop off sharply as alcohol consumption increases beyond the moderate level.

Not all studies that find a drinker's bonus, however, attribute that bonus *solely* to moderate drinking. Two of the authors of the above study using US data update their results in another study (Zarkin et al., 1998) and find that even excessive drinking yields a bonus. Their main result is that male drinkers earn about a 7 percent wage premium relative to male nondrinkers, and this holds true over a wide range of alcohol consumption amounts. They also find a similar result for female drinkers, although the premium is much smaller, suggesting the bonus may be gender specific. Another study (Auld, 2005) finds that while moderate drinking causes a 10 percent increase in income relative to abstinence, heavy drinking causes a 12 percent increase. This also suggests that the drinker's bonus exists across a wide range of alcohol consumption amounts.

If heavy drinking leads to higher earnings than abstinence or moderate drinking does, perhaps it isn't increased productivity that accounts for the drinker's bonus. Another explanation for this phenomenon has to do with the social aspect of drinking. Having the opportunity to drink with your coworkers or clients allows you to get to know them better, and this may give you an advantage in your business dealings with them. Furthermore, even if you are drinking with strangers, you may be developing contacts that can help you in the future. If there is truth to the old saying "It's not what you know, it's who you know," social drinking may help you broaden your contacts. One study (Peters and Stringham, 2006) confirms that drinkers earn more than nondrinkers (with the premium being between 10 and 14 percent), and this holds for both men and women. But to examine the social aspect of drinking, the study compares drinking socially (in bars, for example) to drinking nonsocially and finds that men receive an *additional* wage premium of approximately 7 percent (women receive none).

To further examine the social aspect of drinking, a related follow-up study (Peters, 2009) takes advantage of an interesting data set that includes wages of military officers and enlisted personnel. Looking for the drinker's bonus among military personnel, the study finds that it exists for both officers and enlisted personnel, but the bonuses are not of the same magnitude for each group. The bonus for officers who drink compared to those who do not is larger than the bonus for enlisted personnel who drink compared to those who do not. In explaining this bonus differential, the author turns to the social aspect of drinking. In the military, pay raises are linked to promotions, and promotions for enlisted personnel depend on fairly objective factors, typically based on past performance. For officers, however, promotion is more subjective, as future potential is a key factor. Furthermore, officers considered for promotion are reviewed by other officers, suggesting more of a peer effect than exists with enlisted personnel. The enhanced drinker's bonus for officers may be further evidence of the value of social drinking.

On the other hand, the drinker's bonus may be a myth, yet another example of the difficulty in distinguishing between correlation and causation. There does not seem to be much debate that earnings and alcohol use are positively related, but in what direction does the causation run? For example, it is possible that a person who is hardworking and highly productive deals with much stress while at work and likes to unwind at night with a couple of drinks. In this case, it is not drinking increasing productivity but productivity increasing drinking. Or, even more basically, perhaps increased income leads to increased drinking.

One study (Cook and Peters, 2005) uses data for young adults ages 27 to 34 and examines the impact of alcohol taxes on labor supply and earnings. The authors first confirm, with their particular data set, that the drinker's bonus exists. They then find that increased alcohol prices are associated with higher full-time work participation rates and earnings. In other words, increased alcohol taxes can reduce alcohol consumption, and this leads to improved job market opportunities for full-time workers. How do the authors reconcile *reduced* drinking through taxation leading to higher earnings with a drinker's bonus? The increased earnings of full-time workers also affect alcohol consumption. As these workers become wealthier, their demand for alcohol increases. Thus, a reverse causation problem must be disentangled. Reduced drinking can improve wages (the direct link between alcohol and earnings), but increased earnings can increase alcohol consumption (the direct link between earnings and alcohol). Overall, drinking and earnings are positively related *without* the existence of a drinker's bonus.

Still other studies find inconclusive evidence for the drinker's bonus. One thorough study (Dave and Kaestner, 2001) concludes that because of serious data limitations and methodological problems, the relationship between alcohol consumption and labor market outcomes is weak and indeterminate at best. And an even earlier study (Mullahy and Sindelar, 1993) offers a point that is still valid nearly 20 years later:

> Studies of the effects of alcohol on earnings, income, and productivity have to date yielded conflicting results. The popular view that has been confirmed in several studies is that problem drinking has depressant effects on income. Recently, however, some studies have found insignificant effects or even positive effects of alcohol use. Part of the confusion owes to differences in drinking measures used in these studies. . . . That different studies have employed different measures of labor market success . . . and/or have focused on different populations . . . only serves to compound the confusion. (Mullahy and Sindelar, 1993, 515)

As with all empirical debates, sincere differences in methodological approaches can lead to widely differing results. Yet to the extent that the drinker's bonus exists, it complicates justifying social control policy to protect drinkers from themselves.

Targeting Youths

The usual concern regarding advertising and alcohol is trying to determine how much of an impact advertising has on consumer demand. As with cigarettes, the fundamental debate is whether alcohol advertising increases the aggregate demand for alcohol or whether it simply leads to brand substitution. Here, however, we focus on a different issue. A more specific concern with cigarette, alcohol, and fast-food advertising is how youths are affected by the ads. One study (Nelson, 2006a) provides a different take on the issue. Instead of trying to determine how youths are affected by alcohol advertising, the author examines how alcohol advertising (in magazines) is affected by youths.

Advertisers of many products considered vices are often accused of specifically targeting youths with their ads. Attracting young people to their product is immediately profitable, and it is believed that for addictive goods advertising can hook a consumer for a long time. In 2003 the alcohol beverage industry (beer, wine, and distilled spirits) spent nearly $400 million on magazine advertising (and a total of $1.6 billion in all media outlets). Public concern and several reports by high-profile private institutes led to each branch of the alcohol beverage industry enacting its own guidelines (wine in 2000 and beer and spirits in 2003), including confining advertisers to magazine outlets that had at least a 70 percent adult audience (the previous beer and spirits codes specified a 50 percent adult audience). For many outside the industry, these standards were still not strict enough.

Self-enforced industry standards can be interpreted in different ways. On the one hand, it suggests that the industry is concerned about certain social issues and demonstrating it has a social conscience. On the other hand, maybe it is avoiding state intervention, which may be much stricter and costlier to the industry. Even more cynically, maybe the standards are a clever public relations campaign and irrelevant to actual industry practices. If alcohol producers rarely advertise in magazines that have an adult audience of less than 70 percent or if they don't intentionally target the youth market, the self-imposed standards are meaningless. Thus, how alcohol advertisers choose magazines may tell us something about their actual intentions in terms of the youth market.

The study's data set includes 28 magazines covering a wide variety of subject matter, including news (*Time*, *Newsweek*), sports (*Sports Illustrated*, *ESPN The Magazine*), women's interest (*Cosmopolitan*, *Vogue*), automobiles (*Hot Rod*, *Motor Trend*), and entertainment (*Entertainment Weekly*, *Rolling Stone*). From 2001 to 2003 the magazines with the most alcohol ads are *Sports Illustrated* (446 ads), *Maxim* (453 ads), and *Rolling Stone* (446 ads). The magazines with the greatest percentages of youth audience (defined as number of teens, ages 12 to 19, divided by total audience) are *The Source* (33.3 percent), *Allure* (30.5 percent), and *Spin* (29.3 percent). The magazines with the smallest percentage of youth audience are *Better Homes and Gardens* (4.7 percent), *Newsweek* (8.6 percent), and *Time* (9.8 percent). Other information for each magazine in the data set includes total circulation, ad cost per thousand circulation, and adult median age and real income.

The results of the study suggest that the key variables in determining magazine alcohol advertising are the (real, inflation-adjusted) prices for placing the ads, audience size (where "audience" takes into account readers per copy and not just circulation), and adult demographics. The percentage of youth audience has no effect on the decision to advertise in a specific magazine. Thus, industry self-regulation may have little impact on advertising behavior, and state regulation along the same lines may have little impact. In fact, the main policy conclusion of the author is this:

> Policy makers in the alcohol area would be well advised to turn their attention to discussion of matters of importance for youthful drinking behaviors, rather than decisions made in the market for advertising space. (Nelson, 2006a, 368)

Of course, even if alcohol advertisers have no intention of explicitly targeting the youth audience, that portion of the magazine audience is still being exposed to alcohol ads. If these ads influence youth alcohol consumption, there may still be a social policy issue to consider.

Other studies examine various aspects of youth drinking behavior. One study (Nelson, 2008b) examines the drinking behavior for youths (ages 12 to 17), young adults (ages 18 to 25), and adults (age 26 and above). The study offers several results. First, youth drinking prevalence, young adult drinking prevalence, and adult drinking prevalence show a very strong correlation, with higher correlations applying to young adults and adults. Second, taxes on beer do not appear to change youth or young adult drinking prevalence or binge drinking. It is not so much that youths do not respond to changes in the price of beer but that, in this data set, the variation in price *due to taxes* does not have an effect on drinking behavior.

Third, while higher retail-outlet densities have a positive effect on young adult and adult drinking prevalence, they do not influence youth drinking prevalence or binge drinking. The full cost of purchasing alcohol includes not only the retail price but also the inconvenience costs (travel, time, and so on) of getting to the retail outlet. The more alcohol retail outlets there are in a given geographic area, the lower alcohol's full cost. That these additional costs do not influence youth drinking behaviors suggests that youths are often exposed to alcohol through noncommercial sources, such as at parties or from their parents' liquor cabinets.

Fourth, attendance at major sports events (professional baseball, football, hockey, and basketball) does not have a positive effect on youth drinking prevalence or binge drinking. This result is at odds with the common belief (supported by some other studies) that exposure to alcohol advertising and sponsorship of sporting events encourages youth drinking. Finally, the study finds that certain social control policies do reduce youth and young adult drinking prevalence and binge drinking. The three most effective policies are state monopoly control over retail liquor outlets, bans on Sunday retail outlet alcohol purchases, and a 0.08 percent BAC threshold for drunk driving laws.

Another serious issue concerning youth drinking is the possible association between alcohol abuse and suicide. If drinking increases youth suicide rates, policies that reduce alcohol consumption protect youths from the most self-destructive of all acts. But, as usual, a reverse causation issue must be addressed. Is it that alcohol use increases the likelihood of suicide, or do other factors, such as depression, encourage *both* alcohol use and suicide? One study (Chatterji, Dave, Kaestner, and Markowitz, 2004) finds that alcohol consumption does directly affect youth suicide attempt rates, but in a specific way. Binge drinking does not appear to affect suicide attempt rates, but more persistent alcohol use does.

To identify alcohol abuse and dependency, the study relies on data generated by the Composite International Diagnostic Interview (CIDI), developed by the National Institutes of Health, the World Health Organization, and the University of Michigan:

> The CIDI . . . is a non-clinician administered instrument, which generates psychiatric diagnoses. The CIDI has undergone extensive testing for reliability and validity. Alcohol abuse is defined as either continued use despite knowledge of its adverse effect on health and social functioning or recurrent use in situations when use may be physically hazardous. Alcohol dependence requires the presence of physiological symptoms of tolerance and withdrawal and continued use despite adverse consequences. (Chatterji, Dave, Kaestner, and Markowitz, 2003, 16)

The main result of the study is that there is a causation between alcohol use, defined as abuse or dependence, and suicide attempt rates among young girls (grades 9 through 12) but not among young boys.

Run for the Border

Taxation may be the most common policy tool used to control drinking, but it is a tool that can run into some pragmatic difficulties. When different regions—whether cities, states, or countries—enforce different tax rates, it is possible for people in a high-tax region to purchase alcohol in a bordering low-tax region. Of course, the price differential must be enough to make the journey worthwhile, but if it is, the policy objectives of one region may be partially thwarted by the policies of another.

One study (Beatty, Lasen, and Sommervoll, 2009) examines tax avoidance behavior between Norway, with a relatively high alcohol tax rate, and its neighbor Sweden, with a relatively low tax rate. The authors present evidence that the real price of alcoholic beverages in Norway is 66 percent higher than it is in Sweden. The stated policy of the Norwegian government to reduce alcoholic consumption appears to be reasonably successful, as per capita consumption is lower than in most western European countries and the lowest among Nordic countries. In addition to taxation, Norway imposes personal import quotas on travel abroad, time-of-day restrictions on sales, and age restrictions, and it limits sales of strong alcoholic beverages to state-owned stores.

Although it is legal to bring a certain amount of alcohol purchased outside Norway into the country, the allowable amounts are modest, and there is a strong price incentive to smuggle in a greater amount. The study finds some evidence of such behavior. Retail stores near the Swedish border report lower alcohol sales revenues than stores farther from the border. In addition, households near the border report higher expenditures on alcohol than households farther from the border. These two facts together strongly suggest the existence of a tax-avoidance cross-border purchasing effect. Thus, tax policy in Norway is partially undermined by tax policy in Sweden.

Alcohol and Marijuana

As discussed in chapter 2, a well-intentioned public policy can often have perverse unintended consequences. Separate policies aimed at reducing alcohol consumption and marijuana use may be at cross-purposes. For example, as authorities increase sanctions for marijuana use, that may reduce marijuana use, but it may inadvertently increase alcohol consumption. Likewise, taxes and other policies intended to reduce alcohol consumption may lead to increased marijuana use. Thus, it is important to understand the relationship between alcohol and marijuana use in evaluating the effectiveness of social control policies.

Two basic relationships can exist between alcohol and marijuana (or any two goods for that matter)—they may be *substitutes* or *complements*.

Formally, two goods are substitutes for each other when their *cross-price elasticity of demand* is positive. This means that as the price of marijuana increases, for example, consumption of alcohol *increases*. Marijuana users, facing higher prices, substitute for the now relatively more expensive drug with the relatively less expensive alcohol. Conversely, if the price of marijuana decreases, consumption of alcohol also *decreases* as users substitute it with more marijuana consumption. If users are more concerned with feeling intoxicated and less concerned with precisely how they become intoxicated, alcohol and marijuana may serve a similar purpose and indeed be substitutes.

On the other hand, alcohol and marijuana may be complements, meaning that the cross-price elasticity of demand is negative. If they are complements, as the price of marijuana increases, the consumption of marijuana *and* alcohol decreases. As the price of marijuana decreases, the consumption of both goods increases. Perhaps people, especially when young, who are most likely to experiment with alcohol may also be most likely to experiment with marijuana. If they can directly be discouraged from trying one, they may also indirectly be discouraged from trying the other. Also, some may find that alcohol and marijuana go well together, similar to how smoking cigarettes and drinking in bars are often thought of as complementary activities.

Clearly, the public policy implication of the relationship between alcohol and marijuana use can be profound. If the war on drugs inadvertently leads to increased consumption of alcohol, that is important to consider when evaluating that policy. And while numerous studies attempt to determine the relationship between alcohol and marijuana use, the results, not surprisingly, are mixed. Researchers have to grapple with the usual data and statistical methodology issues, and more fundamentally, there is good reason to believe that alcohol and marijuana are substitutes for some users but complements for others. This further complicates the policy analysis.

One study that finds alcohol and marijuana to be substitutes (DiNardo and Lemieux, 2001) examines the impact of an increase in the MLDA on marijuana use. Using a sample of high school seniors throughout the 1980s, the study found that increasing the MLDA reduced alcohol use but also increased marijuana use. Another study (Chaloupka and Laixuthai, 1997) also finds that alcohol and marijuana are substitutes for high school seniors. This study examines the impact of marijuana decriminalization and prices on drinking behavior. Although decriminalization does not make marijuana legal, reduced sanctions for its use can encourage more consumption. The study finds that youths in states that decriminalized marijuana use consumed alcohol less frequently and were less likely to engage in heavy drinking than youths in states that didn't. As for the marijuana price effect on alcohol consumption (price data collected by the Drug Enforcement Agency), the results generally support the previous result. As the price of marijuana increases, the consumption of marijuana decreases but the consumption of alcohol increases, suggesting they are substitutes.

Two other studies, however, find that alcohol and marijuana are complements. The first study (Pacula, 1998) finds that for young adults, average age 22, as beer taxes increase, marijuana consumption is reduced even more (in percentage terms) than alcohol consumption. Another study (Williams, Pacula, Chaloupka, and Wechsler, 2004) examines alcohol and marijuana use among college students and finds that, as the price of marijuana increases, the consumption of alcohol falls. The authors also find that policies that restrict the use of alcohol on campus and laws that restrict off-campus happy hours (when alcohol is sold at discounted prices) reduce marijuana use. Taken in all, these studies make it difficult to come to a conclusion about the relationship between alcohol and marijuana use, other than noting that policies targeted at one of the substances will likely affect use of the other.

The Hazards of Health Insurance

Let's say there has been a medical breakthrough of immense proportions. Researchers at a pharmaceutical company have designed a pill that completely erases adverse effects of alcohol abuse. You can be a heavy drinker for decades, and just one of these wonder pills rejuvenates you. It would be as if you had never been a drinker at all. In other words, the future costs of current alcohol use have plummeted. This would certainly be wonderful for all the 50-year-old drinkers currently suffering from alcohol-related illnesses. But what would 21-year-old onset drinkers do? A young potential drinker would be aware that she can abuse alcohol for many years while erasing any adverse effects. Knowing the wonder pill is available may increase her likelihood of becoming a drinker or increase the amount of alcohol she consumes throughout her life. The pill, designed to mitigate the adverse effects of alcohol abuse, may also perversely aggravate the adverse effects. The existence of the pill, in other words, affects current behavior.

Although that is an extreme hypothetical example, the existence of health insurance makes possible a similar problem. As long as you continue to pay your insurance premium, some (or most) of your losses will be covered by your insurance provider. Thus, you do not bear the full costs of your behavior. If you are an excessive drinker who will eventually need a liver transplant, you will have the cost of that operation subsidized for you. As with the miracle pill, knowing that you can rejuvenate your liver at relatively low cost to yourself may affect your current drinking behavior. This is an insurance problem known as *moral hazard*.

The concept of moral hazard entails the mere availability of insurance affecting behavior, which stems from two basic conditions. The first is *full insurance*. If you are covered for *all* your losses, in theory you are indifferent as to the losses occurring or not occurring. That is, you no longer care if you suffer adverse health outcomes, and you have no incentive to reduce your likelihood of suffering these losses. Would you be as concerned with preventing yourself from drinking more often if someone else covered your medical expenses? Keep in mind that for now we are discussing a *theoretical* possibility, not a real-world one.

The second condition is *unobservable care*. If the insurance company can observe how much you drink (or smoke or eat or exercise or anything else that affects the probability of suffering losses), it can peg your insurance premium to your behavior. A heavy drinker pays more for insurance, giving him an incentive to reduce alcohol consumption and lower insurance premiums. But if the insurance provider cannot observe how much you drink (or if by law the insurer is prevented from setting different premium rates based on different behaviors), one rate will be set regardless of whether you reduce your consumption of alcohol. With a single rate that cannot adjust, you may lack the incentive to reduce your alcohol consumption.

Moral hazard is a controversial topic, and there have been many studies across many types of behaviors to determine its impact on real-world behavior. One such study (Klick and Stratmann, 2006) considering health insurance and alcohol consumption provides a nice illustration for our purposes. Traditionally, health insurance plans provided stronger coverage for physical ailments than mental illnesses, including addiction treatments. But throughout the 1980s and 1990s, most states enacted mental health parity mandates that required insurance plans to set terms for mental illnesses that were similar to those for physical illnesses. Although the plans varied across the states, the strongest laws required parity in terms of deductibles, co-payments, annual expense caps, and visitation limits. This study examines the period 1988 to 1998, during which 10 states explicitly included substance abuse as part of their parity mandate (Georgia, Kansas, Maryland, Minnesota, Missouri, Montana, New York, North Dakota, South Carolina, and Vermont), and 3 states explicitly excluded substance abuse (Arizona, Colorado, and Texas).

One prediction of the effect of these parity laws is that addicts, appreciating the nature of the laws, will find that future addiction treatment costs have fallen, implying that it is less costly to increase their *current* alcohol consumption. This is a classic example of moral hazard. The study finds that passage of an addiction mandate does lead to increased beer consumption. Quantitatively, the strongest finding is that per capita beer consumption increases by approximately 48 beers (12-ounce beers) per year. While this may not seem like a tremendous increase (about 1 beer per week), in the study's data set per capita beer consumption for those age 14 years or older is approximately 352 beers per year. Thus, the existence of the substance abuse mandate appears to enhance average beer consumption by nearly 14 percent. States that exclude substance abuse from their mandate do not see an increase in per capita beer consumption.

While a thorough discussion of the impact from moral hazard of insurance on health outcomes is beyond the scope of this book, it is important to recognize that policies that reduce addicts' cost of treatment may well increase consumption of the substance. And this holds true for not only drinking but also every type of behavior that adversely affects health. Of course, in the real world the concept of *full* insurance is unlikely to perfectly hold. There are always some losses that are not insured or cannot be insured. And to the extent that a person bears some of his or her own losses, that can mitigate the impact of moral hazard. Still, while the *extent* of the moral hazard problem can be debated, especially in terms of health risks, among economists its existence is widely accepted.

Economists have been studying smoking and drinking behavior for many years, but only relatively recently have they tackled the issue addressed in the next chapter—obesity. While people can live comfortable lives without ever smoking or drinking, everyone needs to eat. Using social policy to control excessive eating or to encourage increased physical activity can be more complex than trying to control smoking and drinking. If you want to use tax policy to reduce smoking, you tax cigarettes. If you want to reduce drinking, you tax alcohol. But if you want to reduce excessive eating, precisely what foods do you tax? And if you want to use social policy to reduce smoking and drinking among youths, age restriction policies are commonly enacted. But can you apply the same type of policy to reduce youth obesity rates? The main focus of the next chapter is to review the economic literature on why obesity rates have skyrocketed over the past few decades, in the United States and many other countries. With an understanding of why people are obese, and becoming more obese, the role of social policy to reduce obesity can be informatively addressed.

Suggested Readings

Papers examining the effect of price changes on alcohol consumption are by Coate and Grossman (1988), Chaloupka and Wechsler (1996), Young and Bielinska (2002), Williams, Chaloupka, and Wechsler (2005), Farrell, Manning, and Finch (2003), Cook, Ostermann, and Sloan (2005a, 2005b), Kenkel (2005), Gallet (2007), Ayyagari et al. (2009), Ludbrook (2009), la Cour and Milhoj (2009), and Asgeirdottir and McGeary (2009).

A substantial review that summarizes many studies on the effect of the MLDA law on alcohol consumption is by Wagenaar and Toomey (2002). Also see the papers by Kaestner (2000), Miron and Tetelbaum (2009), and Fertig and Watson (2009).

Papers on drinking and high school academic performance are by Koch and Ribar (2001), Dee and Evans (2003), DeSimone and Wolaver (2005), Chatterji and DeSimone (2005), Koch and McGeary (2005), Renna (2007, 2008), Gil and Molina (2007), and Sabia (2010). Also see the paper by Cameron and Heckman (1993) on the value of a high school diploma versus a GED. Papers on drinking and college academic performance are by Wolaver (2002), Williams, Powell, and Wechsler (2003), and Powell, Williams, and Wechsler (2004).

Papers on the influence of fraternities and sororities and peer effects on drinking behavior are by Sacerdote (2001), DeSimone (2007, 2009), and Lundborg (2006).

Of the many studies on drinking and risky sexual behavior, some representative ones are by Chesson, Harrison, and Kassler (2000), Rees, Argys, and Averett (2001), Dee (2001), Sen (2002, 2003), Grossman, Kaestner, and Markowitz (2005), Rashad and Kaestner (2004), Markowitz, Kaestner, and Grossman (2005), Grossman and Markowitz (2005), and DeSimone (2010).

The impact of alcohol consumption on wages and job attainment is one of the prominent drinking issues that economists study. The following papers provide a sampling of the literature over the past 20 years: Berger and Leigh (1988), Mullahy and Sindelar (1993), French and Zarkin (1995), Heien (1996), Zarkin et al. (1998), MacDonald and Shields (2001), Dave and Kaestner (2002), van Ours (2004), Auld (2005), Bray (2005), Cook and Peters (2005), Peters and Stringham (2006), Peters (2009), and Keng and Huffman (2010). Also see the paper by Kenkel and Wang (1998).

Papers on the effect of advertising on alcohol consumption are by Nelson (1999, 2005, 2006a, 2008a), Saffer and Dave (2002, 2006), Siegel et al. (2008), Frank (2008), and Rojas and Peterson (2008).

Papers on the relationship between alcohol consumption and marijuana use are by DiNardo and Lemieux (2001), Thies and Register (1993), Chaloupka and Laixuthai (1997), Pacula (1998), and Williams et al. (2004). Similar papers on the relationship between alcohol and tobacco are by Picone, Sloan, and Trogdon (2004), and Pierani and Tiezzi (2009).

Other papers on alcohol issues are by Laixuthai and Chaloupka (1994) on youth alcohol use and public policy; Moore and Cook (1995) on youth alcohol addiction; Dee (1999) on teen drinking and traffic fatalities; Arcidiacono, Sieg, and Sloan (2007) on rational drinking behavior; Chatterji et al. (2004) on drinking and teen suicide; Klick and Stratmann (2006) on health insurance and drinking; Beatty, Larsen, and Sommervoll (2009) on alcohol tax avoidance; Liang and Huang (2008) on zero tolerance laws and drinking and driving behavior; and Dave and Saffer (2008) on drinking and risk preferences. Also see the papers by Delaney, Harmon, and Wall (2008) and Nelson (2008b).

A comprehensive survey on the economics of alcohol is by Cook and Moore (2000). Also see the excellent book by Cook (2007).

4

ALL YOU CAN EAT

One of the best things about being an economist is that we get to raise questions that, to most people, would seem utterly ridiculous. Let's begin this chapter with one such question: Can anyone truly ever be *over*weight? The obvious answer is of course! In 2003 approximately 31 percent of Americans were classified as obese. For a global perspective, rounding out the top five nations with 2003's highest obesity rates are Mexico (24 percent), United Kingdom (23 percent), Slovakia (22 percent), and Greece (22 percent). On the thinner end of the spectrum, Japan and Korea have obesity rates of only 3 percent (http://nationmaster.com/graph/hea_obe-health-obesity).

In addition to the high obesity rates, the *trend* toward obesity has been a concern to many. For example, using data from the United States, the obesity rate climbed from 15 percent in 1980, to 23 percent in 1994, to 27 percent in 1999 (http://www.surgeongeneral.gov/topics/obesity/calltoaction/1_4.htm#fig4). Many other nations have experienced similar trends. Perhaps even more alarming, obesity rates for children have also been on the rise. For children in the United States ages 12 through 19, obesity rates have increased from 5 percent in 1980, to 10 percent in 1994, to 18 percent in 2006 (see http://www.cdc.gov/nchs/data/hestat/obesity_child_07_08/obesity_child_07_08.htm for more statistics on obesity rate trends). Currently, smoking is the number-one cause of death in the United States, with obesity close behind and expected to overtake smoking in the next decade or two. Many consider the obesity problem to be an epidemic:

> *Epidemic*, a word typically used for outbreaks of infectious disease, is now being used by medical professionals to describe the prevalence and rapid rise of obesity in the United States. With over 60 percent of American adults either overweight or obese, the numbers alone support the use of the word. "Obesity is not a benign disorder," says William Dietz, M.D., Ph.D., director of CDC's Division of Nutrition and Physical Activity. "It is a major public health concern because it is associated with chronic diseases including cardiovascular disease, diabetes and some types of cancer." In children, being overweight leads to hypertension, abnormal lipid values, sleep apnea, gallbladder disease, and bony abnormalities—particularly of the legs. Type 2 diabetes, formally called adult onset diabetes, is now occurring in adolescents. (Centers for Disease Control and Prevention [CDC] Foundation, http://www.cdcfoundation .org/healththreats/obesity.aspx)

Although we know being overweight or obese can lead to serious adverse health outcomes, there is still a difficult question to address: Absent a biological predisposition or a medical condition, doesn't one's weight depend on a series of personal *choices*?

How much you weigh primarily depends on two simple things—energy in and energy out. Eating accumulates calories, and physical activity burns calories. How much food do you eat? What type of food do you eat? How much exercising do you do? What type of exercising do you do? In other words, we each choose our weight, so aren't we all, in a manner of speaking, at our correct weight? So maybe being overweight is a personal issue, a problem we have to face on our own. But medical science defines obesity; it is not a personal preference—the medical profession dictates an ideal weight for you. According to the medical definitions of obesity, society has a substantial health issue. So, how is obesity defined?

Who Is Obese?

A common method for measuring whether a person is overweight or obese is to calculate a *body mass index* (BMI). The calculation's simple formula uses your weight and height, in kilograms and meters or pounds and inches. You can take your weight in kilograms and divide by your height in meters squared.

Or take your weight in pounds and divide by your height in inches squared, and multiply all that by 703. The BMI applies to any adult (age 20 or over) of either gender.

The medical profession classifies weight categories in the following way: For a BMI less than 18.5, the person is underweight. For a BMI between 18.5 and 24.9, the person is normal weight. Between 25 and 29.9, the person is overweight, and a BMI of 30 or above is in the obesity category. The CDC offers a handy calculator for determining BMI (http://www.cdc.gov/healthy weight/assessing/bmi/adult_bmi/english_bmi_calculator/bmi_calculator .html). If you plug in a height of, say, 6 feet and a weight of 200 pounds, it displays this message:

> Your BMI is 27.1, indicating your weight is in the overweight category for adults of your height. For your height, a normal weight range would be from 136 to 184 pounds. People who are overweight or obese are at higher risk for chronic conditions such as high blood pressure, diabetes, and high cholesterol. Anyone who is overweight should try to avoid gaining additional weight. Additionally, if you are overweight with other risk factors (such as high LDL cholesterol, low HDL cholesterol, or high blood pressure), you should try to lose weight. Even a small weight loss (just 10% of your current weight) may help lower the risk of disease. Talk with your healthcare provider to determine appropriate ways to lose weight.

The CDC website provides useful information to help the public better understand the potentially adverse health effects of being overweight or obese.

For children and teens, the benchmark BMI weight categories are age and sex specific, and again determined by the medical profession. Those under age 20 are underweight if they are in the lowest 5th percentile of the BMI category for their age and sex group, at a healthy weight if they are between the 5th and 85th percentiles, overweight if they are between the 85th and 95th percentiles, and obese if they are above the 95th percentile. For example, a 9-year-old boy with a BMI of 27.1 would be in the 99th percentile and classified as obese. But a 19-year-old boy with the same BMI would be in the 88th percentile and classified as overweight.

While a convenient measure, BMI is not a perfect indicator of body fatness. As the CDC website points out, for a given BMI women tend to have more body fat than men, older people tend to have more body fat than young adults, and highly trained athletes tend to have less body fat and more muscularity than nonathletes. Several other measures can be used, such as total body fat, percentage body fat, waist circumference, and waist to hip ratio. But in the bulk of the empirical economic research on obesity, BMI, because of its wide availability in data sets, is the measure used.

The Obesity Revolution

In the last two and a half decades of the twentieth century, obesity rates dramatically increased in the United States and in numerous other countries. This trend has continued into the twenty-first century. Many explanations have been put forward to account for the rise in obesity rates. We will start by highlighting the three main ones economists have offered.

Technological Change

One of the first major economic explanations to account for the rise in obesity is also one that is most comfortable for an economist to accept: price changes reduced the cost of consuming calories and increased the cost of expending them (Philipson and Posner, 2003 and 2008, Philipson, 2001, and Lakdawalla and Philipson, 2009). The real price of food (that is, adjusted for inflation) fell throughout the twentieth century because of technological advancements. The increased efficiencies in agricultural and manufacturing production of food reduced the cost of producing and, ultimately, consuming food. Furthermore, as workforce activity shifted from more to less physically demanding labor, the cost of expending calories increased, especially during working hours. When both price effects are in play, they complement each other in a way that leads to rising obesity rates.

As calories become less expensive to consume and more expensive to expend, people do not necessarily become more obese. In a rational eating model, a person chooses her optimal weight. As she expends fewer calories during working hours, she chooses to consume fewer calories even if they are now less expensive to consume. Or she may consume the same or more calories yet counter her sedentary work environment by increasing exercise time or other activities that expend calories. In fact, it is possible that obesity is self-limiting in the sense that once a critical weight is reached, a person will then take measures to lower her weight. But obesity rates increased sharply throughout the 1980s and 1990s. If average calorie intake did not change much during that period, as claimed in the preceding studies, the explanation must be that fewer calories were being expended, especially during work hours.

Division of Labor in Food Preparation

Another technological development that might have led to increased obesity rates has to do with how meals are prepared (Cutler, Glaeser, and Shapiro, 2003). Before the 1970s most meals were prepared at home, often from scratch. That is, cooking at home was fairly labor intensive, and it wasn't unusual for cooking preparation and cleanup time to take a couple of hours. But tremendous technological advancements from the 1970s on greatly reduced the time spent cooking and eating. Such innovations included vacuum packing, deep freezing, improved preservatives, artificial flavors, and microwave ovens. As the time cost of meal preparation falls, we expect the number of meals to increase, whether or not calories *per meal* increase. Furthermore, a larger variety of food items may be more accessible than ever before. Both of these effects may lead to increased calorie intake and, as a result, increased obesity rates.

The authors support this explanation by examining a few implications of their theory. First, they find that food items with large amounts of commercial preparation have increased in consumption between 1970 and 1999, while food items with less commercial preparation have fallen in consumption during the same time. Snack foods represent the greatest increase in calorie intake; they are usually highly densely caloric (that is, high in calories per pound). Easily accessible snack foods mean people eat more often during the day and consume more calories, and obesity rates increase.

Further support for this explanation comes from examining the demographic group predicted to be most affected by the reduction in food preparation costs—women. Women have been most affected by the reduction in meal preparation time, and it is women who have seen the greatest increase in BMI. But even without partitioning the data by gender, the authors find that for each 30 minutes' reduction in meal preparation time, BMI increases on average approximately 0.5 points.

Finally, international comparisons further support this explanation for the change in obesity rates. Countries that have not embraced the technological innovations to the extent that other countries have, have seen smaller changes in obesity rates. For example, Italians have been much less enthused about microwave cooking, with only about 14 percent of Italian households owning a microwave, compared to 80 percent of American households. Obesity rates in Italy are far lower than those rates in the United States. Countries with stricter pesticide and preservative food regulations than the United States also tend to have lower obesity rates. The authors believe that their explanation not only has strong commonsense appeal but also nicely fits the available data.

Working Women and Restaurant Growth

In the 25-year period between 1972 and 1997, the number of restaurants in the United States grew substantially. During that period, the per capita number of fast-food restaurants doubled and the per capita number of full-service restaurants increased by 35 percent. Fast-food restaurants, in particular, serve relatively inexpensive food with a high caloric density, and this may lead to increased calorie consumption and obesity (Chou, Grossman, and Saffer, 2004, Rashad and Grossman, 2004, and Rashad, Grossman, and Chou, 2006). As these restaurants expand to new areas, more people have easier access to them and the restaurants' effect on obesity rates increases.

However, and importantly, these restaurants don't appear out of thin air—they grow in response to customer demand. While restaurants were experiencing substantial growth, labor-force participation rates also grew, primarily from women entering the workforce. With more hours spent at work and far less time spent at home, wage earners and their families demanded more convenient fast-food options. Furthermore, more time spent at work also meant less time available for exercise and recreational activities, not allowing for a calorie expenditure offset to the increased calorie consumption. Thus, it is easy to blame fast-food and other restaurants for increasing obesity rates, but other circumstances must also be considered.

While debate continues about the relevance of each of the main theories to explain increased obesity rates, likely all three theories are correct at least in part. But there is some tension between the theories. For example, proponents of the technological change theory suggest that calorie intake has been relatively stable over time. The authors of the division of labor theory suggest that calorie intake has increased over time. Which is it? Although this seems to be a factual issue, it is not that simple to resolve. Data are not always accurate, and different samples may yield different results. But in this case, a possible explanation simultaneously accounts for *both* claims. Over the course of many years, a very small increase in daily calorie intake, even just 100 extra calories a day (just a half can of soda or a couple of cookies) that are *not* expended, can largely explain the increase in obesity rates. This small amount of calories can be interpreted both ways—calorie intake has remained fairly stable, or it has increased. However you classify the change, it can still be causing significant changes in body weight over the long run.

If increased calorie intake is not the main cause of rising obesity rates, it must be caused by a reduction in energy expenditure. The technological change theory accounts for this effect by arguing that work has become more sedentary over time. This may be the case, but it is likely this explanation had more relevance earlier in the twentieth century than during the last 30 years or so. Furthermore, children and the elderly have also experienced rising obesity rates, yet both of these groups are not often part of the labor force. As for changes in physical activity away from the workplace, the evidence is mixed. Are people, especially children, watching more television and playing more video games during leisure hours? Are people participating in more outdoor activities and sports? Depending on the study and the questions asked of respondents, evidence supports *or* refutes increased leisure-time energy expenditure.

A number of interesting empirical studies have added to our understanding of rising obesity rates. One thorough study (Cawley and Liu, 2007) examines the effect of maternal employment on childhood obesity. Using data covering the 2003 to 2006 period, the study makes several findings that lend empirical support to some of the main theories presented above. Maternal employment is associated with a lower probability of grocery shopping and cooking, less time spent on these activities, and a higher probability of purchasing prepared foods. Working mothers are also likely to spend less time with their children. The study finds that working mothers are less likely to eat with their children, are less likely to engage in physical activities with them, and spend less time engaged in child care and supervision. All are predicted to cause increased childhood obesity rates.

Another study (Courtemanche, 2009) looks at working hours for men and women, to examine the link between work hours and their own weight and their children's weight. The main result is that an increase in work hours is associated with increases in a person's BMI and with the probability of being obese. Also, an increase in a mother's work hours, but not her spouse's, is associated with higher probability for an overweight child. For growth in obesity rates from the 1960s to the early 2000s, the increase in adults' work hours accounts for just 1.4 percent of the increase in adult obesity but for 10.4 percent of the increase in overweight children. Thus, while a longer work week affects the weight of both those who work and their children, the children are far more adversely affected.

One of the difficulties in examining the relationship of restaurant availability to obesity, as mentioned above, is determining whether growth in availability causes obesity or demand from consumers causes growth in availability. One study (Anderson and Matsa, 2011) cleverly distinguishes between these two effects. When new highways are built through rural areas, new restaurants cluster near the exits to serve travelers. Local residents also patronize these restaurants, thus, so the theory goes, facilitating less healthy eating away from home. Yet this increase in restaurant availability is *not* caused by local consumer demand but instead by the location of the new highways. The study can thus isolate causation from restaurant availability to obesity rates.

Local residents who live closer to the highways are expected to visit the restaurants more than residents who live farther away. Yet this study finds no difference in how the presence of these restaurants affected the BMI of residents closer or farther away. This result casts doubt on the theory that restaurant availability influences obesity rates and on the belief that these restaurants' large portions contribute to the obesity problem. First, they find that those who eat at restaurants also tend to have a high calorie intake when they eat at home. Second, people who eat large portions at restaurants tend to reduce their calorie intake during the rest of the day. The authors conclude that combating obesity with policies that target restaurants may be ineffective.

Growth in Explanations to Account for Growth in Obesity Rates

Owing to an unbounded curiosity and, more importantly, a wealth of interesting and available data, economists have offered a wide variety of additional explanations to account for the growth in obesity rates over the past few decades. In fact, the economics of obesity has developed into a substantial field of research in its own right. Here are some of the highlights.

Income Effects

Individual or family income changes can have several possible effects on weight. If you wanted to make some fairly general statements based on available data, you could claim that there is a positive correlation between income and BMI; the prevalence of obesity is greater in developed countries than in less developed countries; in less developed nations those with higher incomes are more likely to be obese, but in the United States those with higher incomes may or may not be more likely to be obese; and in the United States income affects weight differently for men than it does for women. For example, using US data from 2005 (Schmeiser, 2009), as household income rises, the prevalence of overweight men increases and the prevalence of obese men remains fairly constant, but the prevalence of overweight women remains fairly constant and the prevalence of obese women *falls* sharply.

So while the basic economic prediction is that increased wealth leads to increased food consumption and increased calorie intake, it may not be that simple. At low income levels, you may be eating less food but choosing food of high caloric density. Perhaps as you get wealthier you do eat more food, but it is healthier (and often more expensive) food. Or increased wealth may lead to increased opportunities for physical activities, such as purchasing a gym membership or undertaking more expensive physical activities. Or the causation may be the other way around. Some evidence suggests that employers in some professions place emphasis on aesthetic attributes when hiring, meaning that to become wealthy requires controlling your weight.

One study (Schmeiser, 2009) uses the federal Earned Income Tax Credit (EITC) to examine the effect of income on body weight. The EITC was enacted in 1975 to offset payroll taxes with income subsidies for low-income workers with the intention of encouraging more people to enter the labor force. In effect, it is an antipoverty program for adult nonelderly Americans. The study finds that this increased income has no effect on men's BMI, but it increases women's BMI and their obesity prevalence. They find that an additional $1,000 of family income is associated with an average weight increase of approximately one pound. The average increase in annual family income in their sample (using data from 2002) led to an increase of 1.5 to 3.5 pounds, accounting for approximately 10 to 20 percent of BMI increase for women throughout the 1990s.

On the other hand, a study (Garcia Villar and Quintana-Domeque, 2009) using data from nine European Union countries (Austria, Belgium, Denmark, Finland, Greece, Ireland, Italy, Portugal, and Spain) also finds that income does not affect men's BMI, but it finds that it negatively affects women's. That is, this study finds that BMI of women declines with rising income, in contrast to the results of the previous study. Of course, these two studies use very different data sets representing different regions of the world, yet the difference in their main results indicates how careful one must be when making broad generalizations about income and weight.

The authors offer one explanation as to why women's BMI may decline with income, relating to the reverse causation problem mentioned above. It is possible that overweight or obese women have a difficult time finding or keeping high-income jobs. This may happen for two main reasons. First, if increasing weight lowers productivity, women with higher BMI would earn lower wages. Second, some employers may discriminate against overweight or obese women, making it difficult for them to earn high wages. To examine this effect, the authors compare the relationship of income earned by the women (thus allowing for the possibility of discrimination) to income earned by others in the household. They find evidence that the women's income is negatively related to BMI, but they find very little evidence that other family members' income is related to BMI in any way. Another study using US data (Cawley, 2004) finds that for white women an increase in weight of 64 pounds leads to a 9 percent reduction in wages. To give this result some perspective, that would be the same as having one and a half year's less education or three years' less work experience than an average woman. So the relationship between income and weight, especially for women in these studies, can be complex.

Another study (Cawley, Moran, and Simon, 2010) examines how income influences the weight of elderly Americans. The elderly have also had large increases in obesity rates. For men between ages 60 and 74, obesity rates skyrocketed, from 8.4 percent in the early 1960s to 35.8 percent in the late 1990s. For women in the same age range during the same period, the increase was not as pronounced but still quite large: from 26.2 percent to 39.6 percent. Weight gain by the elderly has important public policy implications, as a disproportionate amount of health care expenditure is devoted to that group. As the elderly become a larger percentage of the population and as life expectancy increases, elderly health care will receive more prominence.

The authors take advantage of a quirk in a 1972 amendment of the Social Security Act in which an error occurred. Workers in a particular birth cohort were doubly indexed for inflation, which provided them with a relatively large windfall income gain (especially with the high rates of inflation experienced shortly after the amendment was enacted). Although the error was corrected in 1977, cohorts born before 1917 retained the increased benefits because of a grandfather provision. This data set allows the authors to examine groups of elderly who are very similar in many dimensions but differ in income levels because of a factor completely out of their control. Did this additional income affect the body weight of the group that received it relative to the weight of the group that did not?

The results of the study suggest that this additional income had no effect on the probability of the elderly being overweight or obese. It also had no effect on the probability of the elderly being underweight or at a healthy weight. For this sample of elderly Americans, the study finds no relationship at all between income and body weight. Amid concerns about the future of the social security system, this study concludes that one concern should not be about how changes in benefits will change the weight of the elderly.

Rapid income changes in developing countries may lead to changes in diet and body weight. One study (Du et al., 2004) examines this effect for China for 1987–1997. Throughout the 1980s and 1990s, China saw phenomenal growth rates in its gross domestic product, and this greatly reduced the proportion of the population who were classified as absolutely poor or extremely poor. These income increases, however, had an adverse impact on body weight, particularly for low- and middle-income groups. As these groups' income increased, their diet shifted from traditional foods, such as rice and wheat products, to high-density-caloric and low-fiber foods. Furthermore, energy expenditure appeared to decrease as advances in technology and transportation reduced physical activities in daily life. These changes led to higher overweight and obesity rates, as well as increased morbidity and mortality rates. In this case, income growth associated with new development had an adverse impact on health.

Food Stamps

The Food Stamp Program (FSP) is a major policy effort by the federal government to assist low-income individuals and families in avoiding undernutrition. In 2003, for example, over 20 million people received food stamps. Although the main goal of the FSP is to prevent hunger and starvation, there has been concern that the program may perversely lead to increased obesity rates.

The main explanation as to how the FSP may encourage obesity is that recipients of food stamps may be spending more on food and consuming more calories than they otherwise would be if, for example, they were given cash subsidies instead. Food stamps can be used to purchase only food. Someone who has $50, for example, in food stamps and needs only $40 worth of food might exhaust the extra $10 in stamps on items that are highly caloric, such as soda or candy. Or even if not using the excess to purchase unhealthy food, food stamp recipients may simply be consuming more food than they would with a cash equivalent.

In the late 1980s the Food and Consumer Service of the US Department of Agriculture (USDA) conducted experiments that substituted cash subsidies for food stamps (Fraker, Martini, and Ohls, 1995). A comparison of food expenditures by households receiving food stamps to those given cash equivalents shows that food expenditures significantly decreased as food stamps were replaced with cash. This lends some support to the link between food stamps and increased calorie consumption.

Another study (Kaushal, 2007), however, cleverly tests for the link between food stamps and obesity. Before 1996 all legal low-income immigrants were eligible to participate in the FSP. But in 1996 US federal law was changed to deny eligibility for food stamps to noncitizens. Several states circumvented this federal policy and continued to provide aid to at least some of the now-excluded group, and over the following years federal policy restored eligibility to many. During these policy changes, some immigrants were eligible for food stamp assistance and some were not, and this allows the researchers to compare the two groups. The study finds no significant difference in BMI for immigrants eligible for assistance relative to immigrants not eligible, and concludes that the FSP is not likely to be a big factor in explaining increased obesity rates.

Although several studies have examined the link between the FSP and obesity, a comprehensive review of these studies commissioned by the USDA (ver Ploeg and Ralston, 2008) finds that food stamps just slightly increase body weight. The real complication lies in the FSP having differing effects on the body weight of different gender and age groups. The BMI of nonelderly women appears to be adversely affected by food stamps, but that of children, nonelderly men, and the elderly is not. As food stamps are issued to households, and not to individuals, how the FSP affects obesity rates remains unclear. The review concludes that the FSP is not likely to be a large factor in explaining the tremendous growth in obesity rates over the last few decades.

Cigarette Prices

As we have seen in previous chapters, one complication in implementing social control policy to reduce the consumption of addictive goods is that controlling the use of one product may have adverse effects on the use of another product. The classic example of this involves the link between cigarette smoking and obesity. Ample evidence suggests that smoking and obesity are inversely related. Although many of the reasons for this are highly technical, some are easy to understand. The nicotine in cigarettes can raise the metabolic rate of smokers, often to an unhealthy level. Quitting smoking often lowers the metabolic rate, leading to less burning of calories. Quitting smoking may also lead to an increased appetite, a common withdrawal symptom, and an increased desire for sweets. Sense of taste and smell can improve, affecting one's desire for food. Furthermore, there may be a link between smoking cessation and increased alcohol use, and alcohol can be highly caloric. Finally, someone who smokes for oral gratification may increase eating simply as an oral substitute. Whatever the underlying reasons for the inverse relationship, policies that reduce the incidence of smoking, such as increased cigarette taxation, may have the perverse effect of increasing obesity.

If price changes did not affect smoking, there would be no link between cigarette tax policy and obesity. But as discussed in chapter 2, increased cigarette prices generally do negatively affect smoking. What remains to be seen is whether reduced smoking positively affects obesity. Numerous studies in the economics literature have investigated the smoking-obesity link. One study (Chou, Grossman, and Saffer, 2004) finds a link between increased cigarette prices and increased BMI. They conclude that the widespread federal and state antismoking campaigns and policies, including tax increases, antismoking messages, and a substantial tort settlement tobacco companies must pay to alleviate state Medicaid costs, might have had a serious unintended consequence of contributing to the obesity problem.

Another study (Gruber and Frakes, 2006), however, argues that cigarette prices may be a difficult measure to use because changes in cigarette prices can be caused by many factors that may themselves also lead to changes in smoking and eating behavior. This study instead looks at changes in cigarette *taxes*, as a possibly more direct link between smoking behavior and obesity. The results are strikingly different from the previous study's, finding that increased cigarette taxes lead to *reduced* BMI; that is, higher taxes reduce smoking, and this leads to reduced body weight. But as the authors point out, the results of both studies are tenuous because of methodological issues.

A more recent study (Baum, 2009) offers an empirical examination of the link between US cigarette prices and obesity. First, the author looks at the *correlation* (as opposed to *causation*) between cigarette prices and obesity. Breaking the sample into obese and nonobese groups, the author finds that cigarette taxes average around 67¢ for the obese and 60¢ for the nonobese group. Also, the obese group averages about 4.8 cigarettes a day, while the nonobese average about 5.9. Cigarette smoking, then, appears to be related to a lower level of obesity.

In terms of causation, the author finds that an increase in the cost of a pack of cigarettes does indeed have a significant positive impact on weight. Looking at a proposed policy of increasing cigarette taxes by 77¢ per pack, the author finds that it will lead to an approximate 3 percent increase in the prevalence of obesity. He also finds that the effect of price on obesity is larger for lower-income and younger groups, because they tend to be more sensitive to cigarette price changes (thus smoking less and eating more relative to others).

Other studies find that the effect of cigarette prices on obesity rates may be short-lived. One study (Nonnemaker et al., 2009) examines how increased cigarette prices affect smokers who have recently quit compared to those who kicked the habit longer ago. If weight gain as a result of increased cigarette prices is a short-lived phenomenon, recent quitters should show a greater change in BMI than the second group. Looking at younger former smokers (ages 18 to 29) versus older former smokers (ages 29 to 65), who are likely to have quit much less recently, the study finds that the former group has a significantly larger weight gain due to rising cigarette prices than does the latter group. The study finds that rising cigarette prices do not seem to affect current smokers' BMI and have only a modest impact on all former smokers' BMI.

One other study (Courtemanche, 2007), also examining the short-run versus long-run effect of cigarette prices on body weight, finds, unusually, that rising cigarettes prices lead to *reduced* body weight in the long run. Quantitatively, the study finds that for every one-dollar increase in cigarette prices, there is, in the long run, an annual savings of nearly nine thousand lives due to weight loss. The author explains this result by suggesting that, after quitting smoking and adjusting to being former smokers, the former smokers may begin to make other healthy life decisions regarding eating and exercising.

Fast-Food Price Promotions

Fast-food marketing strategies are often criticized for seducing consumers into purchasing unhealthy products, which exacerbates the obesity problem. But exactly how marketing affects consumption behavior must be given careful consideration. As discussed in chapter 2 in terms of cigarette advertising, does fast-food marketing increase the amount of fast food consumed in the aggregate, or is it just bouncing customers between establishments, with little impact on overall consumption? If fast-food marketing has little impact on aggregate consumption, there is less justification for its restriction in an effort to curb the obesity problem. But if fast-food marketing causes more consumers to make unhealthy food choices or encourages those who already eat at these restaurants to eat more, restricting marketing practices may help fight obesity. One study (Richards and Padilla, 2009) attempts to sort this out by looking at fast-food restaurants in Canada and a particular form of promotional activity there—price promotion.

Fast-food restaurants often use price specials to attract customers. In fact, price promotions are a growing marketing strategy. According to the authors, of the $478 billion devoted to marketing in the United States in 2004, over 52 percent was for price promotion while only 38 percent was for advertising. But if McDonald's has a special deal, two for one, for example, does it attract new customers from other fast-food restaurants, does it attract new customers to fast food in general, or does it make current customers consume more? The authors' main result is that approximately two-thirds of the effect of price promotions is to increase the quantity of fast food consumed, while only one-third involves consumers switching restaurants. Thus, price promotions encourage more fast-food consumption in the aggregate.

Television Advertising

Television is believed to increase the childhood obesity rate through two main avenues: encouraging a sedentary lifestyle among children who prefer to watch television rather than participate in physical activities and encouraging poor eating habits through the demand-enhancing effects of snack food and fast-food restaurant commercials. The effect of fast-food restaurant television advertising on childhood obesity is the focus of one interesting empirical study

(Chou, Rashad, and Grossman, 2008). Using local (or "spot) advertising data from 75 market areas, regions composed primarily of US counties that define television markets, the authors examine what effect a complete fast-food restaurant advertising ban would have on childhood obesity.

The results are striking. The authors find that a complete ban would reduce the number of overweight children ages 3 to 11 by 18 percent; for adolescents ages 12 to 18 the corresponding reduction would be 14 percent. Furthermore, these reductions may be *under*stated. The authors focus on local advertising because it varies from market to market, a necessary condition for performing statistical analysis. But, of course, many fast-food restaurants use additional television advertising sources, such as national network and cable stations, and this advertising can further exacerbate the obesity effect. By not being able to take this type of additional advertising into account, the authors underestimate the effect.

It is also possible that the authors' results may be *over*stated. Even with a complete television advertising ban, other media outlets would be available for fast-food restaurant advertising messages. Radio, magazines, newspapers, billboards, and so on provide additional ways to reach children. Granted, these other media outlets may not be as effective as television, but they would still have some effect. On the other hand, television advertising may be less important in the future as the Internet's use of advertising and other marketing techniques grows, phenomenally increasing product exposure, especially to children. The authors don't examine the impact of these other outlets.

Given that the First Amendment may prohibit banning television fast-food restaurant advertising (hardly an impossible hurdle, given such a ban on cigarette advertising) or that political and practical reasons may make a complete ban difficult, the authors examine an alternative policy option. If fast-food restaurants are prevented from deducting their food advertising expenses from their corporate income tax returns, advertising costs will be higher, which will decrease advertising expenditures. The authors estimate that these decreases would shrink the number of messages seen by children and adolescents by 40 percent and 33 percent, respectively, reducing the number of overweight children by 7 percent and the number of overweight adolescents by 5 percent. These reductions are not as large as those found in the complete advertising ban option, but they offer policy makers an alternative route to tackle the problem of childhood obesity, if such a policy goal is desired.

Proximity of Fast Food to School

If fast-food restaurants contribute to the obesity problem, it may not only be because of the food they serve but also because of their numerous and convenient locations. A McDonald's one block from a school may entice more children to eat there than at one several miles away. As we have seen, part of the cost of eating at a restaurant is the travel cost of getting there, and wide availability of fast-food restaurants greatly reduces this cost. A study (Currie et al., 2010) attempts to link geographic location of fast-food restaurants to obesity rates for schoolchildren.

The schoolchildren data the authors use includes ninth graders from California public schools between 1999 and 2007. The fast-food restaurants in the study include the top ten fast-food chains (McDonald's, Subway, Burger King, Taco Bell, Pizza Hut, Little Caesars, KFC, Wendy's, Domino's Pizza, and Jack in the Box). Of the nearly 8,400 schools in their data set, approximately 7 percent of the schools have a fast-food restaurant within one-tenth mile, 28 percent have one within a quarter mile, and 62 percent have one within a half mile. Thus, for many schoolchildren, fast-food restaurants offer reasonably convenient locations. But remember, just because many fast-food restaurants are close to schools does not mean these restaurants *cause* obesity in schoolchildren. That is what the study attempts to address.

The study's main result is that students who attend a school within one-tenth mile of a fast-food restaurant have a 5.2 percent greater incidence of obesity than those who attend a school within a quarter mile. The result is attributed to proximity of the restaurants. Obesity rates of children attending schools farther than one-tenth mile from a fast-food restaurant show no significant change. For the schoolchildren in this study, then, fast-food restaurants very close to their schools are partly responsible for increased obesity rates.

School Finances and Vending Machines

High schools always seem to be looking for ways to raise money. It is not uncommon to see high school students holding signs that say "Free Car Wash," hoping to collect donations for their efforts. Students go door to door selling magazine subscriptions or candy bars. One high school in southeast Ohio, using Las Vegas as its inspiration, occasionally hosts poker nights and takes a percentage of the pot. While high schools have stopped short of putting slot machines in their gymnasiums, other types of machines have been controversially installed—soda and snack-food vending machines.

The availability of snack foods in schools is common. One study (Anderson and Butcher, 2006) that examines the link between vending machines and obesity cites evidence from 2000 that 27 percent of elementary schools, 67 percent of middle schools, and 96 percent of high schools had food and soda vending machines available to students. Furthermore, they provide evidence that vending machine contracts can be financially lucrative. A high school in Beltsville, Maryland, made nearly $100,000 through vending machine contracts and one school district in Colorado negotiated a 10-year beverage contract for over $11 million. This magnitude of money is as hard for schools to resist as it is for students to resist soda and snacks.

The study has three main results. The first is that schools under fiscal pressure are more likely to pursue vending machine contracts than schools that aren't. So it appears it is not *just* revenue generation that schools are pursuing but additional revenue to compensate for a lack of funds. The second result is that there appears to be a slight link between availability of soda and snack foods through vending machines and students' BMI. The authors find that a 10 percent increase in schools that allow vending machines leads to an approximately 1 percent increase in BMI.

The third result is that how vending machines in schools affect body weight depends on the type of student. The study finds that students who have an overweight parent are more susceptible to vending machines than are students who do not have an overweight parent. In fact, there appears to be no link between school vending machines and BMI for students with normal-weight parents. But for students with an overweight parent, a 10 percent increase in the number of schools with vending machines leads to a more than 2 percent increase in BMI. Thus, the link between youth obesity and school vending machines is more subtle than the second result above suggests.

Many states have considered or enacted laws to deal with school vending machine access, as well as other nutritional issues. Such policies include outright banning of snack food and soda vending machines, adopting minimum nutritional standards for food and beverages sold in schools, making available a wider variety of food and beverages to provide students with healthier options, and restricting the times when students could access vending machines. It is important to note, however, that other factors may come into play when considering the efficacy of these policies. Does the increased revenue allow spending for school activities that help students expend calories? Can students easily access snack foods and soda off school property? If the key link between school vending machines and weight involves family characteristics, are these policies addressing that?

Nutritional Labeling

Providing factual nutritional content can aid consumers in choosing foods and combating obesity. Before 1994 food labeling was largely voluntary and fairly haphazard. But in 1994 the Nutritional Labeling and Education Act (NLEA) took effect and the standard nutritional labels you see on foods today became mandatory for most processed foods. Knowing the nutritional facts for food products, consumers can make healthy choices with greater confidence, not having to rely on what may be misinformation. The impetus for mandatory food labeling is simple: better information implies lower obesity rates.

In enacting the NLEA, the Food and Drug Administration (FDA) estimated that the costs of the new regulation, including administrative and enforcement costs, would be in the $2 billion range over a 20-year period, yet the benefits in terms of improved health outcomes would be staggering, possibly as high as $26 billion. Thus, the FDA had high hopes for their new regulation. Yet critics have astutely observed that the growing obesity rates in the decade before the enactment of the act did not slow in the decade after. Thus, on the basis of casual observation, some have argued that the NLEA was largely ineffective in affecting obesity rates.

This casual observation, however, may be wrong. While it is true that obesity rates in the United States continued to increase throughout the late 1990s and early 2000s, to isolate the NLEA's effect the key question that must be addressed is what would the growth in obesity rates have been had the NLEA *not* been enacted? Would obesity growth rates have been even higher without the NLEA? Also, it is possible that the NLEA affects some groups of consumers but not others, making the effect more difficult to detect.

One study (Variyam and Cawley, 2006) examines the impact of the NLEA on obesity rates. On one hand, the benefits of the NLEA are narrow in scope. The study finds that only one demographic group was affected by the NLEA: non-Hispanic white women's BMI and probability of obesity were significantly lower than they would have been in the absence of the act. Other demographic groups studied—non-Hispanic white men, non-Hispanic black men, and non-Hispanic black women—were not affected by the act. Yet even with this narrow result, the authors found that the health and related benefits of lower obesity rates for non-Hispanic white women could be as high as

$166 billion over a 20-year period. This number is substantially larger than the original FDA estimate, even if the FDA possibly overestimated the scope of those who would benefit from the act.

As fast-food restaurants are often considered a major contributor to the obesity problem, a new federal regulation signed by President Obama in 2010 and due to be enacted in 2011 requires restaurant chains to provide nutritional information on their menus, menu boards, and drive-through signs (Schulman, 2010). Restaurants must post calorie content next to item names at the point of purchase, as well as a statement informing consumers of the suggested daily calorie intake. Also, additional nutritional information must be available to consumers on request. The law offers two main avenues for combating obesity. First, many people possibly underestimate the caloric value of fast-food meals, so the information will allow consumers to reconsider their purchases using accurate information. Second, it is expected that the restaurants will respond to the regulation by offering more healthy choices for their now well-informed customers. This new regulation will affect only restaurant chains that have 20 or more outlets, so a large number of restaurants are exempted from the law. Future research will undoubtedly examine the law's effect on reducing obesity.

Impatience

One explanation given for why people consume unhealthy products is that they are, to some extent, impatient. As we saw in chapter 1, the typical addiction scenario is that an impatient person is more concerned with immediate gratification than future health costs. Obesity may certainly fit into this scenario. You overeat today because you enjoy eating foods that are high in calories. Sure, you recognize that this may lead to a health problem in the future, but that's in the future, something you are not too concerned about right now. Thus, it is possible that people who are relatively obese may also be relatively impatient. Furthermore, the trend toward increased obesity rates may be explained by a trend in increased impatience rates, if such a trend exists.

One study (Smith, Bogin, and Bishai, 2005) uses data on savings behavior as a proxy for time-preference rates and examines the relationship between time preference and obesity. Those who are more patient will tend to save more than those who are less patient. Thus, the link between patience levels and obesity may be empirically examined. The authors find a link between time preference and BMI, with less-patient people tending to have a greater

BMI than those who are more patient. Breaking the sample down by gender, their result holds for both men and women, but it is stronger for men.

Unfortunately, as the authors acknowledge, savings behavior may not be a very good proxy for time preference. The reasons for saving or not saving are numerous, and most have little to do with patience levels. Savings depend on interest rates, a person's risk preference, unplanned emergency expenditures, and more. While it is true that, *all else being equal*, more-patient people are likely to save more than the less patient, the authors are unable to account for the many other factors that affect savings. This concern is addressed in another study (Borghans and Golsteyn, 2006).

The authors of the second study use a variety of proxies for time preference, including savings behavior, as well as questions involving several hypothetical scenarios, hoping to provide more reliable results for the relationship between time preference and obesity. As in the previous study, the authors find some evidence of a positive relationship between impatience and BMI, but the relationship is far from robust across the many proxies. In addition, the authors directly examine whether changes in time preference over time can help explain the increase in obesity rates over time. However, the authors find that rates of time preference are fairly constant over the sample time period (1995 to 2004) and so cannot account for increases in BMI over the same period.

Gasoline Prices

Throughout the 1980s and 1990s, while obesity rates in the United States increased, the real price of gasoline fell. One study (Courtemanche, 2008) asks the following question: Does this fall in gasoline prices help explain the rise in obesity rates? The theoretical link between gasoline prices and obesity is easy to understand. As gasoline prices fall, people drive more often and walk or bicycle less often, expending fewer calories. Also, as driving is less costly, people may eat out more often and possibly consume more calories or eat more unhealthy food. Finally, lower gasoline prices may have less-direct effects on eating behavior. For example, as gasoline prices fall, people may have more disposable income and use it to consume more calories. Or lower gasoline prices may lead to lower food prices through lower production and distribution costs, again causing people to possibly consume more calories.

Empirically, the study finds that 8 percent of the rise in obesity rates from 1979 to 2004 can be attributed to the decline in the real price of gasoline during that period. In addition, the study predicts that a permanent one-dollar increase in the price of gasoline would, over a seven-year period, reduce obesity rates by 10 percent, saving 11,000 lives and $11 billion per year. Thus, even something as unpleasant as a rise in the price of gasoline has a potentially substantial offsetting health benefit.

Walmart and "Every Day Low Prices"

Walmart stores come in three basic varieties—the limited grocery discount store, the full grocery superstore, and the warehouse club store. Because of its tremendous buying power, Walmart prides itself on its "every day low prices." Low prices, however, imply increased consumption, and if Walmart shoppers are increasing their calorie intake by consuming more food or more unhealthy food, Walmart may be a contributing factor in explaining increased obesity rates. But there is another side to the story. Walmart's everyday low prices are for not only unhealthy foods but also healthy foods such as fruits and vegetables. Furthermore, as prices of all types of food fall, buying power increases, and with increased *real* wealth, people may have an increased demand for healthier food. It is possible, then, that Walmart's discount prices can induce people to eat healthier food and reduce obesity rates.

One study (Courtemanche and Carden, 2008) examines the effect of Walmart's pricing policies on the prevalence of overweight and obese people and finds that low prices slightly *reduce* their prevalence. More importantly, the study finds no evidence that Walmart's prices lead to increases in overweight and obesity rates. Thus, lower food prices, while often predicted to increase calorie consumption, may lead some people to pursue a healthier diet.

Child-Care Subsidies

In 1996 the Child Care and Development Fund (CCDF) was created to assist current and former welfare-recipient working parents to purchase legal child-care services at a subsidized price. One study (Herbst and Tekin, forthcoming) examines the link between child-care subsidies and children's weight outcomes. The authors see three avenues by which child-care subsidies can influence weight. First, the quality of the care will obviously have some impact, but this could lead to increased or decreased weight. Care providers offering poor nutritional options or not encouraging physical activities may lead to increased children's weight. Second, mothers must be employed to qualify for the subsidies, and as discussed above, increased labor-force participation of women may be a contributing factor to increased obesity rates. Finally, as discussed in other contexts above, if the lower price of child-care services frees up income to be spent elsewhere, that additional spending may lead to reduced weight (more healthy food or increased physical activities) or increased weight (more unhealthy food or increased sedentary activities).

In theory, then, the effect of child-care subsidies on weight is ambiguous. Empirically, the authors find that child-care subsidies increase BMI as well as the likelihood of being overweight and obese. This link appears to be due to enrollment in child-care programs, as opposed to the other two reasons. Because the CCDF allows parents to choose *any* legal child-care program, parents may be choosing child-care services of questionable quality. As is often the case with well-intentioned policies, as the CCDF encourages more low-income mothers to work, there may be offsetting costs associated with the health of their young children.

Urban Sprawl

Obesity rates vary across America, as do how the rates have changed over time. For example, obesity rates are higher in Mississippi than in Colorado, between 1991 and 1998 the obesity rate in Georgia more than doubled, and in Delaware the rate during the same period increased by approximately 10 percent. This variation in obesity rates has led some to argue that obesity can be affected by neighborhood design. In fairly compact neighborhoods and where houses are mixed with retail outlets, people may more often choose to walk than drive, compared to people who live in more sprawling and largely residential areas. This suggests that people who live in more sprawling neighborhoods are more likely to be obese than those who live in more compact neighborhoods.

However, there is a complication with the urban sprawl argument. Do sprawling neighborhoods lead to increased obesity rates, or do people who are obese prefer to live in sprawling neighborhoods? If you prefer to drive rather than walk, for whatever reasons, compact neighborhoods may not be where you want to live as they can be difficult for cars to maneuver. Thus, observing that obesity rates are higher in more sprawling neighborhoods than in more compact ones does not tell us that the neighborhood design *causes* the higher rate.

One study (Eid et al., 2008) attempts to sort out this complication by examining how weight is affected by moves to more sprawling areas and by moves to less sprawling areas. If neighborhood design influences weight, moving to a more sprawling area should cause weight gain, while moving to a less sprawling area should cause weight loss. The study finds that neighborhood design appears to have no impact on weight, either in the short run or after living in the new area for several years. The authors conclude that, to account for the positive correlation between obesity rates and urban sprawl, the causation is that, on average, people who are obese prefer to live in neighborhoods that are sprawling.

Neighborhood Quality

One study (Sen, Mennemeyer, and Gary, 2009) finds a surprising link between a child's weight and an indicator of the quality of the child's neighborhood—police presence in the neighborhood. The study uses survey data to gauge neighborhood quality across several dimensions, such as crime and violence, abandoned and run-down buildings, lack of public transportation, and lack of police protection. While none of the other neighborhood variables appear to have much effect on children's BMI, lack of police protection is associated with increased weight. The authors speculate that this may be due to parents' concerns that the neighborhood is too dangerous for their children to play outside, especially if there are drug dealers, or bullies, or other dangers that are not quite captured with the other neighborhood variables.

Another study (Sandy et al., 2009) also examines neighborhood quality with several measures, including a very detailed look at publicly available recreational amenities and childhood BMI. Using aerial photographs of neighborhoods to identify recreational amenities, including baseball fields, outdoor basketball courts, football fields, kickball fields, playgrounds, swimming pools, soccer fields, tennis courts, and volleyball courts, the authors do not find much relationship between availability of these amenities and childhood weight. The most encouraging results are for kickball fields, volleyball courts, and general fitness areas, as proximity to these appears to lead to reduced weight. But as found in the previous study, most of the neighborhood variables appear to have no impact on childhood weight.

Physical Education Requirements

Another contributing factor offered to explain the rising trend in youth overweight and obesity rates is a reduction in school physical education (PE) hours throughout the 1990s. In 1991 approximately 41 percent of high school students were enrolled in daily PE classes, but that number fell to 28 percent by

2003. Also, there was a general decrease in the minimum number of hours required in PE class. These declining trends in PE participation have led many concerned organizations, both public and private, to call for policies for increased PE participation to help curtail the trend in youth overweight and obesity rates.

One study (Cawley, Meyerhoeffer, and Newhouse, 2007a) examines the link between PE participation hours and youth weight. While it seems sensible to believe that encouraging more PE hours can only help reduce weight, the link may not be so obvious. First, many schools do not comply with state PE regulations (26 percent of schools do not strictly comply according to one estimate). Second, exactly what is done in a PE class varies greatly. Some students get vigorous physical exercise and sports, while others are largely unsupervised and allowed to do as they please. For example, in 12 states, students may earn PE credit through online courses. Finally, even with increased physical activities, the additional energy expenditure may be offset by increased calorie intake outside school. Although the study finds that increased PE requirements do increase physical activities by approximately 30 minutes per week for boys and 37 minutes per week for girls, this increased activity appears to leave BMI unchanged. The study does find, however, that for girls (but not for boys), the increased PE exposure is associated with increased vigorous physical activities, which can lead to health improvements even if it does not affect BMI.

Cold Weather and Exercise

Bad weather gets blamed for many things, but can you blame obesity on bad weather? One study (Eisenberg and Okeke, 2009) finds that you can, as colder weather leads to less outdoor activity and exercise, which then leads to fewer calories expended and increased BMI. Although the study does not directly examine the link between weather conditions and BMI, it does examine the link between weather and exercise. The main result is that a 5 percent decrease in past-month average daily maximum temperature causes a 2.5 percent decrease in the probability of meeting the CDC guidelines for exercise in the past month. This decrease in outdoor activity, however, is somewhat offset by an increase in indoor activity, but this substitution is not as prevalent among low-income people. The authors suggest that policies encouraging more physical activity should consider not only how the weather affects exercise decisions but also how the opportunity for physical activity varies across income groups.

Job Loss Stress

Losing your job, or worrying about losing your job, creates stress. Some people respond to stress by increasing behaviors such as smoking (as discussed in chapter 2), drinking, and overeating. One study (Deb et al., 2009) uses business closings as a way to measure job loss. This is a particularly useful measure as it is generally outside an employee's control. If, for example, job loss were instead measured by dismissal, the characteristics that led to the firing could also explain smoking, drinking, and overeating. In fact, it's possible that excessive drinking, for example, directly led to job loss. In this case, it is not the job loss stress that causes excessive drinking but the other way around. Individual behavior is very unlikely to affect business closings, so it is a cleaner way of measuring job stress and how people respond to such stress. The study finds that most people do not respond to increased job stress by eating more, but an important subgroup does. The small group of those who respond to job stress by overeating are already (that is, before the job loss) in the higher BMI categories. Thus, this study finds that job loss stress may exacerbate a preexisting condition.

Similarly, economic insecurity in general (also discussed in chapter 2) can lead to weight gain. One study (Smith, Stoddard, and Barnes, 2009) argues that fears of economic insecurity cause a "fattening effect," to prepare for future lean times. The authors find that with their measures of economic insecurity (taking into account probabilities of unemployment and income loss), greater insecurity does lead to weight gain. Furthermore, they find that factors that reduce economic insecurity, such as wealth gains due to inheritance or improved access to health insurance, lead to weight loss.

The health insurance aspect is potentially an important factor in accounting for the rising trend in body weight during the 1980s and 1990s. Between 1979 and 2001 the prevalence of health insurance for US workers decreased by approximately 8 percent. During the same period, the average weight of men ages 30 to 39 increased by more than 13 pounds. The authors calculate that these changes in health insurance markets may have accounted for nearly 3 percent of the rising trend in body weight.

Incredibly, the above explanations do not exhaust the complete list of factors that may have contributed to the rising obesity rates in the past few decades. But the goal of demonstrating that there are many potential factors and that the appropriate public policy responses to the obesity problem may not always be obvious has been achieved. To end this chapter, we turn to two further issues: the role of taxes and the use of the courts to combat the obesity problem.

If It's Fat, Tax It

As we saw in chapter 2, taxation is a common policy tool for controlling behavior. To curtail smoking, it is not difficult to decide what to tax—cigarettes. To curtail obesity, however, precisely which products to tax is far more complicated. Many states apply taxes to particular food and beverage products. The most commonly taxed products are soft drink syrup and bottled soft drinks. Some states do not allow food tax exemptions for candy. But these broad product taxes may not be a highly effective way to discourage consumption of the food that contributes most to the obesity problem. For example, soft drinks are high in sugar content but not in fat content. Furthermore, not all soft drinks are high in sugar content. If taxes cover products that range from highly unhealthy to only moderately unhealthy, the taxes do not encourage substitution of healthy products.

One study (Chouinard et al., 2007) recognizes the problem of taxing too broadly in controlling obesity and instead examines a tax policy that targets the fat content of foods more directly by focusing on dairy products. The authors argue that dairy products are a high source of fat in the typical American's diet, contributing 16 percent of total fat, 28 percent of saturated fat, and 17 percent of cholesterol to the US food supply. A tax applied directly to these high-fat-content products could induce consumers to substitute foods lower in fat content.

The authors provide three strong reasons for considering taxing the fat content of dairy products. First, a large majority of American households consume dairy products (97 percent of households purchase milk, and 80 percent purchase cheese), and these products make up more than 10 percent of the typical American's daily calorie intake. Second, these products' high fat content suggests that their consumption can be linked to certain health problems. Third, these products have low-fat substitutes, such as skim milk, low-fat yogurt, or low-fat butter. If high-fat foods become relatively more expensive, consumers are predicted to substitute with these lower-fat alternatives. At least in theory.

Looking at how a tax increase affects consumption for a range of dairy products (milk, cheese, cream, butter, yogurt), the authors do not find much of a decrease in fat intake. These dairy products have inelastic demands, which means (as discussed in chapter 2) that a price increase has little effect on consumption. They find that a 10 percent tax on fat content results in less than a 1 percent reduction in fat consumption for the average household. Even a very large 50 percent tax on fat content is predicted to reduce fat intake by only 3 percent. The study concludes that in terms of controlling individual behavior, a fat tax is not effective. But this is not the end of the story.

As previously discussed in other contexts, a tax on dairy products harms consumers of these products because they now have to pay higher prices for goods they enjoy. Using the 10 percent tax increase as their benchmark, the authors find that this welfare loss is as much as $4.5 billion annually. On the other hand, a tax increase on a product with a relatively inelastic demand tends to raise a lot of revenue. The price increase is accompanied by a small decrease in consumption, a perfect situation if your goal is to raise revenue. The authors find that a 10 percent tax increase yields nearly $4.5 billion annually, perfectly offsetting consumers' welfare loss. If this additional tax revenue is used to combat obesity through other channels, such as improved information, more exercise facilities, and improved access to health care, it may ultimately be effective through these indirect means. Of course, not only do these other means have to themselves be effective ways of reducing obesity rates but the authorities need to use the tax revenue raised through fat taxes for that purpose.

McLawsuit

In 2003 Judge Sweet, a US district court judge in New York State, offered a ruling in a controversial and extremely high-profile case—*Pelman v. McDonald's Corporation* (237 F. Supp. 2d 512)—concerning fast-food restaurants and childhood obesity. The defendant in this case was the global fast-food chain restaurant McDonald's, and the plaintiffs were two minors, Ashley Pelman and Jazlen Bradley. The plaintiffs alleged that by purchasing and consuming McDonald's products they became overweight and developed health problems such as diabetes, high blood pressure, and high cholesterol. In short, the children's health problems were caused by being obese, their obesity was caused by McDonald's products and business practices, and McDonald's should be held liable.

At the heart of the compliant was the allegation that McDonald's was negligent in selling food products that were high in cholesterol, fat, salt, and sugar, all believed to cause obesity or at least detrimental health effects. Mc-Donald's also failed to warn consumers of the unhealthy ingredients and their adverse health effects. If fast-food restaurants can sell unhealthy food, shouldn't they warn their customers of the health risks associated with consuming such products? Could the growing childhood obesity epidemic be curtailed, and possibly even reversed, by holding McDonald's and other fast-food restaurants accountable for their actions? Judge Sweet was not impressed with the complaint, and he dismissed it.

In a carefully written opinion, relying on legal arguments as well as just plain common sense (as he saw it), Judge Sweet systematically dismissed each of the plaintiffs' complaints. In dealing with the claim that McDonald's products are unhealthy, Judge Sweet offered the following argument:

> Many products cannot possibly be made entirely safe for all consumption, and any food or drug necessarily involves some risk of harm, if only from over-consumption. Ordinary sugar is a deadly poison to some diabetics, and castor oil found use under Mussolini as an instrument of torture. This is not what is meant by "unreasonably dangerous." The article sold must be dangerous to an extent beyond that which would be contemplated by the ordinary consumer who purchases it, with the ordinary knowledge common to the community as to its characteristics. Good whiskey is not unreasonably dangerous merely because it makes some people drunk, and is especially dangerous to alcoholics; but bad whiskey, containing a dangerous amount of fuel oil, is unreasonably dangerous. (531)

The judge did not feel that McDonald's products were unreasonably dangerous.

While the judge's opinion does not rule out the link between fast-food restaurants and childhood obesity, it does suggest that we must question the origin of responsibility for one's actions. This is a common criticism of policies designed to protect people from themselves—they circumvent personal responsibility. Yet personal responsibility does not present a strong enough argument on its own to rule out social intervention. Maybe the children who ate at McDonald's were fully aware of the potential health effects of a steady diet of hamburgers and french fries, but what if they were also naive and time inconsistent? McDonald's may not be to blame for their poor diet, but can we alleviate the problem of childhood obesity by regulating the selling and consuming of fast food? And even if we can approach the problem this way, is it desirable to do so? These questions are dealt with in the next chapter.

Suggested Readings

Papers on the three main economic explanations for the rise in obesity rates are by Philipson and Posner (2003, 2008), Philipson (2001), and Lakdawalla and Philipson (2009) on technological change; Cutler, Glaeser, and Shapiro (2003) on the division of labor in food preparation; and Chou, Grossman, and Saffer (2004), Rashad and Grossman (2004), and Rashad, Grossman, and Chou (2006) on working women and restaurant growth.

Papers on the relationship between BMI, income, and other labor market factors are by Cawley (2004), Cawley and Danziger (2004), Du et al. (2004), Conley and Glauber (2006), Schroeter, Lusk, and Tyner (2008), Cawley, Moran, and Simon (2010), Schmeiser (2009), Courtemanche (2009), and Garcia Villar and Quintana-Domeque (2009).

Papers on obesity and the FSP are by Fraker, Martini, and Ohls (1995), Cuellar (2003), Chen, Yen, and Eastwood (2005), Kaushal (2007), and ver Ploeg and Ralston (2008).

Papers on the relationship between body weight and smoking are by Klesges and Shumaker (1992), Grunberg (1992), Pattishall (1992), Cooper et al. (2003), Cawley, Markowitz, and Tauras (2004, 2006), Gruber and Frakes (2006), Courtemanche (2007), Baum (2009), and Nonnemaker et al. (2009).

Other papers on various explanations for the rise in obesity rates are by Chou, Rashad, and Grossman (2008) on fast-food television advertising; Richards and Padilla (2009) on fast-food promotions; Mair, Pierce, and Teret (2005) and Currie et al. (2010) on fast-food restaurant and school proximity; Anderson and Butcher (2006) on school vending machines; Nayga (2001), Variyam and Cawley (2006), Schulman (2010), and Millimet, Tchernis, and Husain (2010) on various aspects of nutrition information; Komlos, Smith, and Bogin (2004), Smith, Bogin, and Bishai (2005), Borghans and Golsteyn (2006), and Scharff (2009) on impatience; Courtemanche (2008) on gasoline prices; Courtemanche and Carden (2008) on Walmart pricing; Herbst and Tekin (forthcoming) on child-care subsidies; Eid et al. (2008) on urban sprawl; Sen, Mennemeyer, and Gary (2009) and Sandy et al. (2009) on neighborhood quality; Cawley, Meyerhoeffer, and Newhouse (2007a, 2007b) and Cawley and Liu (2006) on physical education requirements; Eisenberg and

Okeke (2009) on weather; and Deb et al. (2009) and Smith, Stoddard, and Barnes (2009) on stress and job insecurity.

Papers addressing various aspects of childhood obesity are by Anderson, Butcher, and Levine (2003), Eberstadt (2003), MacInnis and Rausser (2005), Cawley and Liu (2007), Johnson, McInnes, and Shinogle (2006), Wallinga (2010), Frieden, Dietz, and Collins (2010), Bor (2010), Cawley (2010), and Jain (2010).

Other papers on obesity are by Levy (2002), Auld and Grootendorst (2004), Bednarek, Jeitschko, and Pecchenino (2006), Goldfarb, Leonard, and Suranovic (2006), and Richards, Patterson, and Tegene (2007) on eating models and addiction; Guthrie, Lin, and Frazao (2002) on eating at home versus eating out; Kan and Tsai (2004) on risk knowledge; Anderson and Matsa (2011) on fast-food availability; Chouinard et al. (2007) on taxing dairy products; Morris and Gravelle (2008) on general practitioner supply; Oswald and Powdthavee (2007) on affluence; Burkhauser and Cawley (2008) on alternative measures of obesity; Miljkovic, Nganje, and de Chastenet (2008) on economic factors; and Gandal and Shabelansky (2010) on supermarket prices.

Papers on obesity trends and health care costs are by Komlos and Baur (2004), Bhattacharya and Bundorf (2009), Cutler, Glaeser, and Rosen (2007), Michaud, van Soest, and Andreyeva (2007), Ruhm (2007), Bleich et al. (2008), Burkhauser, Cawley, and Schmeiser (2009), and Mehta and Chang (2009).

See Kersh and Morone (2005) for a discussion of obesity and the courts. Surveys and overviews of the economics of obesity are by Finkelstein, Ruhm, and Kosa (2005), Propper (2005), and Rosin (2008). Also see the book edited by Acs and Lyles (2007).

5

WE KNOW WHAT'S BEST FOR YOU

Do you remember Tim from chapter 1? Let's get to know him better. Tim is a heavy smoker and a heavy drinker, and to make matters worse, his body mass index places him firmly in the obese category. If this were all you knew about Tim, his excesses could place him high up on the list of people in need of social policy intervention to protect them from themselves. But this is not all we know about Tim. We also know that he is time consistent. Tim understands that whatever benefits he enjoys from indulging in smoking, drinking, and eating today, he will possibly have substantial future health costs, and he is perfectly informed about all of these costs and benefits over his entire life span. Furthermore, whether Tim plans to continue indulging or eventually refrain from indulging, he will actually follow that path. Because of his time consistency, Tim will never wake up one morning regretting how much he has smoked, drunk, or eaten in the past.

This chapter discusses the justifications for using social policy to protect people from themselves. In Tim's case, there is little (and possibly no) justification because he is fully informed and time consistent. As we will discuss later, economists often use someone such as Tim as an ideal benchmark, and any deviations from his behavior would be considered inefficient. Of course, quite often the fully informed time-consistent benchmark involves a person who does not choose indulgent acts, but as we saw in chapter 1, time consistency does *not* imply nonindulgent behavior. By smoking, drinking, and eating in excess, Tim is choosing to consume the products that satisfy him the most. But there is one important thing about Tim you do not know—Tim is 12 years old.

Protecting the Children

Most people have an extremely difficult time accepting the concept of a *rational* smoking, drinking, and overeating 12-year-old. The social policy debate over paternalistic policies almost always involves the pros and cons of protecting *adults* from themselves. If you favor such policies for adults, you are very likely to favor such policies for children. Even if you strongly oppose them for adults, you may support (or at least not oppose) them for children. But is it so obvious that we should use *social* resources to protect children from certain indulgences? This can be a very important question, because if the justifications for protecting children are weak, that suggests that justifications for protecting adults are even weaker. And even if the justifications for protecting children are strong, we can examine how well these fit with policies targeted at adults.

So let's start with Tim. The key question to raise is this: If all you know about Tim is that he is a perfectly informed, rational, time-consistent addict, is that enough information for you to determine the role of social policies to protect him from himself? If you believe the answer to this question is yes, there is little justification to adopt policies to control Tim's behavior. Whether Tim is 12, 25, or 73 years old, any intervention to push him off his chosen consumption path must, necessarily, reduce his welfare. But what if your answer is no, we need more information about Tim? How does knowing that Tim is 12 years old change things?

What is the difference between a 12-year-old time-consistent addict and a 25-year-old one? Theoretically, there is no difference. Rationality and time consistency are *assumed* to govern their behavior. So the difference must lie in the practicality of the assumption. Let's face it, does anyone believe a 12-year-old has the cognitive ability to make mature, well-informed, patient, time-consistent decisions? Probably not. In other words, a child such as Tim is unlikely to exist in the real world, so he provides us with no guidance when considering controlling adult behavior.

What about time-inconsistent Sophisticated Sophia? Let's assume that she too is 12 years old. Sophia recognizes her time-inconsistency problem and may practice self-control or prefer social policy to help her control her behavior. Thus, the justification for policies to control sophisticated time-inconsistent children may be quite strong. But this level of sophistication is probably well beyond the ability of the typical 12-year-old, and so we can once again conclude that there are unlikely to be many children like Sophia in the real world. The theoretical model discussed in chapter 1 leaves us with one last possibility—12-year-old Naive Nate.

As a naive time-inconsistent child, Nate may regret his current indulgences in the future, yet he doesn't anticipate this regret. Teens who smoke or drink or who are obese have a high probability of becoming adults who smoke or drink or are obese. As adults many of them look back and wish they had not indulged when they were younger. Nate may indulge as a child with the expectation to refrain as an adult, but when he becomes an adult, he no longer finds it in his best interest to refrain. This may be a justifiable setting for social policies to control Nate's behavior.

Yet even if you agree that naiveté justifies policies to control a child's behavior, precisely how should the policies do it? It may not be necessary to rely on social policies to control children because of the existing built-in private paternalistic mechanism—parents. Interestingly, the justifications for social policies to protect naive children may be weaker than the justifications for protecting adults precisely because of the role of parents in the equation. You don't think of the typical 25-year-old adult as subject to his or her parents' rules, but you do think of the typical 12-year-old child as having such constraints.

If parental guidance is a substitute for social policies, it may be best to allow *private* resources to be used to control the indulgences of children. This allows for social resources to be put to other uses. Besides, it may be that some parents don't mind if their children smoke or drink, especially as the children get into their upper teens, and this further reduces the role for social policies to control their behavior. But there is another side to the story. Some may argue that parents, even with the best intentions, are ineffective at controlling their children. Or an even stronger argument in favor of social policies is that parents themselves may recognize their ineffectiveness in controlling their children and *demand* such policies from the state. These parents are similar to the sophisticated time-inconsistent addict who recognizes her lack of self-control and appreciates government intervention. The child may not be sophisticated, but her parents may be.

Parents certainly have the ability to punish children who indulge against their wishes, but the government may be much more effective at controlling such behavior. For example, you may not want your 12-year-old child to buy cigarettes or alcohol, but how do you monitor her every purchase? The government, on the other hand, can make it illegal for vendors to sell such products to children, something parents cannot do. As we saw in chapter 3, the minimum legal drinking age law is one of the key policy instruments used to discourage youth drinking.

As restrictions to prevent children from indulging in various activities are pretty much globally accepted, it may be easiest to conclude that these policies are justified because children lack the ability to know what is best for them. No doubt a very strong justification to protect children from themselves is that they lack or misperceive the information necessary to make fully informed choices. But lack of full information is an old story in economics, and the modern economic research on paternalism doesn't add much to that traditionally well-understood justification for social control policies. (We briefly return to this issue in chapter 6.) But even if fully informed, if children are myopic and naively time inconsistent, they need to have many of their actions controlled—if not by their parents, who often lack the ability to satisfactorily control their behavior, then by public policy. Thus, if myopia and time inconsistency provide the strongest modern justifications for protecting children from themselves, we need to examine these same qualities in adults and ask whether the justifications hold true for them.

Should We Discount Discounting?

As we discussed in great detail in chapter 1, a person's subjective rate of time preference is an important factor to consider when studying addiction. The discount factor, δ, measures a person's impatience level between adjacent time periods, with a smaller δ implying a higher level of impatience (or a lower level of patience). Because the consumption of addictive goods usually involves a trade-off between current gratification and future poor health, it is predicted that more myopic (or less patient) people are more likely to become addicts than less myopic (or more patient) ones. Thus, having a firm idea of what real-world discount factors are would be helpful when considering public policy options to control addictive goods.

An excellent review of the literature (Frederick, Loewenstein, and O'Donoghue, 2002) surveys a very large number of studies attempting to measure the discount factor. The authors present three key observations.

The first is that measures of the discount factor range from very large to very small, pretty much from 0 (perfectly impatient) to 1 (perfectly patient). Second, over the years, with improved statistical techniques and a wider variety of data sets, measures of the discount factor have not converged or narrowed to a tighter range. There seems to be no escaping a very wide range of values. And third, if one tendency shows up in the data more often than others, it is that discount-factor measures can appear to be quite low, suggesting a low level of patience. Too low an estimated discount factor, though, is at odds with some commonsense beliefs about what realistic discount factors are likely to be. For example, if we estimate that you have a very low discount factor and are myopic, how do we account for your saving money in a low-interest-rate account? The problem may lie in the accuracy of our discount factor estimate.

A wide range of measured discount factors can occur for several reasons. Discounting is a subjective concept, and each person can have a unique discount factor. These studies attempt to measure an average discount factor or a range of discount factors, but people show tremendous differences in patience levels and so do estimates of discount factors. Also, different procedures are used for measuring discount factors. Many studies are experimental, where test subjects are given choices involving real or hypothetical rewards. Tests conceptually identical yet implemented differently can yield very different results. Other studies use real-world data collected from situations that involve trade-offs between current and future outcomes.

For example, consumers choosing an appliance must trade off between the current purchase price and the long-term energy costs of running it (Frederick, Loewenstein, and O'Donoghue, 2002). Appliances that are more energy efficient tend to cost more today but save money in the long run. Estimates of discount factors using this type of market data vary widely across different types of appliances. As another example, an interesting study (Warner and Pleeter, 2001) examined retirement options offered to servicemen when downsizing the military was a policy goal. Those eligible for retirement were given a choice between a one-time payment now or a larger *total* payment but paid out in smaller annual portions over a number of years. The government anticipated roughly a 50–50 split between the two options (on the basis of a discount factor prediction of approximately 0.85), but that was not the case— far more retirees chose the one-time immediate payment. This suggests lower discount factors (less patience) than the government predicted.

In addition to the differences among people and in estimation techniques, several confounding factors make isolating a subjective rate of time preference a truly difficult task. In theory, a discount factor is supposed to measure *only* a person's rate of time preference, that is, how patience level affects current versus future choices. But other forces can influence current versus future choices. For example, let's say you prefer $200 today over $250 one year from today. Is that because your discount factor is above .80 (that is, 200 ÷ 250), or is it because you believe you can invest the $200 today and earn more than the additional $50 by one year from today? If it is the latter case, your preference for $200 today is not helping us calculate your true rate of time preference.

Another confounding factor involves uncertainty about future events. You may prefer the $200 today because you are not confident you will actually receive the $250 one year from today. Also, maybe you prefer the $200 today because you believe you will be in a different situation one year from today, such as being employed, and so the extra money in the future means less to you from today's perspective. It is also possible that inflation has you preferring a current amount over a future amount because of the devaluing effect of rising prices. All of these factors influence the way you trade off current versus future dollars for reasons other than your pure rate of time preference. And these other factors may be impossible to take into account in the studies that attempt to estimate a rate of time preference.

In terms of the addiction story, it may be the case that less-patient people are more likely to become addicts than those who are more patient. But even this basic result may present a problem. What if it is the other way around? What if addicts tend to be less patient than nonaddicts *because* of their addiction? Using data from Norway, a study (Bretteville-Jensen, 1999) compares the discount factors of active heroin and amphetamine users with those of nonusers and former users. Asking each respondent to choose between different hypothetical income streams, the study finds that active users have an annual discount factor of .53, for nonusers it is .95, and for former users it is .87. Of these three groups, then, it is the active drug users who are the least patient, and nonusers who are the most patient.

A standard explanation for this result is that drug users tend to be fairly impatient, more interested in current gratification than future health costs, whereas it is just the opposite for nonusers. What is interesting, however, is that *former* drug users are much closer in patience levels to nonusers than to active users. Were they not fairly impatient to have become drug users in the first place? What this simple demonstration may be showing is that active drug users are impatient precisely because they are drug users. If they kick the habit, they can become more patient again. Perhaps initial drug use is more experimental, leading to greater dependency and, therefore, less-patient behavior. This study certainly demonstrates how the causation between impatience and drug use could run in both directions.

We may never know precisely how rates of time preference act on addictive behavior or how to identify myopic people who, it is commonly believed, would most benefit from social control policies. Far too many studies fail to reach even a loose consensus on what a person's or group's discount factor might be. But even with this complication, something more about discounting needs to be addressed. Are people typically time consistent or time inconsistent?

The Importance of Time Inconsistency

Time inconsistency may be the single most important concept in considering justifications for social policy meant to protect people from themselves. A person may make impatient decisions in the short run (starting to smoke), relying on her ability to make patient decisions in the long run (quitting smoking in 10 years), only to find that, when the long run becomes the short run 10 years later, she makes an impatient decision and continues to smoke. Time inconsistency allows *preference reversals*, and it is this conflict between a person's long-run preferences from the current perspective and her short-run preferences in the future that makes for interesting public policy debate.

To empirically verify the existence of time inconsistency, determining the magnitude of the discount factor matters as well as how it changes over time. Typical time-inconsistent behavior has a person being less patient in the short run and more patient over the long run. This implies that the person's discount factor *increases* over time, as the larger the discount factor, the more patient (or less impatient) the person. Many studies, especially experimental ones, find evidence of an increasing discount factor over time. Nevertheless, it is often suggested that while an increasing discount factor may truly involve time inconsistency, it may also involve the confounding factors previously discussed.

For example, one complication in determining if a discount factor is constant over time has to do with people experiencing disutility from receiving future payments for reasons not associated with their rate of time preference. One study (Coller, Harrison, and Rutstrom, 2005), explicitly takes into account this confounding factor. If you are choosing between two payments that *both* occur in the future, the disutility of waiting applies to both payments. But if you are choosing between a current payment and a future payment, the disutility of waiting applies to only the latter payment. The authors set up an experiment that takes the future disutility into account, and the results suggest that if all payoffs occur in the future, the discount factor does not appear to increase over time. But if a current payoff is compared to a future payoff, evidence is that the discount factor increases over the short run. The authors correctly note that in many policy settings people must consider costs and benefits that both occur in the future, and so time consistency may appropriately be used to describe behavior. In an addiction setting, however, immediate gratification is often at issue, and so it may still be reasonable to consider time-inconsistent behavior.

Another way to verify time inconsistency without explicitly measuring the discount factor is to find evidence of preference reversals. As discussed in chapter 1, many experiments have shown that a person may choose A over B when they are future options, but then choose B over A when they become current options in the future. Preference reversal demonstrations are easy to perform, especially with hypothetical choices, but in many cases there is also evidence of people not reversing their preferences. Furthermore, yet again, time inconsistency may not be the only explanation to account for such reversals. Present-oriented behavior may be explained by many factors.

Although time inconsistency is usually thought of as implying a nonconstant discount factor, that is not necessarily what it means. It is common to believe that people have changing discount factors throughout their lifetime. For example, teenagers are thought of as being less patient than middle-aged adults, and middle-aged adults are thought of as being more patient than elderly adults. As you near the end of your life, you are probably much less concerned with future events and more present oriented. In fact, a person can have a different discount factor every year and still not be time inconsistent. An example illustrates this point.

You are 18 years old and fairly impatient between this year and next year. As an 18-year-old thinking of yourself at age 28, you think you are going to be relatively patient between that year and the year you turn 29, but when that time comes you find you are, once again, impatient between the current period and the next. The consumption path you chose when you were 18 is no longer the consumption path you choose now that you are 28. Now think of yourself as being 18 and impatient, but you know that when you are 28 you will be fairly patient because your discount factor will change over time. You are less patient in the short run than in the long run, but in this case when the long run becomes the short run, you truly are patient. Thus, you can make time-consistent decisions with a varying discount factor.

Another common confusion about time inconsistency is that it is often associated with impatience, but that may not be the case. Impatience has to do with the magnitude of the discount factor, even if it is constant. A person can be time consistent yet have a very small discount factor, making him or her very impatient. Impatient time-consistent people may make impetuous choices to smoke, drink, or overeat, but they do so with no regret and no reason to veer from their initial consumption path. Time inconsistency has to do with how a future period is discounted from today's perspective compared to how it is discounted when the person approaches that period. A patient person can be very patient between two future periods when they are both in the future and less patient between them when they become the present, but not less patient by very much. In other words, a fairly patient person can still face preference reversals.

In the end, despite all the formal research attempting to identify time inconsistency, sometimes anecdotal evidence and common sense can go a long way toward demonstrating certain behavior. A time-consistent person, in theory, has no reason to practice self-control, no reason to experience regret for any past decisions. Yet much real-world anecdotal evidence exists for the presence of self-control and regret. Here are two representative quotations:

> I once wrapped packs of cigarettes in a plastic bag and buried them in a flower pot on the back porch so that I would have to dig them up, extract a cigarette, and rebury the pack every time I wanted a smoke. (Pat, Valley Stream, New York, http://www.aolhealth.com/condition-center/smoking-cessation/10-ways-smokers-kicked-the-habit)

> I'm almost 17 and I have been through more than I would think I would ever go through. But I'm an alcoholic. I have done every drug out there, and I love the feel of it. I tell people that I am not in that stuff but the only reason I got in it is to hide all my problems, and I wish that I could have found something else to hide my problems. I hate being me, and every day I wish I could change

that, but I cannot, and it sucks, but I have to deal with it. (Alyse, Aurora, Colorado, http://www.pbs.org/inthemix/shows/pov_drug_abuse.html)

Although relying on anecdotal evidence can be problematic, especially since evidence from a couple of anecdotes doesn't tell you much about the pervasiveness of the behavior, in this case these two quotations are just the tip of the iceberg. It would be easy to document thousands more, but two adequately illustrate the main point—time inconsistency is quite likely a very common behavioral trait.

Paying for Self-Control

Real-world evidence of self-control is easy to come by. Just look at the many products designed to help people control their indulgences, especially smoking and overeating, and the large number of self-help programs, such as 12-step programs. Clearly, people are willing to pay to get help in curbing their indulgences, which is highly inconsistent with time-consistent behavior.

One interesting form of self-control payment has to do with *quantity rationing* of vices. Many products are sold in various package sizes, with quantity discounts quite common. A smoker can buy a single pack of cigarettes or a 10-pack that offers a lower average price for each pack. Unless the smoker has a serious short-term income constraint, it's not likely that lack of funds has the smoker preferring to buy the single pack, especially if likely to buy 9 more packs before too long anyway. Many types of snack foods are now sold in 100-calorie packs, which are typically much more expensive per serving (on average, 142 percent more expensive per ounce by one estimate) than standard packages. For example, 100-calorie Goldfish Pretzels are three times more expensive per ounce than the regular-size package (http://www.cspinet.org/new/pdf/100_cal_chart .pdf). Why don't consumers save money and purchase the larger-quantity packages and then choose to consume smaller portions each time?

One way to practice self-control is to purchase smaller quantities of vices. If they are sold only in large-quantity packages, self-control may require you to not purchase at all. But with smaller, more expensive packages, you control your consumption by reducing the vice available to you. One study (Wertenbroch, 1998) compares consumers' price responsiveness between vice and virtue products to find evidence of self-control. Although the study offers several tests of self-control behavior, one is most instructive.

When comparing a vice product, such as regular cigarettes, to a virtue product, such as light cigarettes, a given consumer will prefer one over the other, but it isn't obvious which. (Keep in mind that "vice" and "virtue" are being used relatively here, as one can think of both types of cigarettes as vices.) When considering short-run gratification, the consumer may prefer the vice product, but when considering the longer-term impact, the consumer may prefer the virtue product. To identify this behavior, the author first puts together a list of 30 matching pairs of relative virtues and vices, such as regular and light salad dressing, ice cream and frozen yogurt, beef bologna and turkey bologna, and sugared fruit drinks and fruit juice. Test subjects were then asked two different questions:

> Question 1: If you were a consumer of each of the following products and consumption of these products entailed identical long-term consequences (such as long-term health or social effects or any other long-term costs and benefits), which of the two products in each pair would you rather consume? To evaluate these short-term effects, think about taste, ease of use, fun, temptation, or anything else that would make consuming the products enjoyable.

> Question 2: If you were a consumer of each of the following products and consumption of these products entailed identical short-term effects (such as taste, ease of use, fun, temptation, or anything else that would affect how much you enjoy consumption in the short run), which of the two products in each pair would you rather consume? To evaluate these long-term effects, think about health or social effects of consumption, etc.

The first question is designed to determine the immediate consequences of consumption assuming identical delayed consequences. If one of the products is preferred, that suggests it is a relative vice. The second question is designed to determine the delayed consequences of consumption assuming identical immediate consequences. If one of the products is preferred, that suggests it is a relative virtue.

By aggregating all the responses for each pair, the study determines that for 21 of the 30 pairs of products, a relative vice can be distinguished from a relative virtue. For example, ice cream and frozen yogurt are found to be significantly different to respondents, with ice cream being the relative vice. But regular cigarettes and light cigarettes are not found to be significantly different in terms of respondents' preferences of one over the other in the short term or long term. Thus, the study can now examine the price responsiveness of pairs of goods that are considered by the respondents to be relative vices and virtues.

The study finds that vices are more expensive than virtues when bought in small packages. However, vices also carry deeper quantity discounts, meaning that sellers have to offer greater discounts to induce consumers to increase their vice purchases. If it were simply a matter of consumers preferring vices to virtues, we would expect them to be higher priced in *all* package sizes, but this is not the case. Finally, consumption of vices is less sensitive to price changes than consumption of virtues (that is, vices have a lower elasticity of demand). This means that, with price reductions, consumers do not increase their consumption of vices as much as they increase their consumption of virtues. Together, these results suggest that consumers are willing to pay higher prices to limit their consumption of vices, which implies self-control behavior.

One interesting side note about quantity rationing has to do with state policies toward cigarette sales. We have seen before how well-intentioned state policies to protect people from themselves may have perverse side effects. Many states have laws that determine how retailers can sell cigarettes. For example, 16 states do not allow retailers to sell single cigarettes (as of June 2009), and many other states do not allow sales in any packaging other than the cigarette manufacturers' original packaging (National Cancer Institute, http://scld-nci.net/linkdocs/products/factsheets157.pdf). The goal of these restrictions is to discourage people who can't afford to buy a whole pack of cigarettes from being able to purchase just a few cigarettes at a time. This is one way to restrict smoking. On the other hand, if a smoker wants to practice self-control by rationing her purchases, the policy is at odds with that behavior. You may want to buy one cigarette a day to smoke just once a day, but if your minimum purchase size is a pack of 20, you may smoke several a day because of lack of self-control.

While paying for self-control appears to be a way of combating indulgences, ironically, the self-control may also not always be in the person's best interest. One fascinating study (Della Vigna and Malmendier, 2006) examines a real-world scenario that clearly illustrates this point. Many people buy gym memberships in an attempt to stay fit or become fit. Typical payment options include an annual membership, a monthly membership (with automatic renewals), or a pay-as-you-go plan (usually a 10-visit pass). As it turns out, the vast majority of members who choose the monthly option end up paying significantly more per visit than they would have with the pay-as-you-go option. The authors claim that a likely explanation for this outcome is that people overestimate their future self-control when they initially choose the longer-run plan. They plan on taking advantage of the gym membership more frequently than they actually do. In general, if a person invests in self-control mechanisms, but the self-control fails because it too is subject to time-inconsistent behavior, the investment may be wasted, imposing additional costs on the person.

A Sophisticated Experiment, and a Naive One

One problem with distinguishing between time-consistent and time-inconsistent behavior has to do with the confounding factor of uncertainty. As discussed above, people may be present biased because of not only their rate of time preference but also the uncertainty of future events. This makes it difficult to isolate a person's pure rate of time preference. The authors of one study (Fernandez-Villaverde and Mukherji, 2002) designed a clever experiment to try to distinguish time-consistent from time-inconsistent behavior. The experimental design allows each subject to choose between the following two options:

> Option A: You get 180 minutes of access to video games that can be played in the laboratory in three consecutive days after some specified date in the future. You get exactly 60 minutes to play on the first day, 60 minutes on the second day, and 60 minutes on the third day. You must show up at the laboratory on all three days and sign an attendance sheet.

> Option B: You get 180 minutes of access to video games that can be played in the laboratory in three consecutive days after some specified date in the future. You can use the 180 minutes any way you choose over the three days, but you must show up at the laboratory on all three days and sign an attendance sheet.

To provide an incentive for the subjects to show up for each of the three days, even if they have previously used all their minutes, subjects receive a payment of $30 if they complete the option they choose.

This experiment has several nice features. First, and most important, its design distinguishes between time-consistent and time-inconsistent behavior.

We expect time-consistent people to choose option B since it has far more flexibility than option A. In fact, A is a subset of B, so a person can formally choose B and still have the option to mimic A. So why would anyone choose option A? The only reason to choose it would be as a self-control mechanism, because A allows for a strict time schedule. For example, if you recognize you have a self-control problem, you may be concerned that you will use all your minutes on the first day, and so you choose A to prevent yourself from over-indulging early on. Or, exhibiting an aspect of time inconsistency we have not examined, if you don't care for video games, you may end up saving up too many minutes for the last day (that is, delaying a bad outcome) if you cannot commit to smoothing out your play over the three days. So whether enjoying video games or not, a sophisticated time-inconsistent person may choose option A as a commitment strategy.

A second feature of this experiment is that it eliminates many confounding factors that can make it difficult to isolate the rate-of-time-preference effect. One factor the authors are particularly interested in involves uncertainty. Because all game play is in the future, regardless of which option is chosen, uncertainty affecting one option but not the other is ruled out. Furthermore, other confounding factors that exist when the options are monetary payments (such as inflation or interest rates or future wealth holdings, all discussed above) are also ruled out owing to the payoffs being nonmonetary, other than the $30 completion payment. But the $30 payment is given to each subject independent of which option he or she chooses. Also, no hidden costs affect one option but not the other. Each subject, to fully complete the experiment, must incur the cost of showing up at the laboratory on three successive days regardless of the option chosen.

Finally, and also importantly for the authors, the experiment does not involve *hypothetical* choices. When the options in these kinds of experiments are not real, the results may be less reliable because subjects may not take their options seriously. If there is nothing real to gain or lose, subjects may be less inclined to make the same choices they would make under real conditions. The choices in this experiment involve real behavior, and the options are easy to understand.

As for the results, 23 subjects participated in the experiment, and 20 chose option B (87 percent) while 3 chose option A (13 percent). The authors interpret this outcome to suggest that this provides only weak evidence of time-inconsistent behavior, especially when compared to the claims of many other researchers. But they also point out an observational problem with their experiment. While choosing the less flexible option A does suggest a preference for self-commitment, *naive* time-inconsistent people may choose option B under the belief that they can follow the consumption path of a time-consistent person. Thus, those who chose option A are sophisticated time-inconsistent people, but they may not be the only time-inconsistent ones who participated in the experiment. It is interesting, however, that even just a handful of students chose the less flexible option. While the authors downplay this as a weak result, it still clearly demonstrates that some sophisticated people recognize their time-inconsistency problem and take actions to buffer its impact on their behavior. This experiment is a useful illustration of how economists try to distinguish between different behaviors that may be quite difficult to confidently identify in the real world.

While identifying people who practice self-control helps us distinguish between time-consistent and sophisticated time-inconsistent people, it doesn't help distinguish between time-consistent and naive time-inconsistent ones. Both Time-Consistent Tim and Naive Nate would not feel the need to practice self-control. One interesting study (Wong, 2008) presents an experiment that attempts to distinguish time-consistent from naive time-inconsistent behavior.

The author surveys his students about their studying plans in his economics class. The types of questions he asks his students are similar to the following. Let's say that his course begins on October 1 and the first exam is scheduled for October 31. He asks students what they believe is the *ideal* date to begin studying for that exam. Assume a student responds with October 24. The instructor then asks his students what day they believe they will start studying for the exam. The same student responds with October 26. Thus, for this student, the *predicted delay* in studying is two days. Predicted delay measures the degree to which a person is aware of her time-inconsistency problem. Thus, while Sophisticated Sophia would have a positive predicted delay, neither Time-Consistent Tim nor Naive Nate will predict delay.

Tim and Nate, however, can be distinguished, because Tim will correctly predict no delay and Nate will incorrectly predict no delay. To do this, on the day of the exam the instructor asks students what day they actually started studying for the exam. Let's say another student had predicted no delay but started studying October 27, three days after the student's previously identified ideal date. For this student, then, the *unexpected delay* is three days. Tim will not have an unexpected delay, but Nate certainly can.

By putting the two questions together, the survey nicely distinguishes between time-consistent, sophisticated time-inconsistent, and naive time-inconsistent behaviors. Only Tim will have no predicted delay and no unexpected delay. Whatever plans he makes for studying, he will perfectly stick to those plans. Only Sophia can have a predicted delay but no unexpected delay. Sophia is time inconsistent and so may delay her studying, but she perfectly recognizes this problem. Finally, only Nate can have no predicted delay and an unexpected delay. Nate does not recognize his time-inconsistency problem, and so his studying delay is not anticipated by him.

The results of the study are that only a minority of the students exhibit time-consistent behavior. Time inconsistency was by far the most common observed behavior, with naive behavior more prevalent than sophisticated behavior. Furthermore, the study finds that time inconsistency is associated with inferior class performances. Of course, as the author notes, other confounding factors may affect student studying behavior, but this study is a useful attempt to empirically verify theoretical behavior in real-world choice situations.

Putting all the previous discussions in this chapter together, one important conclusion jumps out—people are different, possibly very different. While obvious differences discussed throughout this book involve gender, age, race, income, education, and a host of others, the key differences highlighted here are patience versus impatience, time consistency versus time inconsistency, and sophisticated versus naive behavior. Designing public policy for such wide variation is a daunting task. *Justifying* such public policy may be even more daunting.

Come On, Get Happy

When discussing social policy in any context, the starting point is to define a *social objective*. What is the goal of public policy? Let's begin with a simple objective: crafting social policy to make people happier. While that may seem straightforward, it poses difficulties, especially when the policies are meant to protect people from themselves. It all depends on how the people you are trying to make happier respond to the policies.

To give our discussion some context, let's consider a specific, extremely common policy option—raising the tax rate on a pack of cigarettes. How will this affect the well-being of smokers? To address this question, we must think about what types of smokers we are dealing with. If the smoker is a well-informed time-consistent person, such as Tim, he will not appreciate the social intervention. As we have discussed before, Tim perfectly understands all the costs and benefits of his current and future actions, will never regret a past act, and is making smoking decisions that make him unambiguously better off. If the goal of cigarette taxation is to make people such as Tim better off, it fails.

What if the smoker is a sophisticated time-inconsistent person, such as Sophia? This raises more interesting possibilities for social control policies. Sophia recognizes her potential to experience regret and may prefer to self-control her smoking behavior. But self-control may be difficult, costly, and at times impractical. This is where social policy comes into play. Sophia prefers to have the government control her behavior because she knows she lacks the ability to practice self-control. Then again, it is important to recognize that even if she wants to be controlled, the government's policies may not make her happier. Recall from chapter 2 how some smokers support social policies to restrict smoking in certain venues, such as restaurants, hospitals, and the workplace. While this form of social control may be in some smokers' best interests, these same smokers may not appreciate increased cigarette taxes. There is no guarantee that a specific social control policy will enhance the well-being of these smokers. Nevertheless, there are much stronger justifications for protecting people such as Sophia from themselves than for protecting people such as Tim. When smokers *demand* specific social policies, those policies can make them happier.

That now leaves us with the naive time-inconsistent smokers such as Nate. At first blush, these appear to provide a very strong justification for social control policy, as was argued above with respect to protecting children from themselves. By not recognizing what his immediate gratification from smoking does to his future health costs, Nate can easily get to a point in his life when he looks back and says to himself, "Why did I ever smoke so many cigarettes?" If government tax policy reduces the amount of cigarettes Nate smokes throughout his life, he may not ever experience that regret, making him a happier person. But there is a serious problem with this reasoning. If Nate doesn't recognize his potential for future regret, how can he recognize the ultimate benefits of social policies that control his current behavior? He can't, and even the leading scholars who support paternalistic policies recognize this problem:

> Time inconsistent but naive consumers, who have a self-control problem but don't recognize its existence, would not be made better off in their own eyes by higher taxation; such consumers view themselves as time consistent, so . . . they would feel worse off from a tax-induced price rise. Social welfare . . . may rise when taxes increase on naive (time inconsistent) smokers, but their own perceived welfare will not increase. (Gruber and Mullainathan, 2002, 9)

The policy implications of this quotation warrant further scrutiny.

Let's consider a society made up entirely of naive time-inconsistent smokers. The state raises the cigarette tax rate and every single person *perceives* himself or herself to be worse off for having to pay more for an enjoyable activity. If all members of our society believe that their welfare has decreased, how is it possible that *social* welfare may rise? If social welfare is the sum of every person's personal welfare, it cannot increase. It must, by definition, decrease. If the social goal is to make people happier, that goal is not achieved in this society with an increased cigarette tax.

Let's think of the same scenario in a different context. You are a parent with your child at a grocery store, and she wants you to put lots of candy and snack food in the shopping cart. You refuse. She throws a fit. You continue to refuse. Do you believe your actions are making your child happier? Maybe you can say that in the long run your child will be happier without the junk food. But would your child agree with you? Can she appreciate the future benefits she will enjoy by eating healthy food today? While you may be happier with your child eating well, it is not your welfare we are discussing right now—it is your child's. And as your child perceives it, your actions make your child unambiguously worse off.

So is it possible to make someone better off without the person realizing it? It seems that the correct answer to this question is no. If the person does not perceive himself to be happier, he is not happier. But from a public policy perspective, it is not the right question to ask. The right question is this: Can you increase *social welfare* by making someone better off without the person realizing it? And the answer to this question is perfectly clear—it depends. On what it depends is at the heart of the public policy debate over paternalistic social policies.

The Right Question and an Ideal Answer

It seems that understanding the naive time-inconsistent person is the key to understanding the recent economic scholarship recommending, either implicitly or explicitly, paternalistic social policies. Recall time-inconsistent Naive Nate from chapter 1. Nate is fully informed about the costs and benefits of all his current and future actions. He does not behave irrationally when he decides to undertake a current activity. In fact, he calculates the *current value* of all his options and chooses the one that makes him best off from the current perspective. The naive aspect about Nate's behavior is that he doesn't recognize that he is time inconsistent.

Nate recognizes that he is relatively impatient between the current period and the next but relatively patient between two future periods. So if he believes he can make an impetuous decision today relying on his behavior being more patient in the future, he'll be in for a surprise when he experiences a preference reversal. When the two future periods eventually become the current period and the next one, Nate will once again be relatively impatient between the two periods and make an impetuous decision. The strange aspect of naive behavior, however, is that Nate may continue to be naive even after experiencing a preference reversal. When he realizes that his future preferences for a particular choice are not as he anticipated, shouldn't Naive Nate now become Sophisticated Nate? In other words, can Nate truly be naive for very long?

Consider the following example. Nate is determined to lose weight. At the first of the month he will follow a strict diet, but for now he will indulge, taking comfort in his days of being obese being numbered. So Nate gains a few more pounds over the next couple of weeks, wakes up on the first of the month, and decides he will start his strict diet the first of *next* month. This is classic preference reversal, and because Nate did not anticipate his future lack of self-control, we know he is naive. But if he now realizes he does not follow through with his future plans, why does he expect to begin a diet on the first of next month? The answer to this question provides the crucial clue to understanding naive time-inconsistent behavior. Nate is the way he is for a very simple reason—he is *assumed* to be that way.

Some economists are very uncomfortable when considering naive time-inconsistent behavior. It just doesn't seem to make much *economic* sense. Nate doesn't necessarily follow the consumption path he sets out for himself, as

Tim would. Nate also doesn't recognize his potential for preference reversal, as Sophia would. Sophia may have a strange time preference compared to Tim, but economists are pleased that she recognizes her behavioral quirks. But Nate is an economic mess. Even if you are willing to concede that Nate doesn't recognize his time inconsistency right away, how can he still fail to recognize it when it continues to rear its ugly head? How can he be that oblivious to even his own experiences?

The reason why Nate is assumed to be not only initially naive but *always* naive is that he behaves in ways that are commonly thought of as occurring in the real world. How many of us anticipate future behavior, do not follow through, and then at that point, reset our thinking and anticipate future behavior and then, yet again, do not follow through? The greatest defense for the assumption of naive behavior is that it seems to account for much real-world behavior. In fact, most people would probably consider time consistency to be the least observed behavior in the real world. Never veering from a consumption path? Never regretting a decision? That is unrealistic.

It is important to understand that economists do not model the real world. Instead, we model an abstract, primitive version of the real world. By necessity, this is all we can do. The real world is highly complicated. Even when considering the behavior of a single person, many complications could never be perfectly captured in an abstract model. When introducing a person such as Time-Consistent Tim, we don't really believe that precisely such a person exists in the real world, but we do believe that modeling time-consistent behavior can provide us with many insights that allow us to confidently move to the next stage and model slightly more complex behavior, such as time inconsistency. And then after modeling time inconsistency, we can expand the scope of our abstract world and consider further refinements such as sophistication and naiveté.

In making our model more realistic, by assuming naive behavior, for example, we have to sacrifice some abstract conveniences because we now have to consider people in an economic framework who do not understand their own behavior. And this creates a policy paradox. If naive people do not understand that they are time inconsistent, and they lack the ability to ever realize this, how can they ever appreciate social policy designed to protect them? They can't, and so social welfare must be thought of in a way that can justify policy intervention even if it reduces the perceived welfare of those it is meant to help.

Numerous social welfare objectives can be used to justify paternalistic intervention, but one in particular is often applied to policies targeted at naive people. Instead of basing social welfare on actual preferences, people's *ideal preferences* are used. The only problem now is to define "ideal preferences."

Think about Time-Consistent Tim and Naive Nate. Let's assume that these two are identical in every way except one—Tim is time consistent and Nate is not. What this implies is that while they both have identical long-term rates of time preference, their short-term rates differ. For all *future* periods, Tim and Nate are equally patient between any two periods. But between the current period and the next, Tim is more patient than Nate. This difference can lead Nate to make time-inconsistent decisions but not recognize this inconsistency until it is too late. So Nate *believes* he will behave exactly as Tim, although in actuality he won't. If social control policy can get Nate to mimic Tim's behavior, Nate's belief about being like Tim will now be correct. In this setting, Tim's preferences are being used as the ideal benchmark, and so these preferences are being defined as social welfare.

For example, let's say it is Monday and both Tim and Nate are invited to the same party this Saturday night. They know there will be lots of snack food and beer, and they will indulge heavily if they attend. But both also realize that they have an exam next Monday and if they have a hangover and stomachache on Sunday, they will not be able to study effectively. So as of today, they both decide they do not want to attend the party. Now it's Saturday. Tim, being time consistent, still does not want to attend the party. Nate, however, being time inconsistent, was relatively patient between Saturday and Sunday on Monday, but now that it is Saturday, he is relatively impatient about Sunday and so he heavily discounts the costs he will incur after the party. He decides to attend the party. He is in no condition to study on Sunday, he does poorly on his exam, and he regrets ever having gone to the party.

If we can go back in time one week and ask Nate what his preference will be a week from now, he himself will tell us he does *not* want to attend the party. That is his true preference, and it matches Tim's. When Saturday comes along, he has a preference reversal and wants to attend the party. His preference no longer matches Tim's, the ideal preference by definition. If we had the ability to use social policy to prevent Nate from attending the party, all we would be doing is helping him stick to his original plan. And remember, it is *his* original plan. Social control in this example makes Nate better off by forcing him to remain time consistent. The intervention encourages time-consistent, or ideal, behavior. Thus, social welfare will be enhanced.

This view of social welfare contends that Nate's time preference is, in a sense, mistaken. His current short-term relative impatience is matched against a whole future of relative patience. The short-term preference is an anomaly, one that leads to inconsistency and regret. Social policy may be well suited to correct this mistake, but let's consider the party story once again.

Now let's assume that you are the social control agent, and it is your job to follow Nate around and keep him on the ideal path. Early in the week, he has no interest in attending the party, so you telling him he cannot attend will have no effect. Now it's Saturday, and he announces that he is going to attend the party. It is your job to tell him no. How do you think Nate will react? He may say, "Thank you for helping me stick to my original plan." You certainly will be relieved if he says that. But he also may say, "I've changed my mind and now I want to go to the party; get out of my way." That will create some tension. You remind him of how he felt a week ago, how he *truly* felt. He agrees with you, but reminds you that it was a week ago and he truly *now* wants to go to the party. You inform him of all the costs he will bear tomorrow and how that will affect his exam grade. He agrees with you that there will be costs, but because he is relatively impatient between today and tomorrow, he discounts those costs by a greater amount than he did a week ago. His preference now is to attend the party. If you stop him, you will force him to adhere to the ideal path and social welfare will be enhanced, but he may not be happy about it.

It is Nate's unhappiness that leads to a serious criticism of using ideal preferences to define social welfare. Nate can be thought of as two selves—the current self and the future self. There is a tension between the two selves, but that tension is motivated by changing preferences. The current Nate is relatively patient about future events, and the future Nate is relatively impatient when the time arrives. But why can't Nate resolve this problem on his own? Are the authorities in the best position to resolve the tension between the current and future Nates?

Consider the following analogy. You and your wife are newlyweds, about to start living together for the first time. You smoke. She doesn't like secondhand smoke. How will you resolve this problem? You will have to negotiate some outcome that is agreeable to both of you. Maybe you will smoke only outside the home or only when she is not at home. It's possible that you will quit smoking altogether, or that she will learn to live with secondhand smoke.

There are many possible outcomes, but there is one that both of you may not be too excited about—the government stepping in and telling you what the smoking policy in your home will be. If this solution doesn't appeal to you, is it any different from the government stepping in and resolving the tension between the two Nates?

In thinking about a current self negotiating with a future self, some commentators point out that it is not clear which self deserves more consideration. If your current self overeats, he will impose costs on your future self. But if your future self insists on your current self dieting and exercising, then the future self imposes costs on your current self. If social control is directed at protecting your current self, is that the self that you would favor? Is anyone in a better position to resolve this internal struggle than you?

One critic of paternalistic intervention offers the following astute comment about using social policy to keep naive people on their own original consumption path:

> The old paternalism said, "We know what's best for you, and we'll make you do it." The new paternalism says, "*You* know what's best for you, and we'll make you do it." (Whitman, 2006, 2; emphasis in original)

The critics of paternalistic policies argue that, just as the husband and wife can resolve their smoking issue, each person can resolve his or her time-inconsistency problem. But this method is strongest for sophisticated time-inconsistent people, not naive ones. If you don't recognize that you have a time-inconsistency problem, there won't be much of an internal struggle for you to resolve. You believe you are time consistent, so your current self and future self are in harmony. A sophisticated time-inconsistent person may be able to deal with the internal conflict because she recognizes it, but even then she may welcome social control to help her overcome her self-control issues. Arguing that people have the *potential* to balance their current and future behavior does not necessarily rule out the value of social policy, especially for naive people.

But what other problems are there with basing social policy on ideal behavior? One concern is that it may be difficult to design policy that will allow Nate to mimic Tim. Let's return to an example we have previously discussed. Tim decides today to start smoking with the intention of quitting in 10 years. That, by definition, is the ideal behavior in this setting. Nate also believes that he can quit in 10 years, but when the time comes he finds that he no longer wants to quit. How can social policy get Nate to start smoking now and quit in 10 years? Social policy is often much better suited for controlling current behavior than (only) future behavior. Increased taxes may discourage Nate from starting smoking or from smoking a lot, but can it allow Nate to mimic the ideal consumption path? And if Nate chooses not to smoke at all, how does the social welfare of this path compare to that of the ideal path or to that of Nate's original time-inconsistent path? Is a Nate who doesn't smoke a *second-best* ideal outcome?

An even more difficult problem involves identifying the ideal behavior to begin with. In the party example, Nate expresses an early desire not to attend the party. This may be a useful way to determine an ideal benchmark. But can future desires from a current perspective be identified? And if yes, how do we know that the future desire will not eventually be consistently achieved? Perhaps the best way to deal with naive time inconsistency is to gather information on the potential for future regret. For example, suppose a survey of former drug users provides strong evidence that many of them regret having ever decided to consume drugs in the first place. This may not tell us if Nate will eventually regret his current decision to use drugs, but it does suggest that, in this context, regret is a pervasive experience. In fact, the government anticipating future regret accounts for one of the early behavioral economics applications justifying social policy intervention to protect naive time-inconsistent people from themselves. The following is not an addiction story, but it is instructive.

Let's assume that you just graduated from college and you are debt free. You are 25 years old and you begin working at your first full-time job. You realize that in 40 years you will be ready to retire, and you want to save a specific amount for that time. All you need now is a retirement savings plan. You decide you want to have fun while you are young, so you plan on spending every dollar of your disposable income until you are 40 years old. Once you turn 40, you will then save every dollar of your disposable income until you retire at 65. Following this path, you will retire at 65 with precisely the amount of savings you desire. When your first paycheck arrives, however, you discover that the government has a different savings plan for you, and you are required to follow it.

The government plan has you saving at a constant rate throughout your 40 years of employment. When you are ready to retire, this plan also leaves you with the amount of savings you desire, but you don't get to save your way.

How do we evaluate the sense of the government's saving plan? Requiring savings has a tremendous commonsense appeal. People may plan on saving for retirement, only to find that they fall short of their original goal. Time-inconsistent behavior is certainly a problem in this setting. If many people end up at retirement age without the appropriate savings, they will face severe hardships or be a burden to the state. The government may have a substantial amount of evidence that, without required savings, most people do end up short of their goal and experience regret. Thus, the government is only help-ing people achieve goals they themselves want to achieve. You get to age 65, you see a healthy retirement savings, and you are thankful for being forced to save. Or are you unhappy?

Here's the problem. When you get to 65 and have the amount of savings you planned for, you may say to yourself, "I could have done that *my* way and I would have been happier; I didn't need the government to intervene." But let's say we tell you that you couldn't have done it the way you planned. You would have spent wildly for 15 years and then continued to spend wildly because you are time inconsistent and naive. You would not have followed your original path. But how can we convince you of that? The government forced you on a specific savings path and did not allow you to experience regret. As far as you are concerned, you have been made worse off. Unless sometime in your life you had realized that you would not have followed your original path, you will never come to appreciate the intervention. And if you truly are naive, that moment of realization will never materialize.

Justifying a required savings plan, then, either requires people to appreci-ate that they cannot adequately save for their own retirement, that is, they are sophisticated time inconsistent, or to be naive time inconsistent and needing to be held to an ideal savings path. In the former case, social welfare increases directly because people's welfare increases. In the latter case, social welfare in-creases because it is defined in terms of ideal behavior. Ideal preferences thus can have the unusual feature of being defined strictly outside the unknown *true* preferences of the person being protected by social policy.

It is clear, then, that ideal behavior is often identified by what is believed to be socially acceptable behavior. Is it ideal to refrain from smoking, drink-ing, or overeating? Remember, time consistency does not imply that a person won't choose to indulge in these behaviors; it just implies that, whatever con-sumption path he chooses, he will never veer. Perhaps *ideal* would be inter-preted as maintaining a high discount factor, meaning that a person who is relatively myopic (small discount factor, but not necessarily time inconsistent) would be held to the ideal behavior of a more patient person. In short, ideal behavior can be defined as absolutely anything the policy officials want to define it as, and this allows public policy to often be trivially justifiable.

If defining social welfare with ideal preferences makes you uncomfortable, another approach is to count as social welfare the *actual* preferences of everyone affected by the policy. For example, increase the tax on cigarettes and see how it impacts *all* smokers. Policies that are broadly applied and not targeted at specific groups are often criticized for necessarily harming some people. Cigarette taxes will reduce the welfare of time-consistent smokers, even if they do increase the welfare of some time-inconsistent ones. But this criticism is often countered by the correct observation that the objective of maximizing social welfare does not guarantee that everyone is going to be made better off by a particular policy. As long as the welfare gains exceed the welfare losses, the policy enhances the net social welfare. However, applying this observation in a situation in which policy is meant to help naive time-inconsistent people is problematic.

Let's consider a society of only three people—Tim, Sophia, and Nate. All three are smokers, and the authorities are considering a policy of increasing cigarette taxes to control their behavior. Does the proposed policy enhance social welfare? Tim is time consistent and, therefore, made worse off. Sophia is time inconsistent but sophisticated, and let's assume she appreciates the social control and is made better off. Nate is time inconsistent and naive and, as argued above, does not appreciate the control and is made worse off. If Sophia's welfare gains fall short of the *sum* of Tim's and Nate's welfare losses, the policy does not enhance the net social welfare. By this criterion, the policy should not be enacted. This is very traditional social welfare analysis.

From a paternalistic perspective, however, one of the stated goals of social control is to protect naive addicts such as Nate. If social control policies are enacted only when the gains to sophisticated time-inconsistent addicts are large enough to warrant them, naive people will often be left to their own indulgences. So this brings us back to ideal preferences as the surest way to justify social policy to protect the naive.

The main point being made here is *not* that it is difficult to justify social policy to protect naive people from themselves when they don't appreciate the control. The point is that justifying the policy by claiming that the people themselves are better off is not valid. They simply are not better off, but their perceived well-being is not the welfare standard being used. This doesn't dismiss the potential value of such policies; it just suggests we have to consider their justifications carefully.

What Is on Your Mind?

Many of the scholarly economic articles discussed in this book can be difficult to read, not only for the layperson but also for economists who do not specialize in the article's field or who are not comfortable with highly technical research. A typical formal economic article can be jam-packed with complicated mathematical equations, theorems, and proofs. There can also be difficult-to-interpret tables of results and intricate graphs. As challenging as many of these articles are, rarely do they contain anything totally alien to the trained economist. But when reading an economic article that includes a picture of a brain scan with the caption "The human brain with some economically relevant areas marked," we are entering a new economic realm. That realm is known as *neuroeconomics*.

Perhaps the best way to delve into the economics of the brain is to present an experiment that fits perfectly with one of the major themes of this book—time inconsistency. Naive Nate is relatively impatient between the current period and the next one but relatively patient between two future periods. This helps explain why Nate may experience regret when a current consumption path veers in the future from what he originally intended. Many studies attempt to verify the existence of time-inconsistent behavior, but a neuroeconomic study has an additional goal: to explain what is happening in the brain as test subjects make decisions involving current versus future choices.

One study (McClure, Laibson, et al., 2004) nicely illustrates this goal:

> We hypothesize that the discrepancy between short-run and long-run preferences reflects the differential activation of distinguishable neural systems. Specifically, we hypothesize that short-run impatience is driven by the limbic system, which responds preferentially to immediate rewards and is less sensitive to the value of future rewards, whereas long-run patience is mediated by the lateral prefrontal cortex and associated structures, which are able to evaluate trade-offs between abstract rewards in the more distant future. (504)

Then, using brain scan technology, they put their hypothesis to the test.

Experimental subjects were given a series of choices involving real payoffs (between \$5 and \$40) that had them choose between smaller, more immediate rewards versus larger, more delayed rewards. While they were making their choices, their brains were scanned using functional magnetic resonance imaging. Collecting data on which parts of the brain are activated when making a choice, the authors are able to test their hypothesis. The study finds evidence to support its claim that immediate payoffs activate different regions of the brain than delayed payoffs do.

So what now? How does knowing which parts of the brain "light up" under different circumstances further economic analysis? Knowing what part of the brain activates when a person makes impatient decisions allows us to examine other cues that activate the same part of the brain. For example, the authors point out that the sight or smell or touch of a desired object leads to impulsive behavior and activates the brain's limbic system. Thus, maybe these cues act on the portion of the brain that controls impatient behavior. Heroin addicts, for example, in a drug-craving state, tend to be highly impulsive, which activates the limbic system. This activation may be causing myopia. So neuroeconomics may be able to address the issue, discussed earlier, of whether myopia leads to heroin addiction or heroin addiction leads to myopia.

The authors' ultimate conclusion is presented in a way that most economists would find familiar, as they credit neuroeconomics with identifying a trade-off:

> Human behavior is often governed by a competition between lower level, automatic processes that may reflect evolutionary adaptations to particular environments, and the more recently evolved, uniquely human capacity for abstract, domain-general reasoning and future planning. (506)

But for our purposes, an important issue remains. Do the results of neuroeconomic research identify new approaches or justifications for public policy intervention to protect people from themselves?

In chapter 1 we discussed an economic model of addiction that allows addictive behavior to be thought of as a mistake (Bernheim and Rangel, 2004). This model relies heavily on the results of neuroeconomics, and it provides an interesting case for us to consider because the authors present well-thought-out implications of their model for public policy. The authors attempt to show how their model of addiction yields novel insights into public policy considerations.

The most blunt forms of policy controls to restrict the use of addictive goods make them illegal or heavily tax their use. Yet both of these controls require addicts to respond to the resulting increased cost of consuming the goods. If, as the authors argue, addiction is a compulsion, a choice separated from preference, this lapse in rationality will have the addict largely ignore the cost increase and consume a similar amount of the good. In other words, if this model of addiction governs behavior, tax policy will not achieve the goal of reducing the use of addictive goods. This is an important insight, but it can be restated in a more traditional way.

Let's rephrase this discussion using an economic concept introduced in chapter 2—the price elasticity of demand. Consumers who are not very sensitive to price changes (that is, they have low elasticities of demand) will not be much affected by tax or other cost increases. Compulsive behavior may *explain* a low elasticity, but ultimately recognizing that some consumers will not respond much to price changes is a very old story in economics. Does it matter, from a policy perspective, whether addicts are not affected by control measures because they are making choices beyond their immediate control or because of other reasons? *Why* a person has a low elasticity of demand may be of secondary importance to recognizing that it exists.

In a similar vein, consider the role of advertising and other marketing strategies to enhance demand for addictive goods. Advertising can act as a cue that triggers compulsive behavior in addicts. Furthermore, the substantial antismoking messages, for example, on cigarette packages, may act as *countercues* that help addicts resist compulsions. Restricting advertising, then, or promoting countercue messages may be an effective social policy to control addictive behavior. Yet while neuroeconomics is a fairly new field, such social policies have been around for decades. We have known for a very long time that advertising is an attempt to enhance demand, and antismoking, antidrinking, and antidrug campaigns are attempts to reduce demand for these goods. So what does recognizing that addicts are susceptible to cues and countercues add to our understanding of social control policies? Once again, is it important to know *why* advertising enhances demand or to simply recognize that it does? In this case, neuroeconomics may offer some important and novel insights.

An interesting study (McClure, Li, et al., 2004) examines how the brain responds to differently designed taste tests between Coca-Cola and Pepsi-Cola soft drinks. In a blind taste test, approximately half the subjects (who were having their brains scanned at the time of the test) chose Pepsi. This choice is based on preference alone as no other information is given. But when the same subjects repeated the test knowing which of the drinks was Coke, approximately 75 percent chose Coke. Different parts of the brain responded to the different tests. In the first test, the response was in the part of the brain related to feelings of reward (the ventromedial prefrontal cortex). In the second test, the response was in the part of the brain related to higher cognitive thinking and memory (the lateral prefrontal cortex and hippocampus). Thus, on preference alone, Coke and Pepsi should have shared the market equally. But Coke's brand recognition gave Coke a three-to-one market share advantage. While some subjects *preferred* Pepsi based on taste, they *chose* Coke instead because of Coke's marketing strategies.

How the results of studies like these can be used to justify or design social policy remains an open and intriguing question. For example, as discussed in chapter 2, many countries have advertising restrictions on cigarettes, but these restrictions often fall short of being comprehensive bans. There are different types of advertising and marketing techniques. Maybe some affect different parts of the brain than others. Maybe some countercues affect different parts of the brains than others. Perhaps neuroeconomics can help design social control policies that can target specific types of advertising and promote the specific types of countercues that most effectively reduce addictive behavior.

Perhaps the greatest indication that social policy needs to consider the results of neuroeconomics (and neuroscience in general) is that firms are beginning to develop *neuromarketing* strategies. For example, movie studios are using brain imaging to determine the effectiveness of movie trailers in attracting viewers (Jain, 2010). If advertisers are using neuromarketing strategies to enhance the demand for products that social policy prefers to restrict, authorities must better understand neuroscience to develop effective policy options.

Among economists, neuroeconomics has its strong supporters, its harsh critics, but mostly a lot of scholars who either aren't interested in the field or don't know enough about it to decide one way or the other what its contributions to economics are or will be. One of the profession's leading and most-respected theorists, Drew Fudenberg, has this to say about neuroeconomics:

> It seems too early to know just how much impact this will have on most economics, but the potential impact is large, and the research under way is

fascinating. Thus, while I don't think that every economist ought to take up neuroeconomics, I do think that anyone interested in individual choice and decision making ought to keep an eye on how it develops. (2006, 707)

As of now, it is perhaps premature to praise *or* criticize neuroeconomics too enthusiastically. But keeping an open mind and using extreme caution in advising social policy is always sound advice with this, or any other, approach to economic analysis.

Suggested Readings

There is a phenomenally large literature on time preference and discounting. The place to start is the excellent paper by Frederick, Loewenstein, and O'Donoghue (2002), which provides a thorough and thoughtful survey on the massive literature. For just a small sampling of the literature, see the papers by Fishburn and Rubinstein (1982), Loewenstein and Thaler (1989), Mischel, Shoda, and Rodriguez (1989), Benzion, Rapoport, and Yagil (1989), Loewenstein and Prelec (1991, 1992), Becker and Mulligan (1997), Bretteville-Jensen (1999), Angeletos et al. (2001), Bickel and Marsch (2001), Warner and Pleeter (2001), Fehr (2002), Fernandez-Villaverde and Mukherji (2002), Diamond and Koszegi (2003), Rubinstein (2003), Gruber and Koszegi (2004), Dasgupta and Maskin (2005), McClure, Laibson, et al. (2004), Soman et al. (2005), Coller, Harrison, and Rutstrom (2005), Shapiro (2005), Sopher and Sheth (2005), Hansen (2006), Benhabib, Bisin, and Schotter (2010), Winkler (2006), Eisenhauer and Ventura (2006), Frederick (2006), Blondel, Loheac, and Rinaudo (2007), McClure et al. (2007), Bettinger and Slonim (2007), Khwaja, Silverman, and Sloan (2007), Rasmusen (2008a), Andersen et al. (2008), Wong (2008), Ida and Goto (2009), Grignon (2009), Noor (2009), and Andreoni and Sprenger (2010a, 2010b).

The best place to start learning about neuroeconomics is the excellent survey paper by Camerer, Loewenstein, and Prelec (2005). Other papers favorable to the new field are by Bernheim and Rangel (2005), Camerer (2006, 2008), Jamison (2008), McCabe (2008), and Spiegler (2008). Papers critical of the new field are by Gul and Pesendorfer (2008), Rubinstein (2008), and Harrison (2008a, 2008b).

Papers on neuromarketing are by Jain (2009) and McClure, Li, et al. (2004).

Papers on self-control are by Thaler and Shefrin (1981), Schelling (1984), Cowen (1991), Wertenbroch (1998), Ariely and Wertenbroch (2002), Benabou and Tirole (2004), Read (2006), Della Vigna and Malmendier (2006), Ameriks, Caplin, Leahy, and Tyler (2007), and Heidhues and Koszegi (2009).

A few papers that deal with the economics of happiness are by Ng (2003), Gruber and Mullainathan (2005), Dolan, Peasgood, and White (2008), and Barrotta (2008).

There is an industry of research debating the pros and cons of behavioral economics and paternalistic social policies. Some of these papers choose sides, some of them present both sides, and all of them present interesting and challenging viewpoints on these relatively new fields. For just a sampling of this literature, see the papers by Sunstein (1986), Burrows (1993, 1995), Conlisk (1996), Blackmar (1998), Jolls, Sunstein, and Thaler (1998a, 1998b), Posner (1998), Rabin (1998), Zamir (1998), McFadden (1999), Korobkin and Ulen (2000), Leonard, Goldfarb, and Suranovic (2000), Rubinstein (2001), Mitchell (2002, 2005), Benjamin and Laibson (2003), Camerer et al. (2003), O'Donoghue and Rabin (2003, 2006), Rachlinski (2003, 2006), Sunstein and Thaler (2003), Thaler and Sunstein (2003), Thaler and Benartzi (2004), Harrison (2005), Benjamin, Brown, and Shapiro (2006), Epstein (2006), Fudenberg (2006), Glaeser (2006), Jolls and Sunstein (2006), Loewenstein and O'Donoghue (2006), Pesendorfer (2006), Rubinstein (2006), Whitman (2006), Berg and Gigerenzer (2007), and Levine (2009).

6

THE NEW PATERNALISM

Final Observations

Throughout this book, several themes have been emphasized. This chapter sums up those themes and briefly discusses the role of economic analysis in approaching social issues, especially from a paternalistic perspective.

It Is Rational to Assume Rationality

While it may seem unusual to see the words *rational* and *addiction* combined, rational behavior is at the heart of most economic models of addiction. Rationality does not imply perfection. If you are an addict, rationality simply requires you to do the best you can, given whatever conditions you face. Whether you are Time-Consistent Tim, Naive Nate, or Sophisticated Sophia, you behave rationally when deciding on your consumption path, even though your consumption path can vary depending on who you are. Are you poorly informed? Are you time inconsistent? Do you recognize that you are time inconsistent? These conditions pose different constraints, and it is these constraints that may be used to justify social policy intervention to protect you from yourself.

Even the strongest supporters of paternalistic policies appreciate the value of the fully rational, time-consistent person. Time-Consistent Tim is commonly used as a benchmark for ideal behavior, while Naive Nate is used as a reasonable representation of real-world behavior, which generally veers from the ideal. Perhaps it is just slightly ironic that Tim has lost favor in economic models by being unrealistic, Nate has gained favor by being realistic, and yet it is the unrealistic behavior that the realistic person is being held to for social welfare analysis.

As an abstract ideal benchmark, or as a possible true description of real-world behavior, economic analysis is centered on the concept of the perfectly rational person. If we model economic behavior by starting with the assumption of irrationality, it is difficult to refine the model and arrive at behavior that reflects perfect rationality. But if we start with perfect rationality, we can easily add refinements that allow behavior to reflect, if not irrationality, at least rationality that faces substantial constraints. Economic analysis of addictive and indulgent behavior can begin with rationality, but it does not have to end there.

Patience Is a Preference, Not a Virtue

Perhaps the single most important point to stress when analyzing addictive behavior is that impatience, while often considered a character flaw, is nevertheless a *preference*. So many studies recommend policy intervention to protect myopic people from themselves, with very little acknowledgment that myopia itself in no way represents irrationality. At times, it appears that impatience and time inconsistency are considered to be one and the same, but they are not. At other times, impatience is correctly understood, yet still vilified. In economic models of addiction, impatience is often used as a predictor of indulgent behavior because it offers a simple explanation as to why addicts trade off current benefits against future health costs. But there is a big difference between *explaining* addiction and *condemning* it. Perhaps the condemnation is a consequence of thinking of social welfare with ideal preferences.

Two time-consistent people with different levels of impatience can choose completely different consumption paths. If one is relatively patient and decides to refrain from smoking and the other is relatively impatient and decides to start smoking, in what sense is refraining the better choice? If it is considered the ideal choice, the ideal is being defined as a specific socially acceptable act completely independent of true time-consistent preferences. This represents the slippery slope of using ideal preferences as a benchmark: once that door is opened, a wide range of behaviors can be classified as ideal.

The myopia justification for policy intervention holds up best when trying to protect children from themselves. But is it because children are myopic or is it because they lack the cognitive maturity to appreciate what it means to be myopic that justifies the policy intervention? If we can determine when a person is mature enough to adopt fully realized preferences, we can no longer consider him or her a child. It doesn't mean that we can't justify social policy to control the behavior of myopic adults, but it does mean that the matter deserves careful thought.

Compared to myopia, time inconsistency presents a stronger case for social control. While still falling under the category of preferences, time inconsistency presents some interesting complications. To some scholars, preference reversal due to time inconsistency represents an error. Your long-run preferences, from today's perspective, will not hold up when the future arrives, and thus you don't follow through with what you yourself planned to do. Other scholars feel that time inconsistency is nothing more than a tension between two selves—the current self and the future self. And as with many other trade-offs you have to consider daily, there is no reason why you can't resolve them yourself. But policy analysts must notice whether you appreciate your time inconsistency (Sophisticated Sophia) or you are completely unaware of it (Naive Nate). Furthermore, if you are naive, you cannot, by definition, appreciate social control policy aimed to protect you from yourself. Precisely how social welfare responds to the policy in this setting depends strictly on how it is defined. While time-inconsistent behavior does not unambiguously justify social policy intervention, it is certainly one of the most useful concepts for analyzing addiction that has come out of the field of behavioral economics.

Good Health, Well-Being, and the Complexities of Policy Analysis

An unusual aspect of some of the modern economic research on addiction is the objective of using social policy to encourage good health. Consider this astute observation from the authors of a leading survey on the economics of smoking:

> The objective of much of the research is now to determine how to harness economic forces and logic, how to use economic tools, to decrease smoking, with the ultimate goal being to reduce the toll of tobacco. (Chaloupka and Warner, 2000, 1542)

How can anyone argue with such a commonsense goal? Now consider a footnote in the same survey:

> Not all of the research is motivated by a desire to decrease smoking. Some
> authors express the opinion that more respect should be accorded consumer
> sovereignty, despite the issues of addiction and youthful initiation of smoking
> that have led many economists to perceive the market for cigarettes as suffer-
> ing from important market imperfections. (1542)

There is no confusion here. The goal is to decrease smoking. As for the benefits smokers receive from cigarettes, they are briefly mentioned in a footnote
and then the authors move on. Why can this be thought of as unusual?

While it is perfectly legitimate to consider improvements in health as a
social objective, it is by no means the only, or best, objective. Economists tend
to be expansive in their thinking when it comes to what makes people better
off. Well-being is a broad concept, much broader than good health, and it is
a highly subjective concept. Better health may improve a person's well-being,
but depending on how the better health is achieved and maintained, it also
may reduce it.

To ignore the benefits of smoking, excessive drinking, overeating, or drug
use in a social welfare analysis is a legitimate approach, but it doesn't get
around the criticism that you are ignoring benefits in a cost-*benefit* calculation. If you begin your analysis by assuming that certain behaviors are bad,
the public policy debate tends to focus on which policies to enact, rather than
on whether there is sense in not enacting any policies at all. People routinely
trade off the benefits of certain activities, such as participating in sports,
against the health costs, such as suffering an injury. It may be a more comfortable calculation to compare the benefits of sports with the health risks of
being injured than to compare the benefits of smoking with the health risks
of contracting lung cancer, yet it is still fundamentally the same calculation—
you compare benefits with costs.

The economic approach to cost-benefit public policy analysis can be
thought of as involving three steps. The first is the theoretical step of identifying all the relevant costs and benefits of whatever policy is being considered.
At this stage, there is no reason to be narrow in your analysis. Look for all the
trade-offs you can find, from the obvious to the improbable.

The next step is to try to measure the costs and benefits, and this is a very
tricky step. As we have seen many times throughout this book, empirical
results vary widely across studies. Even if there is a strong consensus on the
costs and benefits that have been identified, statistical analysis does not lend
itself well to reaching a similar consensus on their measurement. Results can

vary because of sincere differences across studies. Different data sets can be used to examine similar issues. Often specific data needed to account for all the costs and benefits are not available or proxies for unobservable variables are used, each yielding different results. Several statistical techniques can be used, each legitimate but possibly yielding different results. There is no such thing as a definitive empirical result, and there is rarely such a thing as a consensus empirical result. This lack of agreement has nothing to do with economic reasoning—it is simply the nature of empirical analysis.

The final step is to recommend or, if you are in the position to do so, implement policy. This is by far the most complicated step. As we have seen, defining a social welfare objective is a subjective exercise, as anything you want to include or exclude can be rationalized. Even if you are able to perfectly identify every potential cost and benefit and measure them without any controversy, there is still the question of which to include in the social welfare objective. It is perfectly legitimate to exclude the benefits of indulgent behaviors, just as it is perfectly legitimate to include them. But in general, it is impossible to accurately measure all the costs and benefits, even if you can identify them. How, then, can economic analysis be used to advise public policy?

Let's take as an example a result from chapter 4, the study (Courtemanche, 2008) that finds that an increase in the price of gasoline can reduce the incidence of obesity. The first step toward public policy is done cleverly here, finding a link between obesity and gas prices. Certainly, from a theoretical point of view, it may be that higher gas prices lead to more walking and less driving to restaurants, and this helps reduce the obesity rate. The author in the second step finds an empirical link between gas prices and obesity and between gas prices and walking and eating out. He then presents a benefit calculation of a permanent $1-per-gallon increase in gas prices and finds that it leads to a savings of $11 billion per year due to the reduced obesity rates. He then moves on to step three, offering the following conclusion:

> It is possible that revenue-neutral policies designed to alter gas price in such a way as to induce healthier eating and exercise decisions may improve social welfare. An example would be increasing gasoline taxes while subsidizing mass transit or reducing payroll taxes. However, given the recent sharp increases in gas prices, such a policy proposal is unlikely to be politically viable. An alternative would be to alter federal tax rates in such a way as to establish a gas price floor. (Courtemanche, 2008, 23)

No doubt the author's results warrant the policy conclusion, but the conclusion rests on very tenuous empirical results, with the caveats carefully identified by the author himself.

This is a typical public policy–based economic research paper. How seriously the policy conclusion should be taken by those in the position to enact policy can be debated, but the policy implication is clearly identified. Of course, a $1 increase in the price of gas would have tremendous economy-wide impact, well beyond reducing the obesity rate, and the study does not address the full impact of the proposed policy (rightly so, given the objective of the study). Furthermore, as we saw in chapter 4, there are many potential explanations for the increase in obesity rates, suggesting that there are many possible avenues for policy responses. How does the gas price increase fare relative to these other options?

Some economists try to avoid explicitly identifying policy conclusions in their research, leaving it to the reader to draw those links. Others explicitly offer policy implications but generally make it clear that these are *implications*, not findings of fact. And then there are those who not only explicitly offer policy conclusions but are extremely proactive in trying to get their recommendations enacted. There is no one correct approach here; it's all a matter of what you, as a scholar, are comfortable doing with your results. But as we have seen time and time again throughout this book, the nature of statistical analysis makes confidence in the empirical results of any single study, or body of research, difficult to come by. Still, the more pieces of the puzzle we can fit together, the clearer the picture is going to be, even when some of the pieces don't seem to fit well together. The best economic policy advice is meant to give policy officials more to think about, so that their policy choices can be based on as much information as is currently available.

It's All about the Differences

Undoubtedly, the most challenging aspect of implementing paternalistic social policies is dealing with the tremendous degree of differences among people. A cigarette tax, for example, affects *all* smokers (who purchase cigarettes legally), yet not all smokers will respond in the same way to the tax. Some may be price sensitive and be largely affected by the tax, and others may be price insensitive and not much affected. And there is no easy way to distinguish between smokers on the basis of price sensitivity. Are there predictable differences based on age, gender, race, income, smoking intensity, and so on? How do you set a tax rate that controls the behavior of those most in need of protection but is not too heavy a burden on those not in need?

In addition to those differences, the main one that we have focused on here is based on time preference, and even this one trait has several characteristics. People can be divided into the patient and the impatient (and into many degrees of impatience), the time consistent and time inconsistent, and the sophisticated and naive. And there are many other distinctions based on several other models of addictive behavior. All these differences make it extremely difficult to design social policies and determine their social welfare effect.

The new paternalists, however, offer an intriguing approach to circumventing the difficulties involved in designing policies that affect a widely diverse group of people. They refer to their approach as *asymmetric paternalism* (Camerer et al., 2003):

> Paternalism treads on consumer sovereignty by forcing, or preventing, choices for the individual's own good, much as when parents limit their child's freedom to skip school or eat candy for dinner. Recent research in behavioral economics has identified a variety of decision-making errors that may expand the scope of paternalistic regulation. To the extent that the errors identified by behavioral research lead people not to behave in their own best interests, paternalism may prove useful. But, to the extent that paternalism prevents people from behaving in their own best interests, paternalism may prove costly. Our purpose in this Article is to argue that in many cases it is possible to have one's cake and eat it too. We propose an approach to evaluating paternalistic regulations and doctrines that we call "asymmetric paternalism." A regulation is asymmetrically paternalistic if it creates large benefits for those who make errors, while imposing little or no harm on those who are fully rational. Such regulations are relatively harmless to those who reliably make decisions in their best interest, while at the same time advantageous to those making suboptimal choices. (1211–1212)

A brief example illustrates their main idea: Suppose that one of the main reasons why many people smoke is that they underestimate the risks of smoking. To counter this problem, the authorities design policies that inform smokers of the true risks of their behavior. For example, the state may require cigarette packages to have warning labels, or it may publish and distribute pamphlets explaining the risks, or it may design websites that are easy to access and navigate, or it may use various media to relay informative messages. The advantage of information-enhancing policies is that they should have virtually no impact on smokers who are already perfectly informed. Without having to explicitly identify different groups of smokers, those who can benefit from the information will be affected and those who can't benefit won't be affected. Compared to a tax increase that affects all smokers, the asymmetric policy *self-selects* those most in need of it.

This policy approach has some difficulties, however. Most obviously, for information-enhancing policies to be effective, an informational deficiency must be causing the problem in the first place. If instead the problem is time inconsistency, providing smoking risk information will do little to correct that behavior. Furthermore, providing information is not a costless policy. The information must be gathered and distributed. Determining all the true risks of smoking may be a daunting task, and resources will also be needed to get that information into the hands of those who lack it. If the government requires private firms to provide that information to consumers, and the costs of production increase, then there may be price increases for all consumers, not just those who need the information.

Also, it is difficult to determine how even the correct information will be interpreted. If you are told that smoking one pack of cigarettes a week for 30 years means you have a 1 in 12 chance of developing lung cancer, how will that information affect your behavior? Would it be more effective to provide less precise information such as "smoking causes lung cancer"? And what if your problem is that you *over*estimate the risk of smoking? As discussed in chapter 2, is the social goal to have you perfectly informed or to reduce your smoking? If you overestimate the risks of smoking, you are already smoking too little from a perfect information perspective, so correcting your informational deficiency may have you increase your smoking.

No doubt, social control policies targeting those most in need of control have advantages over policies applied more broadly across an eclectic group of people. But paternalistic intervention, as the above quote clearly points out, always has the potential to do more harm than good. Fortunately, there is one reassuring aspect in trying to justify social policy to protect people from themselves—the justifications are likely to be unnecessary.

Protecting Us from Them

Nearly every policy proposed or implemented to protect people from themselves can be justified far more traditionally with *external cost* arguments. We don't have to justify cigarette taxes by claiming they will discourage smokers from harming themselves. Instead, we can claim that they will discourage smokers from harming *others*. When *private* actions impose *social* costs, corrective social policies are commonly proposed. And there are a variety of social costs associated with the behaviors discussed throughout this book: the danger or cost to others of secondhand smoke; drunk drivers causing automobile accidents; violent behavior linked to alcohol abuse, especially in domestic settings; obesity, which imposes substantial health care costs on state and private insurance pools; crimes committed by drug users to support their habit; and so on. While analyses of social policies to protect people from others has been the subject of countless academic papers and books, it is not the focus of this book. Still, some points are worth highlighting.

Protecting people from others is a strong justification for social control policy, but there are still many interesting issues to consider. If reducing the impact of secondhand smoke is the goal, how do you balance the benefits smokers enjoy against the costs they impose on nonsmokers? Can restaurants, bars, and other public venues determine their own smoking policies to satisfy their customers, or should the government mandate where smoking will be allowed? If reducing the impact of drunk driving accidents is the goal, should the state use policies to restrict access to alcohol or should the act of driving while intoxicated be targeted instead? If unhealthy behavior imposes substantial costs on others in public and private insurance pools, should those who indulge in these acts have extremely high insurance premiums or even be denied insurance altogether? Finally, do drug users commit property and violent crimes to get the funds to purchase drugs *because* drugs are illegal and therefore costly both in terms of dollars and criminal punishment? These are just a few examples of the complications in dealing with social policies to protect people from others. Perhaps because these policies were proposed and enacted long before the recent paternalistic arguments gained popularity among some scholars, economists tend to be far more comfortable with this justification for social policy than the one that involves protecting people from themselves. The paternalistic arguments seem to be at their strongest when they add further support to the traditional arguments in recommending policies to control indulgent behavior. While the debate over the relative merits of different economic approaches to justifying social policy will rage on indefinitely, it serves the profession well to face substantial, and sometimes radical, new challenges.

Suggested Reading

For a more comprehensive discussion of the economic approach to social issues, especially in terms of using social policies to protect people from others, see Winter (2005).

REFERENCES

Acs, Z. J., and Lyles, A., eds. (2007). *Obesity, Business and Public Policy*, Cheltenham, UK: Edward Elgar.

Adda, J., and Cornaglia, F. (2006). "Taxes, Cigarette Consumption, and Smoking Intensity," *American Economic Review*, 96:1013–1028.

Adda, J., and Lechene, V. (2001). "Smoking and Endogenous Mortality: Does Heterogeneity in Life Expectancy Explain Differences in Smoking Behavior?," Working Paper, University College London.

Alamar, B., and Glantz, S. A. (2006). "Modeling Addictive Consumption as an Infectious Disease," *Contributions to Economic Analysis and Policy*, 5:1–22.

Ameriks, J., Caplin, A., Leahy, J., and Tyler, T. (2007). "Measuring Self-Control Problems," *American Economic Review*, 97:966–972.

Andersen, S., Harrison, G. W., Lau, M. I., and Rutstrom, E. E. (2008). "Eliciting Risk and Time Preferences," *Econometrica*, 76:583–618.

Anderson, M., and Matsa, D. A. (2011). "Are Restaurants Really Supersizing America?," *American Economic Journal: Applied Microeconomics*, 3:152–188.

Anderson, P. M., and Butcher, K. F. (2006). "Reading, Writing and Refreshments: Are School Finances Contributing to Children's Obesity?," *Journal of Human Resources*, 41:467–494.

Anderson, P. M., Butcher, K. F., and Levine, P. B. (2003). "Economic Perspectives on Childhood Obesity," *Economic Perspectives, Federal Reserve Bank of Chicago*, 3Q: 30–48.

Andreoni, J., and Sprenger, C. (2010a). "Risk Preferences Are Not Time Preferences," NBER Working Paper 16348.

———. (2010b). "Estimating Time Preferences from Convex Budgets," NBER Working Paper 16347.

Angeletos, G., Laibson, D., Repetto, A., Tobacman, J., and Weinberg, S. (2001). "The Hyperbolic Consumption Model: Calibration, Simulation, and Empirical Evaluation," *Journal of Economic Perspectives*, 15:47–68.

Arcidiacono, P., Sieg, H., and Sloan, F. (2007). "Living Rationally under the Volcano? An Empirical Analysis of Heavy Drinking and Smoking," *International Economic Review*, 48:37–65.

Ariely, D., and Wertenbroch, K. (2002). "Procrastination, Deadline, and Performance: Self-Control by Precommitment," *Psychological Science*, 13:219–224.

Asgeirsdottir, T. L., and McGeary, K. A. (2009). "Alcohol and Labor Supply: The Case of Iceland," *European Journal of Health Economics*, 10:455–465.

Auld, M. C. (2005). "Smoking, Drinking, and Income," *Journal of Human Resources*, 40:505–518.

Auld, M. C., and Grootendorst, P. (2004). "An Empirical Analysis of Milk Addiction," *Journal of Health Economics*, 23:1117–1133.

Ayyagari, P., Deb, P., Fletcher, J., Gallo, W. T., and Sindelar, J. L. (2009). "Sin Taxes: Do Heterogeneous Responses Undercut Their Value?," NBER Working Paper 15124.

Ayyagari, P., and Sindelar, J. L. (2010). "The Impact of Job Stress on Smoking and Quitting: Evidence from the HRS," *B.E. Journal of Economic Analysis and Policy*, 10:1–30.

Barnes, M. G., and Smith, T. G. (2009). "Tobacco Use as Response to Economic Insecurity: Evidence from the National Longitudinal Survey of Youth," *B.E. Journal of Economic Analysis and Policy*, 9:1–27.

Barrotta, P. (2008). "Why Economists Should Be Unhappy with the Economics of Happiness," *Economics and Philosophy*, 24:143–165.

Baum, C. L. (2009). "The Effects of Cigarette Costs on BMI and Obesity," *Health Economics*, 18:3–19.

Beatty, T. K. M., Larsen, E. R., and Sommervoll, D. E. (2009). "Driven to Drink: Sin Taxes near a Border," *Journal of Health Economics*, 28:1175–1184.

Becker, G. S., Grossman, M., and Murphy, K. M. (1991). "Rational Addiction and the Effect of Price on Consumption," *AEA Papers and Proceedings*, 81:237–241.

Becker, G. S., and Mulligan, C. B. (1997). "The Endogenous Determination of Time Preference," *Quarterly Journal of Economics*, 112:729–758.

Becker, G. S., and Murphy, K. M. (1988). "A Theory of Rational Addiction," *Journal of Political Economy*, 96:675–700.

Bednarek, H., Jeitschko, T. D., and Pecchenino, R. A. (2006). "Gluttony and Sloth: Symptoms of Trouble or Signs of Bliss? A Theory of Choice in the Presence of Behavioral Adjustment Costs," *Contributions to Economic Analysis and Policy*, 5:1–42.

Benabou, R., and Tirole, J. (2004). "Willpower and Personal Rules," *Journal of Political Economy*, 112:848–886.

Benhabib, J., Bisin, A., and Schotter, A. (2010). "Present-Bias, Quasi Hyperbolic Discounting, and Fixed Costs," *Games and Economic Behavior*, 69:205–223.

Benjamin, D. J., Brown, S. A., and Shapiro, J. M. (2006). "Who Is Behavioral? Cognitive Ability and Anomalous Preferences," Working Paper, Harvard University.

Benjamin, D. J., and Laibson, D. I. (2003). "Good Policies for Bad Governments: Behavioral Political Economy," Working Paper, Harvard University.

Benzion, U., Rapoport, A., and Yagil, J. (1989). "Discount Rates Inferred from Decisions: An Experimental Study," *Management Science*, 35:270–284.

Berg, N., and Gigerenzer, G. (2007). "Psychology Implies Paternalism? Bounded Rationality May Reduce the Rationale to Regulate Risk-Taking," *Social Choice and Welfare*, 28:337–359.

Berger, M. C., and Leigh, J. P. (1988). "The Effect of Alcohol Use on Wages," *Applied Economics*, 20:1343–1351.

Bernheim, B. D., and Rangel, A. (2004). "Addiction and Cue-Triggered Decision Processes," *American Economic Review*, 94:1558–1590.

———. (2005). "From Neuroscience to Public Policy: A New Economic View of Addiction," *Swedish Economic Policy Review*, 12:11–56.

Beshears, J., Choi, J. J., Laibson, D., and Madrian, B. C. (2006). "Early Decisions: A Regulatory Framework," NBER Working Paper 11920.

Bettinger, E., and Slonim, R. (2007). "Patience among Children," *Journal of Public Economics*, 91:343–363.

Bhattacharya, J., and Bundorf, M. K. (2009). "The Incidence of the Health Care Costs of Obesity," *Journal of Health Economics*, 28:649–658.

Bickel, W. K., and Marsch, L. A. (2001). "Toward a Behavioral Economic Understanding of Drug Dependence: Delay Discounting Processes," *Addiction*, 96:73–86.

Bitler, M. P., Carpenter, C., and Zavodny, M. (2010). "Effects of Venue-Specific State Clean Air Laws on Smoking-Related Outcomes," *Health Economics*, 19:1425–1440.

Blackmar, T. M. (1998). "*Perez v. Brown & Williamson Tobacco Corp.*: The Validity of Seeking Protection from Ourselves," *University of Toledo Law Review*, 29:727–752.

Blecher, E. (2008). "The Impact of Tobacco Advertising Bans on Consumption in Developing Countries," *Journal of Health Economics*, 27:930–942.

Bleich, S., Cutler, D., Murray, C., and Adams, A. (2008). "Why Is the Developed World Obese?," *Annual Review of Public Health*, 29:273–295.

Blondel, S., Loheac, Y., and Rinaudo, S. (2007). "Rationality and Drug Use: An Experimental Approach," *Journal of Health Economics*, 26:643–658.

Bor, J. (2010). "The Science of Childhood Obesity," *Health Affairs*, 29:393–397.

Borghans, L., and Golsteyn, H. H. (2006). "Time Discounting and the Body Mass Index: Evidence from the Netherlands," *Economics and Human Biology*, 4:39–61.

Bray, J. W. (2005). "Alcohol Use, Human Capital, and Wages," *Journal of Labor Economics*, 23:279–312.

Bretteville-Jensen, A. L. (1999). "Addiction and Discounting," *Journal of Health Economics*, 18:393–407.

Burkhauser, R. V., and Cawley, J. (2008). "Beyond BMI: The Value of More Accurate Measures of Fatness and Obesity in Social Science Research," *Journal of Health Economics*, 27:519–529.

Burkhauser, R. V., Cawley, J., and Schmeiser, M. D. (2009). "Differences in the U.S. Trends in the Prevalence of Obesity Based on Body Mass Index and Skinfold Thickness," NBER Working Paper 15005.

Burrows, P. (1993). "Patronising Paternalism," *Oxford Economic Papers*, 45:542–572.

———. (1995). "Analyzing Legal Paternalism," *International Review of Law and Economics*, 15:489–508.

Camerer, C. F. (2006). "Wanting, Liking, and Learning: Neuroscience and Paternalism," *University of Chicago Law Review*, 73:87–110.

———. (2008). "The Potential of Neuroeconomics," *Economics and Philosophy*, 24:369–379.

Camerer, C., Issacharoff, S., Loewenstein, G., O'Donoghue, T., and Rabin, M. (2003). "Regulation for Conservatives: Behavioral Economics and the Case for 'Asymmetric Paternalism,'" *University of Pennsylvania Law Review*, 151:1211–1254.

Camerer, C., Loewenstein, G., and Prelec, D. (2005). "Neuroeconomics: How Neuroscience Can Inform Economics," *Journal of Economic Literature*, 43:9–64.

Cameron, S. V., and Heckman, J. J. (1993). "The Nonequivalence of High School Equivalents," *Journal of Labor Economics*, 11:1–47.

Carbone, J. C., Kverndokk, S., and Rogeberg, O. J. (2005). "Smoking, Health, Risk, and Perception," *Journal of Health Economics*, 24:631–653.

Card, D., and Lemieux, T. (2001). "Going to College to Avoid the Draft: The Unintended Legacy of the Vietnam War," *AEA Papers and Proceedings*, 91:97–102.

Carpenter, C., and Cook, P. J. (2008). "Cigarette Taxes and Youth Smoking: New Evidence from National, State, and Local Youth Risk Behavior Surveys, *Journal of Health Economics*, 27:287–299.

Carrillo, J. D. (2005). "To Be Consumed with Moderation," *European Economic Review*, 49:99–111.

Cawley, J. (2004). "The Impact of Obesity on Wages," *Journal of Human Resources*, 39:451–474.

———. (2010). "The Economics of Childhood Obesity," *Health Affairs*, 29:364–371.

Cawley, J., and Danzinger, S. (2004). "Obesity as a Barrier to the Transition from Welfare to Work," NBER Working Paper 10508.

Cawley, J., and Liu, F. (2006). "Correlates of State Legislative Action to Prevent Childhood Obesity," *Obesity*, 16:162–167.

———. (2007). "Maternal Employment and Childhood Obesity: A Search for Mechanisms in Time Use Data," NBER Working Paper 13600.

Cawley, J., Markowitz, S., and Tauras, J. (2004). "Lighting Up and Slimming Down: The Effects of Body Weight and Cigarette Prices on Adolescent Smoking Initiation," *Journal of Health Economics*, 23:293–311.

———. (2006). "Obesity, Cigarette Prices, Youth Access Laws and Adolescent Smoking Initiation," *Eastern Economic Journal*, 32:149–170.

Cawley, J., Meyerhoeffer, C., and Newhouse, D. (2007a). "The Impact of State Physical Education Requirements on Youth Physical Activity and Overweight," *Health Economics*, 16:1287–1301.

———. (2007b). "The Correlation of Youth Physical Activity with State Policies," *Contemporary Economic Policy*, 25:506–517.

Cawley, J., Moran, J. R., and Simon, K. I. (2010). "The Impact of Income on the Weight of Elderly Americans," *Health Economics*, 19:979–993.

CDC. (2009). "Summary Health Statistics for U.S. Adults: National Health Interview Survey, 2008," Centers for Disease Control and Prevention, http://www.cdc.gov/nchs/data/series/sr_10/sr10_242.pdf, pp. 70–73.

———. (2011). "Smoking and Tobacco Use," Centers for Disease Control and Prevention, http://www.cdc.gov/tobacco/data_statistics/fact_sheets/smokeless/smokeless_facts/index.htm.

Chaloupka, F. (1991). "Rational Addictive Behavior and Cigarette Smoking," *Journal of Political Economy*, 99:722–742.

Chaloupka, F. J., and Laixuthai, A. (1997). "Do Youths Substitute Alcohol and Marijuana? Some Econometric Evidence," *Eastern Economic Journal*, 23:253–276.

Chaloupka, F. J., Tauras, J. A., and Grossman, M. (1997). "Public Policy and Youth Smokeless Tobacco Use," *Southern Economic Journal*, 64:503–516.

Chaloupka, F. J., and Warner, K. E. (2000). "The Economics of Smoking," in A. J. Cuyler and J. P. Newhouse, eds., *Handbook of Health Economics*, Amsterdam: Elsevier, 1541–1627.

Chaloupka, F. J., and Wechsler, H. (1996). "Binge Drinking in College: The Impact of Price, Availability, and Alcohol Control Policies," *Contemporary Economic Policy*, 14:112–124.

———. (1997). "Price, Tobacco Control Policies and Smoking among Young Adults," *Journal of Health Economics*, 16:359–373.

Chapman, S., and Richardson, J. (1990). "Tobacco Excise and Declining Tobacco Consumption: The Case of Papua New Guinea," *American Journal of Public Health*, 80:537–540.

Chatterji, P., Dave, D., Kaestner, R., and Markowitz, S. (2003). "Alcohol Abuse and Suicide Attempts among Youth: Correlation or Causation?," NBER Working Paper 9638.

———. (2004). "Alcohol Abuse and Suicide Attempts among Youth: Correlation or Causation?," *Economics and Human Biology*, 2:159–180.

Chatterji, P., and DeSimone, J. (2005). "Adolescent Drinking and High School Dropout," NBER Working Paper 11337.

Chen, Z., Yen, S. T., and Eastwood, D. B. (2005). "Effects of Food Stamp Participation on Body Weight and Obesity," *American Journal of Agricultural Economics*, 87:1167–1173.

Chesson, H., Harrison, P. and Kassler, W. J. (2000). "Sex under the Influence: The Effect of Alcohol Policy on Sexually Transmitted Disease Rates in the United States," *Journal of Law and Economics*, 43:215–238.

Chou, S., Grossman, M., and Saffer, H. (2004). "An Economic Analysis of Adult Obesity: Results from the Behavioral Risk Factor Surveillance System," *Journal of Health Economics*, 23:565–587.

Chou, S., Rashad, I., and Grossman, M. (2008). "Fast-Food Restaurant Advertising on Television and Its Influence on Childhood Obesity," *Journal of Law and Economics*, 51:599–618.

Chouinard, H. H., Davis, D. E., LaFrance, J. T., and Perloff, J. M. (2007). "Fat Taxes: Big Money for Small Change," *Forum for Health Economics and Policy*, 10:1–28.

Clark, A., and Etile, F. (2002). "Do Health Changes Affect Smoking? Evidence from British Panel Data," *Journal of Health Economics*, 21:533–562.

Coate, D., and Grossman, M. (1988). "Effects of Alcoholic Beverage Prices and Legal Drinking Ages on Youth Alcohol Use," *Journal of Law and Economics*, 31:145–171.

Coller, M., Harrison, G. W., and Rutstrom, E. E. (2005). "Are Discount Rates Constant? Reconciling Theory and Observation," Working Paper, University of South Carolina.

Conley, D., and Glauber, R. (2006). "Gender, Body Mass and Economic Status," *Advances in Health Economics and Health Sciences Research*, 17:253–275.

Conlisk, J. (1996). "Why Bounded Rationality?," *Journal of Economic Literature*, 34:669–700.

Cook, P. J. (2007). *Paying the Tab: The Costs and Benefits of Alcohol Control*, Princeton, NJ: Princeton University Press.

Cook, P. J., and Hutchinson, R. (2007). "Smoke Signals: Adolescent Smoking and School Continuation," *Advances in Austrian Economics*, 10:157–186.

Cook, P. J., and Moore, M. J. (2000). "Alcohol," in A. J. Cuyler and J. P. Newhouse, eds., *Handbook of Health Economics*, Amsterdam: Elsevier, 1629–1673.

Cook, P. J., Ostermann, J., and Sloan, F. A. (2005a). "Are Alcohol Excise Taxes Good for Us? Short- and Long-Term Effects on Mortality Rates," NBER Working Paper 11138.

———. (2005b). "The Net Effect of an Alcohol Tax Increase on Death Rates in Middle Age," *AEA Papers and Proceedings*, 95:278–281.

Cook, P. J., and Peters, B. (2005). "The Myth of the Drinkers' Bonus," NBER Working Paper 11902.

Cooper, T. V., Klesges, R. C., Robinson, L. A., and Zbikowski, S. M. (2003). "A Prospective Equilibrium of the Relationships between Smoking Dosage and Body Mass Index in an Adolescent, Biracial Cohort," *Addictive Behaviors*, 28:501–512.

Courtemanche, C. (2007). "Rising Cigarette Prices and Rising Obesity: Coincidence or Unintended Consequence?," *Journal of Health Economics*, 28:781–798.

———. (2008). "A Silver Lining? The Connection between Gasoline Prices and Obesity," Working Paper, University of North Carolina at Greensboro.

———. (2009). "Longer Hours and Larger Waistlines? The Relationship between Work Hours and Obesity," *Forum for Health Economics and Policy*, 12:1–31.

Courtemanche, C., and Carden, A. (2008). "The Skinny on Big-Box Retailing: Wal-Mart, Warehouse Clubs, and Obesity." Working Paper, University of North Carolina at Greensboro.

Cowen, T. (1991). "Self-Constraint versus Self-Liberation," *Ethics*, 101:360–373.

Cuellar, S. (2003). "Do Food Stamps Cause an Over-Consumption of Food?," Working Paper, Sonoma State University.

Currie, J., Della Vigna, S., Moretti, E., and Pathania, V. (2010). "The Effect of Fast Food Restaurants on Obesity," *American Economic Journal: Economic Policy*, 2:32–63.

Cutler, D., and Glaeser, E. (2005). "What Explains Differences in Smoking, Drinking and Other Health-Related Behaviors?," *AEA Papers and Proceedings*, 95:238–242.

Cutler, D. M., Glaeser, E. L., and Rosen, A. B. (2007). "Is the US Population Behaving Healthier?," NBER Working Paper 13013.

Cutler, D. M., Glaeser, E. L., and Shapiro, J. M. (2003). "Why Have Americans Become More Obese?," *Journal of Economic Perspectives*, 17:93–118.

Czart, V., Pacula, R. L., Chaloupka, F. J., and Wechsler, H. (2001). "The Impact of Prices and Control Policies on Cigarette Smoking among College Students," *Contemporary Economic Policy*, 19:135–149.

Dasgupta, P., and Maskin, E. (2005). "Uncertainty and Hyperbolic Discounting," *American Economic Review*, 95:1290–1299.

Dave, D., and Kaestner, R. (2002). "Alcohol Taxes and Labor Market Outcomes," *Journal of Health Economics*, 21:357–371.

Dave, D., and Saffer, H. (2008). "Alcohol Demand and Risk Preference," *Journal of Economic Psychology*, 29:810–831.

De Walque, D. (2007). "Does Education Affect Smoking Behaviors? Evidence Using the Vietnam Draft as an Instrument for College Education," *Journal of Health Economics*, 26:877–895.

Deb, P., Gallo, W. T., Ayyagari, P., Fletcher, J. M., and Sindelar, J. L. (2009). "Job Loss: Eat, Drink and Try to Be Merry?," NBER Working Paper 15122.

DeCicca, P., Kenkel, D., and Mathios, A. (2000). "Racial Difference in the Determinants of Smoking Onset," *Journal of Risk and Uncertainty*, 21:311–340.

———. (2002). "Putting Out the Fires: Will Higher Taxes Reduce the Onset of Youth Smoking?," *Journal of Political Economy*, 110:144–169.

———. (2008). "Cigarette Taxes and the Transition from Youth to Adult Smoking: Smoking Initiation, Cessation, and Participation," *Journal of Health Economics*, 27:904–917.

DeCicca, P., Kenkel, D., Mathios, A., Shin, Y., and Lim, J. (2008). "Youth Smoking, Cigarette Prices, and Anti-Smoking Sentiment," *Health Economics*, 17:733–749.

DeCicca, P., and McLeod, L. (2008). "Cigarette Taxes and Older Adult Smoking: Evidence from Recent Large Tax Increases," *Journal of Health Economics*, 27:918–929.

Decker, S. L., and Schwartz, A. E. (2000). "Cigarettes and Alcohol: Substitutes or Complements?," NBER Working Paper 7535.

Dee, T. S. (1999). "State Alcohol Policies, Teen Drinking and Traffic Fatalities," *Journal of Public Economics*, 72:289–315.

———. (2001). "The Effects of Minimum Legal Drinking Ages on Teen Childbearing," *Journal of Human Resources*, 36:823–838.

Dee, T. S., and Evans, W. N. (2003). "Teen Drinking and Educational Attainment: Evidence from Two-Sample Instrumental Variables Estimates," *Journal of Labor Economics*, 21:178–209.

Delaney, L., Harmon, C., and Wall, P. (2008). "Behavioral Economics and Drinking Behavior: Preliminary Results from an Irish College Study," *Economic Inquiry*, 46:29–36.

Della Vigna, S., and Malmendier, U. (2006). "Paying Not to Go to the Gym," *American Economic Review*, 96:694–719.

DeSimone, J. (2007). "Fraternity Membership and Binge Drinking," *Journal of Health Economics*, 26:950–967.

———. (2009). "Fraternity Membership and Drinking Behavior," *Economic Inquiry*, 47:337–350.

DeSimone, J. S. (2010). "Binge Drinking and Risky Sex among College Students," NBER Working Paper 15953.

DeSimone, J., and Wolaver, A. (2005). "Drinking and Academic Performance in High School," NBER Working Paper 11035.

Diamond, P., and Koszegi, B. (2003). "Quasi-Hyperbolic Discounting and Retirement," *Journal of Public Economics*, 87:1839–1872.

Diamond, P., and Vartiainen, H., eds. (2007). *Behavioral Economics and Its Applications*, Princeton, NJ: Princeton University Press.

DiNardo, J., and Lemieux, T. (2001). "Alcohol, Marijuana, and American Youth: The Unintended Effects of Government Regulation," *Journal of Health Economics*, 20:991–1010.

Dockner, E. J., and Feichtinger, G. (1993). "Cyclical Consumption Patterns and Rational Addiction," *American Economic Review*, 83:256–263.

Dolan, P., Peasgood, T., and White, M. (2008). "Do We Really Know What Makes Us Happy? A Review of the Economic Literature on the Factors Associated with Subjective Well-Being," *Journal of Economic Psychology*, 29:94–122.

Du, S., Mroz, T. A., Zhai, F., and Popkin, B. M. (2004). "Rapid Income Growth Adversely Affects Diet in China—Particularly for the Poor," *Social Science and Medicine*, 59:1505–1515.

Eberstadt, M. (2003). "The Child-Fat Problem," *Policy Review*, February and March: 3–19.

Eid, J., Overman, H. G., Puga, D., and Turner, M. A. (2008). "Fat City: Questioning the Relationship between Urban Sprawl and Obesity," *Journal of Urban Economics*, 63:385–404.

Eisenberg, D., and Okeke, E. (2009). "Too Cold for a Jog? Weather, Exercise, and Socio-economic Status," *B.E. Journal of Economic Analysis and Policy*, 9:1–30.

Eisenberg, D., and Rowe, B. (2009). "The Effect of Smoking in Young Adulthood on Smoking Later in Life: Evidence Based on the Vietnam Era Draft Lottery," *Forum for Health Economics and Policy*, 12:1–32.

Eisenhauer, J. G., and Ventura, L. (2006). "The Prevalence of Hyperbolic Discounting: Some European Evidence," *Applied Economics*, 38:1223–1234.

Emery, S., White, M. M., and Pierce, J. P. (2001). "Does Cigarette Price Influence Adolescent Experimentation?," *Journal of Health Economics*, 20:261–270.

Epstein, R. A. (2006). "Behavioral Economics: Human Errors and Market Corrections," *University of Chicago Law Review*, 73:111–132.

Evans, W. N., and Farrelly, M. C. (1998). "The Compensating Behavior of Smokers: Taxes, Tar, and Nicotine," *RAND Journal of Economics*, 29:578–595.

Farrell, S., Manning, W. G., and Finch, M. D. (2003). "Alcohol Dependence and the Price of Alcoholic Beverages," *Journal of Health Economics*, 22:117–147.

Farrelly, M. C., Bray, J. W., Pechacek, T., and Woollery, T. (2001). "Response by Adults to Increases in Cigarette Prices by Sociodemographic Characteristics," *Southern Economic Journal*, 68:156–165.

Farrelly, M. C., Nimsch, C. T., Hyland, A., and Cummings, M. (2004). "The Effects of Higher Cigarette Prices on Tar and Nicotine Consumption in a Cohort of Adult Smokers," *Health Economics*, 13:49–58.

Fehr, E. (2002). "The Economics of Impatience," *Nature*, 415:269–272.

Fenn, A. J., Antonovitz, F., and Schroeter, J. R. (2001). "Cigarettes and Addiction Information: New Evidence in Support of the Rational Addiction Model," *Economics Letters*, 72:39–45.

Ferguson, B. S. (2000). "Interpreting the Rational Addiction Model," *Addiction*, 9:587–598.

Fernandez-Villaverde, J., and Mukherji, A. (2002). "Can We Really Observe Hyperbolic Discounting?," Working Paper, University of Pennsylvania.

Fertig, A. R., and Watson, T. (2009). "Minimum Drinking Age Laws and Infant Health Outcomes," *Journal of Health Economics*, 28:737–747.

Finkelstein, E. A., Ruhm, C. J., and Kosa, K. M. (2005). "Economic Causes and Consequences of Obesity," *Annual Review of Public Health*, 26:239–257.

Fishburn, P. C., and Rubinstein, A. (1982). "Time Preference," *International Economic Review*, 23:677–694.

Fletcher, J. M., Deb, P., and Sindelar, J. L. (2009). "Tobacco Use, Taxation and Self Control in Adolescence," NBER Working Paper 15130.

Fraker, T. M., Martini, A. P., and Ohls, J. C. (1995). "The Effect of Food Stamp Cashout on Food Expenditures: An Assessment of the Findings from Four Demonstrations," *Journal of Human Resources*, 30:633–649.

Frank, M. W. (2008). "Media Substitution in Advertising: A Spirited Case Study," *International Journal of Industrial Organization*, 26:308–326.

Frederick, S. (2006). "Valuing Future Life and Future Lives: A Framework for Understanding Discounting," *Journal of Economic Psychology*, 27:667–680.

Frederick, S., Loewenstein, G., and O'Donoghue, T. (2002). "Time Discounting and Time Preference: A Critical Review," *Journal of Economic Literature*, 40:351–401.

French, M. T., and Zarkin, G. A. (1995). "Is Moderate Alcohol Use Related to Wages? Evidence from Four Worksites," *Journal of Health Economics*, 14:319–344.

Frieden, T. R., Dietz, W., and Collins, J. (2010). "Reducing Childhood Obesity through Policy Change: Acting Now to Prevent Obesity," *Health Affairs*, 29:357–363.

Fudenberg, D. (2006). "Advancing beyond *Advances in Behavioral Economics*," *Journal of Economic Literature*, 44:694–711.

Fudenberg, D., and Levine, D. K. (2006). "A Dual-Self Model of Impulse Control," *American Economic Review*, 96:1449–1476.

Gallet, C. A. (2003). "Advertising and Restrictions in the Cigarette Industry: Evidence of State-by-State Variation," *Contemporary Economic Policy*, 21:338–348.

———. (2007). "The Demand for Alcohol: A Meta-Analysis of Elasticities," *Australian Journal of Agricultural and Resource Economics*, 51:121–135.

Gandal, N., and Shabelansky, A. (2010). "Obesity and Price Sensitivity at the Supermarket," *Forum for Health Economics and Policy*, 2:1–19.

Garcia Villar, J. G., and Quintana-Domeque, C. (2009). "Income and Body Mass Index in Europe," *Economics and Human Biology*, 7:73–83.

Gil, A. I., and Molina, J. A. (2007). "Human Development and Alcohol Abuse in Adolescence," *Applied Economics*, 39:1315–1323.

Gilpatric, S. M. (2009). "Present-Biased Preferences and Rebate Redemption," *Journal of Economic Behavior and Organization*, 67:735–754.

Glaeser, E. L. (2006). "Paternalism and Psychology," *University of Chicago Law Review*, 73:133–156.

Glazer, J., and Weiss, A. M. (2007). "A Model of Dysfunctional Urges and Addiction with an Application to Cigarette Smoking," *B.E. Journal of Economic Analysis and Policy*, 7:1–20.

Goel, R. K. (2009). "Cigarette Advertising and U.S. Cigarette Demand: A Policy Assessment," *Journal of Policy Modeling*, 31:351–357.

Goel, R. K., and Nelson, M. A. (2006). "The Effectiveness of Anti-Smoking Legislation: A Review," *Journal of Economic Surveys*, 20:325–355.

Goldfarb, R. S., Leonard, T. C., and Suranovic, S. (2006). "Modeling Alternative Motives for Dieting," *Eastern Economic Journal*, 32:115–131.

Grignon, M. (2009). "An Empirical Investigation of Heterogeneity in Time Preferences and Smoking Behaviors," *Journal of Socio-Economics*, 38:739–751.

Grimard, F., and Parent, D. (2007). "Education and Smoking: Were Vietnam War Draft Avoiders Also More Likely to Avoid Smoking?," *Journal of Health Economics*, 26:896–926.

Grossman, M., Kaestner, R., and Markowitz, S. (2005). "An Investigation of the Effects of Alcohol Policies on Youth STDs," *AEA Papers and Proceedings*, 95:263–266.

Grossman, M., and Markowitz, S. (2005). "I Did What Last Night?! Adolescent Risky Sexual Behaviors and Substance Use," *Eastern Economic Journal*, 31:383–405.

Gruber, J. (2001). "Youth Smoking in the 1990's: Why Did It Rise and What Are the Long-Run Implications?," *AEA Papers and Proceedings*, 91:85–90.

Gruber, J., and Frakes, M. (2006). "Does Falling Smoking Lead to Rising Obesity?," *Journal of Health Economics*, 25:183–197.

Gruber, J., and Koszegi, B. (2001). "Is Addiction 'Rational'? Theory and Evidence," *Quarterly Journal of Economics*, 116:1261–1303.

———. (2004). "Tax Incidence When Individuals Are Time-Inconsistent: The Case of Cigarette Excise Taxes," *Journal of Public Economics*, 88:1959–1987.

Gruber, J., and Mullainathan, S. (2002). "Do Cigarette Taxes Make Smokers Happier?," NBER Working Paper 8872.

———. (2005). "Do Cigarette Taxes Make Smokers Happier?," *Advances in Economic Analysis and Policy*, 5:1–43.

Grunberg, N. E. (1992). "Cigarette Smoking and Body Weight: A Personal Journey through a Complex Field," *Health Psychology*, 11:26–31.

Gul, F., and Pesendorfer, W. (2001). "Temptation and Self-Control," *Econometrica*, 69:1403–1435.

———. (2007). "Harmful Addiction," *Review of Economic Studies*, 74:147–172.

———. (2008). "The Case for Mindless Economics," in A. Caplan and A. Shotter, eds., *The Foundations of Positive and Normative Economics*, New York: Oxford University Press.

Guthrie, J. F., Lin, B., and Frazao, E. (2002). "Role of Food Prepared Away from Home in the American Diet, 1977–78 versus 1994–96: Changes and Consequences," *Journal of Nutrition Education and Behavior*, 34:140–150.

Hammar, H., and Carlsson, F. (2005). "Smokers' Expectations to Quit Smoking," *Health Economics*, 14:257–267.

Hammar, H., and Johansson-Stenman, O. (2004). "The Value of Risk-Free Cigarettes: Do Smokers Underestimate the Risk?," *Health Economics*, 13:59–71.

Hammitt, J. K., and Graham, J. D. (1999). "Willingness to Pay for Health Protection: Inadequate Sensitivity to Probability?," *Journal of Risk and Uncertainty*, 8:33–62.

Hansen, A. C. (2006). "Do Declining Discount Rates Lead to Time Inconsistent Economic Advice?," *Ecological Economics*, 60:138–144.

Harrison, G. W. (2005). "Book Review: *Advances in Behavioral Economics*," *Journal of Economic Psychology*, 26:793–795.

———. (2008a). "Neuroeconomics: A Critical Reconsideration," *Economics and Philosophy*, 24:303–344.

———. (2008b). "Neuroeconomics: A Rejoinder," *Economics and Philosophy*, 24:533–544.

Heckman, J. J., Flyer, F., and Loughlin, C. (2008). "An Assessment of Causal Inference in Smoking Initiation Research and a Framework for Future Research," *Economic Inquiry*, 46:37–44.

Heidhues, P., and Koszegi, B. (2009). "Futile Attempts at Self-Control," *Journal of the European Economic Association*, 7:423–434.

Heien, D. M. (1996). "Do Drinkers Earn Less?," *Southern Economic Journal*, 63:60–68.

Herbst, C. M., and Tekin, E. (forthcoming). "Child Care Subsidies and Childhood Obesity," *Review of Economics of the Household*.

Hersch, J. (2000). "Gender, Income Levels, and the Demand for Cigarettes," *Journal of Risk and Uncertainty*, 21:263–282.

———. (2005). "Smoking Restrictions as a Self-Control Mechanism," *Journal of Risk and Uncertainty*, 31:5–21.

Hersch, J., Del Rossi, A. F., and Viscusi, W. K. (2004). "Voter Preferences and State Regulation of Smoking," *Economic Inquiry*, 42:455–468.

Hsieh, C., Yen, L., Liu, J., and Lin, C. J. (1996). "Smoking, Health Knowledge, and Anti-Smoking Campaigns: An Empirical Study in Taiwan," *Journal of Health Economics*, 15:87–104.

Ida, T., and Goto, R. (2009). "Interdependency among Addictive Behaviours and Time/Risk Preferences: Discrete Choice Model Analysis of Smoking, Drinking, and Gambling," *Journal of Economic Psychology*, 30:608–621.

Iwasaki, N., Tremblay, C. H., and Tremblay, V. J. (2006). "Advertising Restrictions and Cigarette Smoking: Evidence from Myopic and Rational Addiction Models," *Contemporary Economic Policy*, 24:370–381.

Jain, A. (2010). "Temptations in Cyberspace: New Battlefields in Childhood Obesity," *Health Affairs*, 29:425–429.

Jain, S. (2009). "Self-Control and Optimal Goals: A Theoretical Analysis," *Marketing Science*, 28:1027–1045.

Jamison, J. C. (2008). "Well-Being and Neuroeconomics," *Economics and Philosophy*, 24:407–418.

Jehiel, P., and Lilico, A. (2010). "Smoking Today and Stopping Tomorrow: A Limited Foresight Perspective," *Cesifo Studies*, 56:141–164.

Johnson, E., McInnes, M. M., and Shinogle, J. A. (2006). "What Is the Economic Cost of Overweight Children?," *Eastern Economic Journal*, 32:171–187.

Jolls, C., and Sunstein, C. R. (2006). "Debiasing through Law," *Journal of Legal Studies*, 35:199–241.

Jolls, C., Sunstein, C. R., and Thaler, R. (1998a). "A Behavioral Approach to Law and Economics," *Stanford Law Review*, 50:1471–1550.

———. (1998b). "Theories and Tropes: A Reply to Posner and Kelman," *Stanford Law Review*, 50:1593–1608.

Kaestner, R. (2000). "A Note on the Effect of Minimum Drinking Age Laws on Youth Alcohol Consumption," *Contemporary Economic Policy*, 18:315–325.

Kan, K. (2007). "Cigarette Smoking and Self-Control," *Journal of Health Economics*, 26:61–81.

Kan, K., and Tsai, W. (2004). "Obesity and Risk Knowledge," *Journal of Health Economics*, 23:907–934.

Kaushal, N. (2007). "Do Food Stamps Cause Obesity? Evidence from Immigrant Experience," *Journal of Health Economics*, 26:968–991.

Keeler, T. E., Marciniak, M., and Hu, T. (1999). "Rational Addiction and Smoking Cessation: An Empirical Study," *Journal of Socio-Economics*, 28:633–643.

Keng, S., and Huffman, W. E. (2010). "Binge Drinking and Labor Market Success: A Longitudinal Study on Young People," *Journal of Population Economics*, 23:303–322.

Kenkel, D. S. (2005). "Are Alcohol and Tax Hikes Fully Passed Through to Prices? Evidence from Alaska," *AEA Papers and Proceedings*, 95:273–277.

Kenkel, D., and Wang, P. (1998). "Are Alcoholics in Bad Jobs?," NBER Working Paper 6401.

Kersh, R., and Morone, J. A. (2005). "Obesity, Courts, and the New Politics of Public Health," *Journal of Health Politics, Policy and Law*, 30:839–868.

Khwaja, A., Silverman, D., and Sloan, F. (2007). "Time Preference, Time Discounting, and Smoking Decisions," *Journal of Health Economics*, 26:927–949.

Khwaja, A., Silverman, D., Sloan, F., and Wang, Y. (2009). "Are Mature Smokers Misinformed?," *Journal of Health Economics*, 28:385–397.

Khwaja, A., Sloan, F., and Chung, S. (2006). "Learning about Individual Risk and the Decision to Smoke," *International Journal of Industrial Organization*, 24:683–699.

Khwaja, A., Sloan, F., and Salm, M. (2006). "Evidence on Preferences and Subjective Beliefs of Risk Takers: The Case of Smoking," *International Journal of Industrial Organization*, 24:667–682.

Klesges, R. C., and Shumaker, S. A. (1992). "Understanding the Relations between Smoking and Body Weight and Their Importance to Smoking Cessation and Relapse," *Health Psychology*, 11:1–3.

Klick, J., and Stratmann, T. (2006). "Subsidizing Addiction: Do State Health Insurance Mandates Increase Alcohol Consumption?," *Journal of Legal Studies*, 35:175–198.

Koch, S. F., and McGeary, A. (2005). "The Effect of Youth Alcohol Initiation on High School Completion," *Economic Inquiry*, 43:750–765.

Koch, S. F., and Ribar, D. C. (2001). "A Siblings Analysis of the Effects of Alcohol Consumption Onset on Educational Attainment," *Contemporary Economic Policy*, 19:162–174.

Komlos, J., and Baur, M. (2004). "From the Tallest to (One of) the Fattest: The Enigmatic Fate of the American Population in the 20th Century," *Economics and Human Biology*, 2:57–74.

Komlos, J., Smith, P. K., and Bogin, B. (2004). "Obesity and the Rate of Time Preference: Is There a Connection?," *Journal of Biosocial Science*, 36:209–219.

Korobkin, R. B., and Ulen, T. S. (2000). "Law and Behavioral Science: Removing the Rationality Assumption from Law and Economics," *California Law Review*, 88:1051–1144.

Kostova, D., Ross, H., Blecher, E., and Markowitz, S. (2010). "Prices and Cigarette Demand: Evidence from Youth Tobacco Use in Developing Countries," NBER Working Paper 15781.

La Cour, L., and Milhoj, A. (2009). "The Sale of Alcohol in Denmark: Recent Developments and Dependencies on Prices/Taxes," *Applied Economics*, 41:1089–1103.

Laibson, D. (2001). "A Cue Theory of Consumption," *Quarterly Journal of Economics*, 116:81–119.

Laixuthai, A., and Chaloupka, F. J. (1994). "Youth Alcohol Use and Public Policy," *Contemporary Policy Issues*, 11:69–81.

Lakdawalla, D., and Philipson, T. (2009). "The Growth of Obesity and Technological Change: A Theoretical and Empirical Examination," *Economics and Human Biology*, 7:283–293.

Lance, P. M., Akin, J. S., Dow, W. H., and Loh, C. (2004). "Is Cigarette Smoking in Poorer Nations Highly Sensitive to Price? Evidence from Russia and China," *Journal of Health Economics*, 23:173–189.

Laux, F. L. (2000). "Addiction as a Market Failure: Using Rational Addiction Results to Justify Tobacco Regulation," *Journal of Health Economics*, 19:421–437.

Leonard, T. C., Goldfarb, R. S., and Suranovic, S. M. (2000). "New on Paternalism and Public Policy," *Economics and Philosophy*, 16:323–331.

Levine, D. K. (2009). "Is Behavioral Economics Doomed? The Ordinary versus the Extraordinary," Working Paper, Washington University at St. Louis.

Levy, A. (2002). "Rational Eating: Can It Lead to Overweightness or Underweightness?," *Journal of Health Economics*, 21:887–899.

Liang, L., and Huang, J. (2008). "Go Out or Stay In? The Effects of Zero Tolerance Laws on Alcohol Use and Drinking and Driving Patterns among College Students," *Health Economics*, 17:1261–1275.

Loewenstein, G. (1996). "Out of Control: Visceral Influences on Behavior," *Organizational Behavior and Human Decision Processes*, 65:272–292.

Loewenstein, G., and O'Donoghue, T. (2006). "'We Can Do This the Easy Way or the Hard Way': Negative Emotions, Self-Regulation, and the Law." *University of Chicago Law Review*, 73:183–206.

Loewenstein, G., O'Donoghue, T., and Rabin, M. (2003). "Projection Bias in Predicting Future Utility," *Quarterly Journal of Economics*, 118:1209–1248.

Loewenstein, G., and Prelec, D. (1991). "Negative Time Preference," *AEA Papers and Proceedings*, 81:347–352.

———. (1992). "Anomalies in Intertemporal Choice: Evidence and an Interpretation," *Quarterly Journal of Economics*, 107:573–597.

Loewenstein, G., and Rabin, M., eds. (2003). *Advances in Behavioral Economics*, Princeton, NJ: Princeton University Press.

Loewenstein, G., and Thaler, R. H. (1989). "Intertemporal Choice," *Journal of Economic Perspectives*, 3:181–193.

Ludbrook, A. (2009). "Minimum Pricing of Alcohol," *Health Economics*, 18:1357–1360.

Lundborg, P. (2006). "Having the Wrong Friends," *Journal of Health Economics*, 25:214–233.

Lundborg, P., and Andersson, H. (2008). "Gender, Risk Perceptions, and Smoking Behavior," *Journal of Health Economics*, 27:1299–1311.

MacDonald, Z., and Shields, M. A. (2001). "The Impact of Alcohol Consumption on Occupational Attainment in England," *Economica*, 68:427–453.

MacInnis, B., and Rausser, G. (2005). "Does Food Processing Contribute to Childhood Obesity Disparities?," *American Journal of Agricultural Economics*, 87:1154–1158.

Mair, J. S., Pierce, M. W., and Teret, S. P. (2005). "The Use of Zoning to Restrict Fast Food Outlets: A Potential Strategy to Combat Obesity," Working Paper, Center for Law and the Public's Health at Johns Hopkins and Georgetown Universities.

Manzini, P., and Mariotti, M. (2006). "A Vague Theory of Choice over Time," *Advances in Theoretical Economics*, 6:1–27.

Markowitz, S., Kaestner, R., and Grossman, M. (2005). "An Investigation of the Effects of Alcohol Consumption and Alcohol Policies on Youth Risky Sexual Behaviors," *AEA Papers and Proceedings*, 95:263–266.

McCabe, K. A. (2008). "Neuroeconomics and the Economic Sciences," *Economics and Philosophy*, 24:345–368.

McClure, S. M., Ericson, K. M., Laibson, D. I., Loewenstein, G., and Cohen, J. D. (2007). "Time Discounting for Primary Rewards," *Journal of Neuroscience*, 27:5796–5804.

McClure, S. M., Laibson, D. I., Loewenstein, G., and Cohen, J. D. (2004). "Separate Neural Systems Value Immediate and Delayed Monetary Rewards," *Science*, 306:503–507.

McClure, S. M., Li, J., Tomlin, D., Cypert, K. S., Montague, M., and Montague, P. R. (2004). "Neural Correlates of Behavioral Preference for Culturally Familiar Drinks," *Neuron*, 44:379–387.

McFadden, D. (1999). "Rationality for Economists?," *Journal of Risk and Uncertainty*, 19:73–105.

Mehta, N. K., and Chang, V. W. (2009). "Mortality Attributable to Obesity among Middle-Aged Adults in the United States," *Demography*, 46:851–872.

Michaud, P. C., Soest, A. H. O., and Andreyeva, T. (2007). "Cross-County Variations in Obesity Patterns among Older Americans and Europeans," *Forum for Health Economics and Policy*, 10:1–30.

Miljkovic, D., Nganje, W., and de Chastenet, H. (2008). "Economic Factors Affecting the Increase in Obesity in the United States: Differential Response to Price," *Food Policy*, 33:48–60.

Millimet, D. L., Tchernis, R., and Husain, M. (2010). "School Nutrition Programs and the Incidence of Childhood Obesity," *Journal of Human Resources*, 45:640–654.

Miron, J. A., and Tetelbaum, E. (2009). "Does the Minimum Legal Drinking Age Save Lives?," *Economic Inquiry*, 47:317–336.

Mischel, W., Shoda, Y., and Rodriguez, M. L. (1989). "Delay of Gratification in Children," *Science*, 244:933–938.

Mitchell, G. (2002). "Why Law and Economics' Perfect Rationality Should Not Be Traded for Behavioral Law and Economics' Equal Incompetence," *Georgetown Law Journal*, 91:67–167.

———. (2005). "Libertarian Paternalism Is an Oxymoron," *Northwestern University Law Review*, 99:1245–1277.

Moore, M. J., and Cook, P. J. (1995). "Habit and Heterogeneity in the Youthful Demand for Alcohol," NBER Working Paper 5152.

Morris, S., and Gravelle, H. (2008). "GP Supply and Obesity." *Journal of Health Economics*, 27:1357–1367.

Mullahy, J., and Sindelar, J. L. (1993). "Alcoholism, Work, and Income," *Journal of Labor Economics*, 11:494–520.

Naurath, N., and Jones, J. M. (2007). "Smoking Rates around the World—How Do Americans Compare?," Gallup, http://www.gallup.com/poll/28432/smoking-rates-around-world-how-americans-compare.aspx.

Nayga, R. M., Jr. (2001). "Effect of Schooling on Obesity: Is Health Knowledge a Moderating Factor?," *Education Economics*, 9:129–137.

Nelson, J. P. (1999). "Broadcast Advertising and U.S. Demand for Alcoholic Beverages," *Southern Economic Journal*, 65:774–790.

———. (2005). "Beer Advertising and Marketing Update: Structure, Conduct, and Social Costs," *Review of Industrial Organization*, 26:269–306.

———. (2006a). "Alcohol Advertising in Magazines: Do Beer, Wine, and Spirit Ads Target Youth?," *Contemporary Economic Policy*, 24:357–369.

———. (2006b). "Cigarette Advertising Regulation: A Meta-Analysis," *International Review of Law and Economics*, 26:195–226.

———. (2008a). "Reply to Siegel et al.: Alcohol Advertising in Magazines and Disproportionate Exposure," *Contemporary Economic Policy*, 26:493–504.

———. (2008b). "How Similar Are Youth and Adult Alcohol Behaviors? Panel Results for Excise Taxes and Outlet Density," *Atlantic Economic Journal*, 36:89–104.

Ng, Y. (2003). "From Preference to Happiness: Towards a More Complete Welfare Economics," *Social Choice and Welfare*, 20:307–350.

Nonnemaker, J., Finkelstein, E., Engelen, M., Hoerger, T., and Farrelly, M. (2009). "Have Efforts to Reduce Smoking Really Contributed to the Obesity Epidemic?," *Economic Inquiry*, 47:366–376.

Noor, J. (2009). "Hyperbolic Discounting and the Standard Model: Eliciting Discount Functions," *Journal of Economic Theory*, 144:2077–2083.

O'Donoghue, T., and Rabin, M. (1999a). "Doing It Now or Later," *American Economic Review*, 89:103–124.

———. (1999b). "Addiction and Self-Control," in J. Elster, ed., *Addiction: Entries and Exits*, New York: Russell Sage Foundation Press.

———. (2000). "The Economics of Immediate Gratification," *Journal of Behavioral Decision Making*, 13:233–250.

———. (2001a). "Choice and Procrastination," *Quarterly Journal of Economics*, 116:121–160.

———. (2001b). "Self Awareness and Self Control," in R. Baumeister, G. Loewenstein, and D. Read, eds., *Now or Later: Economic and Psychological Perspective on Intertemporal Choice*, New York: Russell Sage Foundation Press.

———. (2002). "Addiction and Present-Biased Preferences," Working Paper, Cornell University.

———. (2003). "Studying Optimal Paternalism, Illustrated by a Model of Sin Taxes," *AEA Papers and Proceedings*, 93:186–191.

———. (2006). "Optimal Sin Taxes," *Journal of Public Economics*, 90:1825–1849.

Ohsfeldt, R. L., Boyle, R. G., and Capilouto, E. (1997). "Effects of Tobacco Excise Taxes on the Use of Smokeless Tobacco Products in the USA," *Health Economics Letters*, 6:525–531.

Orphanides, A., and Zervos, D. (1995). "Rational Addiction with Learning and Regret," *Journal of Political Economy*, 103:739–758.

———. (1998). "Myopia and Addictive Behaviour," *Economic Journal*, 108:75–91.

Oswald, A. J., and Powdthavee, N. (2007). "Obesity, Unhappiness, and the Challenge of Affluence: Theory and Evidence," *Economic Journal*, 117:441–454.

Pacula, R. L. (1998). "Does Increasing the Beer Tax Reduce Marijuana Consumption?," *Journal of Health Economics*, 17:557–585.

Pattishall, E. G. (1992). "Smoking and Body Weight: Reactions and Perspectives," *Health Psychology*, 11:32–33.

Pesendorfer, W. (2006). "Behavioral Economics Comes of Age: A Review Essay on Advances in Behavioral Economics," *Journal of Economic Literature*, 44:712–721.

Peters, B. L. (2009). "The Drinkers' Bonus in the Military: Officers versus Enlisted Personnel," *Applied Economics*, 41:2211–2220.

Peters, B. L., and Stringham, E. (2006). "No Booze? You May Lose: Why Drinkers Earn More Money than Nondrinkers," *Journal of Labor Research*, 27:411–421.

Philipson, T. (2001). "The World-Wide Growth in Obesity: An Economic Research Agenda," *Health Economics*, 10:1–7.

Philipson, T., and Posner, R. (2003). "The Long-Run Growth in Obesity as a Function of Technological Change," *Perspectives in Biology and Medicine*, 46:87–108.

———. (2008). "Is the Obesity Epidemic a Public Health Problem? A Decade of Research on the Economics of Obesity," *Journal of Economic Literature*, 46:974–982.

Picone, G. A., Sloan, F., and Trogdon, J. G. (2004). "The Effect of the Tobacco Settlement and Smoking Bans on Alcohol Consumption," *Health Economics*, 13:1063–1080.

Pierani, P., and Tiezzi, S. (2009). "Addiction and Interaction between Alcohol and Tobacco Consumption," *Empirical Economics*, 37:1–23.

Posner, R. A. (1998). "Rational Choice, Behavioral Economics, and the Law," *Stanford Law Review*, 50:1551–1575.

Powell, L. M., and Chaloupka, F. J. (2005). "Parents, Public Policy, and Youth Smoking," *Journal of Policy Analysis and Management*, 24:93–112.

Powell, L. M., Tauras, J. A., and Ross, H. (2005). "The Importance of Peer Effects, Cigarette Prices and Tobacco Control Policies for Youth Smoking Behavior," *Journal of Health Economics*, 24:950–968.

Powell, L. M., Williams, J., and Wechsler, H. (2004). "Study Habits and the Level of Alcohol Use among College Students," *Education Economics*, 12:135–149.

Propper, C. (2005). "Why Economics Is Good for Your Health: 2004 Royal Economics Society Public Lecture," *Health Economics*, 14:987–997.

Quiggin, J. (2001). "Does Rational Addiction Imply Irrational Non-Addiction?," Working Paper 411, Australian National University.

Rabin, M. (1998). "Psychology and Economics," *Journal of Economic Literature*, 36:11–46.

Rachlinski, J. J. (2003). "The Uncertain Psychological Case for Paternalism," *Northwestern University Law Review*, 97:1165–1225.

———. (2006). "Cognitive Errors, Individual Differences, and Paternalism," *University of Chicago Law Review*, 73:207–229.

Raptou, E., Mattas, K., and Katrakilidis, C. (2009). "Investigating Smoker's Profile: The Role of Psychosocial Characteristics and the Effectiveness of Tobacco Policy Tools," *American Journal of Economics and Sociology*, 68:603–638.

Rashad, I., and Grossman, M. (2004). "The Economics of Obesity," *The Public Interest*, Summer: 104–112.

Rashad, I., Grossman, M., and Chou, S. (2006). "The Super Size of America: An Economic Estimation of Body Mass Index and Obesity in Adults," *Eastern Economic Journal*, 32:133–148.

Rashad, I., and Kaestner, R. (2004). "Teenage Sex, Drugs and Alcohol Use: Problems Identifying the Cause of Risky Behaviors," *Journal of Health Economics*, 23:493–503.

Rasmusen, E. (2008a). "Some Common Confusions about Hyperbolic Discounting," Working Paper, Indiana University.

———. (2008b). "Internalities and Paternalism: Applying the Compensation Criterion to Multiple Selves across Time," Working Paper, Indiana University.

Read, D. (2006). "Which Side Are You On? The Ethics of Self-Command," *Journal of Economic Psychology*, 27:681–693.

Rees, D. I., Argys, L. M., and Averett, S. L. (2001). "New Evidence on the Relationship between Substance Use and Adolescent Sexual Behavior," *Journal of Health Economics*, 20:835–845.

Renna, F. (2007). "The Economic Cost of Teen Drinking: Late Graduation and Lowered Earnings," *Health Economics*, 16:407–419.

———. (2008). "Teens' Alcohol Consumption and Schooling," *Economics of Education Review*, 27:69–78.

Richards, T. J., and Padilla, L. (2009). "Promotion and Fast Food Demand," *American Journal of Agricultural Economics*, 91:168–183.

Richards, T. J., Patterson, P. M., and Tegene, A. (2007). "Obesity and Nutrient Consumption: A Rational Addiction?," *Contemporary Economic Policy*, 25:309–324.

Rogeberg, O. (2004). "Taking Absurd Theories Seriously: Economics and the Case of Rational Addiction Theories," *Philosophy of Science*, 71:263–285.

Rojas, C., and Peterson, E. B. (2008). "Demand for Differentiated Products: Price and Advertising Evidence from the U.S. Beer Market," *International Journal of Industrial Organization*, 26:288–307.

Rosin, O. (2008). "The Economic Causes of Obesity: A Survey," *Journal of Economic Surveys*, 22:617–647.

Ross, H., Chaloupka, F. J., and Wakefield, M. (2006). "Youth Smoking Uptake Progress: Price and Public Policy Effects," *Eastern Economic Journal*, 32:355–367.

Rubinstein, A. (2001). "A Theorist's View of Experiments," *European Economic Review*, 45:615–628.

———. (2003). "'Economics and Psychology': The Case of Hyperbolic Discounting," *International Economic Review*, 44:1207–1216.

———. (2006). "Discussion of 'Behavioral Economics'," in R. Blundell, W. K. Newey, and T. Persson, eds., *Advances in Economic Theory*, Cambridge: Cambridge University Press.

———. (2008). "Comments on Neuroeconomics," *Economics and Philosophy*, 24:485–494.

Ruhm, C. J. (2007). "Current and Future Prevalence of Obesity and Severe Obesity in the United States," *Forum for Health Economics and Policy*, 10:1–26.

Sabia, J. J. (2010). "Wastin' Away in Margaritaville? New Evidence on the Academic Effects of Teenage Binge Drinking," *Contemporary Economic Policy*, 28:1–22.

Sacerdote, B. (2001). "Peer Effects with Random Assignment: Results for Dartmouth Roommates," *Quarterly Journal of Economics*, 116:681–704.

Saffer, H., and Chaloupka, F. (2000). "The Effect of Tobacco Advertising Bans on Tobacco Consumption," *Journal of Health Economics*, 19:1117–1137.

Saffer, H., and Dave, D. (2002). "Alcohol Consumption and Alcohol Advertising Bans," *Applied Economics*, 34:1325–1334.

———. (2005). "Mental Illness and the Demand for Alcohol, Cocaine, and Cigarettes," *Economic Inquiry*, 43:229–246.

———. (2006). "Alcohol Advertising and Alcohol Consumption by Adolescents," *Health Economics*, 15:617–637.

Sandy, R., Liu, F., Ottensmann, J., Tchernis, R., Wilson, J., and Ford, O. T. (2009). "Studying the Child Obesity Epidemic with Natural Experiments," NBER Working Paper 14989.

Scharff, R. L. (2009). "Obesity and Hyperbolic Discounting: Evidence," *Journal of Consumer Policy*, 32:3–21.

Schelling, T. C. (1984). "Self-Command in Practice, in Policy, and in a Theory of Rational Choice," *AEA Papers and Proceedings*, 74:1–11.

Schmeiser, M. D. (2009). "Expanding Wallets and Waistlines: The Impact of Family Income on the BMI of Women and Men Eligible for the Earned Income Tax Credit," *Health Economics*, 18:1277–1294.

Schroeter, C., Lusk, J., and Tyner, W. (2008). "Determining the Impact of Food Price and Income Changes on Body Weight," *Journal of Health Economics*, 27:45–68.

Schulman, T. (2010). "Menu Labeling: Knowledge for a Healthier America," *Harvard Journal on Legislation*, 47:587–610.

Sen, B. (2002). "Does Alcohol-Use Increase the Risk of Sexual Intercourse among Adolescents? Evidence from the NLSY97," *Journal of Health Economics*, 21:1085–1093.

———. (2003). "Can Beer Taxes Affect Teen Pregnancy? Evidence Based on Teen Abortion Rates and Birth Rates," *Southern Economic Journal*, 70:328–343.

Sen, B., Mennemeyer, S., and Gary, L. C. (2009). "The Relationship between Neighborhood Quality and Obesity among Children," NBER Working Paper 14985.

Shapiro, J. M. (2005). "Is There a Daily Discount Rate? Evidence from the Food Stamp Nutrition Cycle," *Journal of Public Economics*, 89:303–325.

Showalter, M. H. (1999). "Firm Behavior in a Market with Addiction: The Case of Cigarettes," *Journal of Health Economics*, 18:409–427.

Siegel, M., King, C., Ostroff, J., Ross, C., Dixon, K., and Jernigan, D. H. (2008). "Comment—Alcohol Advertising in Magazines and Youth Readership: Are Youths Disproportionately Exposed?," *Contemporary Economic Policy*, 26:482–492.

Skog, O. (1999). "Hyperbolic Discounting, Willpower, and Addiction," in J. Elster, ed., *Addiction: Entries and Exits*, New York: Russell Sage Foundation Press.

Sloan, F. A., Smith, V. K., and Taylor, D. H., Jr. (2002). "Information, Addiction, and 'Bad Choices': Lessons from a Century of Cigarettes," *Economics Letters*, 77:147–155.

Slovic, P. (1998). "Do Adolescent Smokers Know the Risks?," *Duke Law Journal*, 47:1133–1138.

———. (2000a). "What Does It Mean to Know a Cumulative Risk? Adolescents' Perceptions of Short-Term and Long-Term Consequences of Smoking," *Journal of Behavioral Decision Making*, 13:259–266.

———. (2000b). "Rejoinder: The Perils of Viscusi's Analyses of Smoking Risk Perceptions," *Journal of Behavioral Decision Making*, 13:273–276.

Smith, P. K., Bogin, B., and Bishai, D. (2005). "Are Time Preference and Body Mass Index Associated? Evidence from the National Longitudinal Survey of Youth," *Economics and Human Biology*, 3:259–270.

Smith, T. G., Stoddard, C., and Barnes, M. G. (2009). "Why the Poor Get Fat: Weight Gain and Economic Insecurity," *Forum for Health Economics and Policy*, 12:1–29.

Soman, D., Ainslie, G., Frederick, S., Li, X., Lynch, J., Moreau, P., Mitchell, A., Read, D., Sawyer, A., Trope, Y., Wertenbroch, K., and Zauberman, G. (2005). "The Psychology of Intertemporal Discounting: Why Are Distant Events Valued Differently from Proximal Ones?," *Marketing Letters*, 16:347–360.

Sopher, B., and Sheth, A. (2005). "A Deeper Look at Hyperbolic Discounting," *Theory and Decision*, 60:219–255.

Spiegler, R. (2008). "Comments on the Potential Significance of Neuroeconomics for Economic Theory," *Economics and Philosophy*, 24:515–521.

Stehr, M. (2005). "Cigarette Tax Avoidance and Evasion," *Journal of Health Economics*, 24:277–297.

———. (2007). "The Effect of Cigarette Taxes on Smoking among Men and Women," *Health Economics*, 16:1333–1343.

Sunstein, C. R. (1986). "Legal Interference with Private Preferences," *University of Chicago Law Review*, 53:1129–1174.

Sunstein, C. R., and Thaler, R. H. (2003). "Libertarian Paternalism Is Not an Oxymoron," *University of Chicago Law Review*, 70:1159–1202.

Thaler, R. H., and Sunstein, C. R. (2003). "Libertarian Paternalism," *AEA Papers and Proceedings*, 93:175–179.

Tauras, J. A. (2005a). "Can Public Policy Deter Smoking Escalation among Young Adults?," *Journal of Policy Analysis and Management*, 24:771–784.

———. (2005b). "An Empirical Analysis of Adult Cigarette Demand," *Eastern Economic Journal*, 31:361–375.

———. (2006). "Smoke-Free Laws, Cigarette Prices, and Adult Cigarette Demand," *Economic Inquiry*, 44:333–342.

Tauras, J., Powell, L., Chaloupka, F., and Ross, H. (2007). "The Demand for Smokeless Tobacco among Male High School Students in the United States: The Impact of Taxes, Prices and Policies," *Applied Economics*, 39:31–41.

Tekin, E., Mocan, N., and Liang, L. (2009). "Do Adolescents with Emotional or Behavioral Problems Respond to Cigarette Prices?," *Southern Economic Journal*, 76:67–85.

Thaler, R. H., and Benartzi, S. (2004). "Save More Tomorrow: Using Behavioral Economics to Increase Employee Saving," *Journal of Political Economy*, 112: S164–S187.

Thaler, R. H., and Shefrin, H. M. (1981). "An Economic Theory of Self-Control," *Journal of Political Economy*, 89:392–406.

Thies, C. F., and Register, C. A. (1993). "Decriminalization of Marijuana and the Demand for Alcohol, Marijuana, and Cocaine," *Social Science Journal*, 30:385–399.

Townsend, J., Roderick, P., and Cooper, J. (1994). "Cigarette Smoking by Socioeconomic Group, Sex, and Age: Effects of Price, Income, and Health Publicity," *British Medical Journal*, 309:923–927.

Van Ours, J. C. (2004). "A Pint a Day Raises a Man's Pay; But Smoking Blows That Gain Away," *Journal of Health Economics*, 23:863–886.

Variyam, J. N., and Cawley, J. (2006). "Nutrition Labels and Obesity," NBER Working Paper 11956.

Ver Ploeg, M., and Ralston, K. (2008). "Food Stamps and Obesity: What Do We Know?," United States Department of Agriculture, Economic Information Bulletin Number 34.

Viscusi, W. K. (1990). "Do Smokers Underestimate Risks?," *Journal of Political Economy*, 98:1253–1269.

———. (1991). "Age Variations in Risk Perceptions and Smoking Decisions," *Review of Economics and Statistics*, 53:577–588.

———. (1998). "Constructive Cigarette Regulation," *Duke Law Journal*, 47:1095–1131.

———. (2000). "Comment: The Perils of Qualitative Smoking Risk Measure," *Journal of Behavioral Decision Making*, 13:267–271.

Viscusi, W. K., and Hakes, J. K. (2008). "Risk Beliefs and Smoking Behavior," *Economic Inquiry*, 46:45–59.

Viscusi, W. K., and Hersch, J. (2008). "The Mortality Cost to Smokers," *Journal of Health Economics*, 27:45–59.

Wagenaar, A. C., and Toomey, T. I. (2002). "Effects of Minimum Drinking Age Laws: Review and Analyses of the Literature from 1960 to 2000," *Journal of Studies on Alcohol*, Supp. 14:206–225.

Wallinga, D. (2010). "Agricultural Policy and Childhood Obesity: A Food Systems and Public Health Commentary," *Health Affairs*, 29:405–410.

Wan, J. (2006). "Cigarette Tax Revenues and Tobacco Control in Japan," *Applied Economics*, 38:1663–1675.

Wang, R. (2007). "The Optimal Consumption and the Quitting of Harmful Addictive Goods," *B.E. Journal of Economic Analysis and Policy*, 7:1–36.

Warner, J. T., and Pleeter, S. (2001). "The Personal Discount Rate: Evidence from Military Downsizing Programs," *American Economic Review*, 91:33–53.

Warner, K. E. (1990). "Tobacco Taxation as Health Policy in the Third World," *American Journal of Public Health*, 80:529–531.

Weimer, D. L., Vining, A. R., and Thomas, R. K. (2009). "Cost-Benefit Analysis Involving Addictive Goods: Contingent Valuation to Estimate Willingness-to-Pay for Smoking Cessation," *Health Economics*, 18:181–202.

Wertenbroch, K. (1998). "Consumption Self-Control by Rationing Purchase Quantities of Virtue and Vice," *Marketing Science*, 17:317–337.

Whitman, G. (2006). "Against the New Paternalism," *Policy Analysis*, February: 1–16.

Williams, J., Chaloupka, F. J., and Wechsler, H. (2005). "Are There Differential Effects of Price and Policy on College Students' Drinking Intensity?," *Contemporary Economic Policy*, 23:78–90.

Williams, J., Pacula, R. L., Chaloupka, F. J., and Wechsler, H. (2004). "Alcohol and Marijuana Use among College Students: Economic Complements or Substitutes?," *Health Economics*, 13:825–843.

Williams, J., Powell, L. M., and Wechsler, H. (2003). "Does Alcohol Consumption Reduce Human Capital Accumulation? Evidence from the College Alcohol Study," *Applied Economics*, 35:1227–1239.

Winkler, R. (2006). "Does 'Better' Discounting Lead to 'Worse' Outcomes in Long-Run Decisions? The Dilemma of Hyperbolic Discounting," *Ecological Economics*, 57:573–582.

Winter, H. (2005). *Trade-Offs: An Introduction to Economic Reasoning and Social Issues*, Chicago: University of Chicago Press.

———. (2008). *The Economics of Crime: An Introduction to Rational Crime Analysis*, London: Routledge.

Wolaver, A. (2002). "Effects of Heavy Drinking in College on Study Effort, Grade Point Average, and Major Choice," *Contemporary Economic Policy*, 20:415–428.

Wong, W. (2008). "How Much Time-Inconsistency Is There and Does It Matter? Evidence on Self-Awareness, Size, and Effects," *Journal of Economic Behavior and Organization*, 68:645–656.

Young, D. J., and Bielinska, A. (2002). "Alcohol Taxes and Beverage Prices," *National Tax Journal*, 55:57–73.

Yuengert, A. M. (2006). "Model Selection and Multiple Research Goals: The Case of Rational Addiction," *Journal of Economic Methodology*, 13:77–96.

Zamir, E. (1998). "The Efficiency of Paternalism," *Virginia Law Review*, 84:229–286.

Zarkin, G. A., French, M. T., Mroz, T., and Bray, J. W. (1998). "Alcohol Use and Wages: New Results from the National Household Survey on Drug Abuse," *Journal of Health Economics*, 17:53–68.

INDEX